Books by Florence A. Merriam.

BIRDS THROUGH AN OPERA-GLASS. In Riverside Library for Young People. Illustrated. 16mo, 75 cents.

MY SUMMER IN A MORMON VILLAGE. With an Illustration. 16mo, $1.00.

A-BIRDING ON A BRONCO. Illustrated. 16mo, $1.25.

BIRDS OF VILLAGE AND FIELD. A Bird Book for Beginners. Fully illustrated. 12mo, $2.00.

HOUGHTON, MIFFLIN & CO.
BOSTON AND NEW YORK.

PLATE I. — GOLDFINCH

(Page 145)

BIRDS
OF VILLAGE AND FIELD

A Bird Book for Beginners

BY

FLORENCE A. MERRIAM Bailey

ILLUSTRATED

BOSTON AND NEW YORK
HOUGHTON, MIFFLIN AND COMPANY
The Riverside Press, Cambridge
1900

Copyright, 1898,
By FLORENCE A. MERRIAM.

All rights reserved.

PREFATORY NOTE

In this day of outdoor and nature interest, we are coming to realize that to the birds as well as the flowers we owe much of the beauty and charm of country life; and if it could be accomplished within the narrow margins of our busy lives, we would gladly know more of the songsters.

Their prevalence, though often unsuspected, helps render this possible; for they are to be found in villages and cities as well as in the fields. In a shrubby back yard in Chicago, close to one of the main thoroughfares, Mrs. Sara Hubbard has seen fifty-seven species in a year, and her record for ten years was a hundred species. In an orchard in Brattleboro', Vermont, Mrs. E. B. Davenport has noted seventy-nine species in a year. And within the limits of Portland, Connecticut, Mr. John H. Sage has known ninety-nine kinds of birds to nest (see Appendix, p. 388). In the larger cities, cemeteries and parks offer rare opportunities for bird study. Dr. W. C. Braislin gives a list of seventy-six species for

Prospect Park, Brooklyn; while Mr. H. E. Parkhurst has himself seen ninety-four species in Central Park, and as many as a hundred and forty-two have been recorded altogether.

The question, then, is not one of finding birds, but of knowing their names when they are found; and here the way of the beginner is hard. Years of experience with field classes of such beginners has made me appreciate the peculiar disadvantages under which they labor, and I have written this book to make it possible for them to know the birds without shooting them. I have done this by borrowing only necessary statistics from the ornithologies, giving untechnical descriptions, and illustrated keys based on such colors and markings as any one can note in the field; for I have written for those who do not know a Crow or a Robin as well as for boys who would get a start in bird-work, and teachers who would prepare themselves for this increasingly popular branch of nature study.

To open the way for more intimate acquaintance after the formalities of introduction are over, I have offered suggestions on how to observe in the field (see Appendix, p. 380), hoping that the friendship thus acquired by seeing the songsters in their homes may urge the student to go on and gain for himself the delights of a deeper study of birds.

In the preparation of the Keys for this book, I have been largely helped by my brother, Dr. C. Hart Merriam; and at other points have been kindly assisted by Miss Isabel Eaton, Mrs. G. C. Maynard, Mr. Robert Ridgway, Mr. Frank M. Chapman, Mr. John H. Sage, Dr. A. K. Fisher, Dr. T. S. Palmer, Prof. F. E. L. Beal, and Mr. Sylvester Judd. The ranges given are from Chapman's Handbook, with additional notes by Dr. A. K. Fisher; the measurements are taken from the Handbook, but are given in round numbers of quarter inches. Of the migration and winter bird lists (see Appendix, pp. 369–379), the Washington ones have been kindly made by Mr. William Palmer; the St. Louis migration list has been compiled from notes by Mr. Otto Widmann in the files of the Biological Survey; and the Portland lists, together with that of birds known to nest in Portland, have been kindly supplied by Mr. John H. Sage.

The pictures of birds are from drawings by Ernest Seton Thompson, Louis Agassiz Fuertes, and John L. Ridgway. For the use of drawings of birds, insects, and plants which have previously appeared in the publications of the Department of Agriculture and the National Museum, I am indebted to the courtesy of Dr. L. O. Howard, Chief of the Division of Entomology; Mr. F. V. Coville, Chief of the Division of Botany; and Dr. C. Hart Merriam, Chief of the Biological Survey of the Department of Agriculture; and to Mr. F. A. Lucas, Curator of Comparative Anatomy in the National Museum. For the use of cuts previously published in the 'Auk,' the 'Osprey,' and a report of the Illinois State Laboratory of Natural History, I am indebted to the courtesy of Dr. J. A. Allen, Mr. Walter A. Johnson, and Prof. S. A. Forbes.

FLORENCE A. MERRIAM.

WASHINGTON, D. C., June 1, 1897.

CONTENTS

	PAGE
INTRODUCTION.	
How to find a Bird's Name	xiii
Where to find Birds	xiv
How to watch Birds	xv
How Birds affect Village Trees, Gardens, and Farms	xv
How to keep Birds about our Houses	xxiv
General Key to Birds mentioned in Book (Illustrated)	xxix
HUMMINGBIRD	1
CATBIRD	6
AMERICAN CROW	11
FISH CROW	16
ROBIN	17
WOOD THRUSH	22
CHIMNEY SWIFT	23
MOURNING DOVE	29
GROUND DOVE	31
RUFFED GROUSE	32
BOB-WHITE	37
Key to Grouse and Quail	40
BLUEBIRD	41
HOUSE WREN	44
PURPLE MARTIN	48
BARN SWALLOW	49
EAVE SWALLOW	52
BANK SWALLOW	54
BALTIMORE ORIOLE	56
ORCHARD ORIOLE	61
MOCKINGBIRD	63
CARDINAL	65
CHICKADEE	67
CAROLINA CHICKADEE	71
WHITE-BREASTED NUTHATCH	73

CONTENTS

RED-BREASTED NUTHATCH	76
PASSENGER PIGEON	78
Key to Pigeons and Doves	80
LEAST FLYCATCHER	80
KINGBIRD	83
PHŒBE	87
WOOD PEWEE	90
CROW BLACKBIRD	93
RED-WINGED BLACKBIRD	96
COWBIRD	98
RUSTY BLACKBIRD	101
BOBOLINK	103
MEADOWLARK	106
Key to Blackbirds and Orioles	111
CHIPPING SPARROW	113
SONG SPARROW	116
VESPER SPARROW	119
RED-EYED VIREO	120
WARBLING VIREO	126
FLICKER	127
RED-HEADED WOODPECKER	131
HAIRY WOODPECKER	135
DOWNY WOODPECKER	137
WAXWING	141
GOLDFINCH	145
PURPLE FINCH	148
INDIGO BUNTING	149
TUFTED TITMOUSE	151
Key to Nuthatches and Tits	152
BLUE JAY	154
BELTED KINGFISHER	157
YELLOW-BILLED CUCKOO	160
BLACK-BILLED CUCKOO	163
Key to Cuckoos and Kingfishers	165
ROSE-BREASTED GROSBEAK	166
SCARLET TANAGER	170
SUMMER TANAGER	173
Key to Tanagers	174
WHITE-THROATED SPARROW	174

CONTENTS ix

WHITE-CROWNED SPARROW	176
BROWN THRASHER	177
CHEWINK	181
FIELD SPARROW	183
WHIP-POOR-WILL	185
NIGHTHAWK	188
Key to Goatsuckers, Hummingbirds, Swifts	193
WHITE-BELLIED SWALLOW	194
ROUGH-WINGED SWALLOW	195
Key to Swallows	196
WINTER WREN	197
CAROLINA WREN	199
BEWICK'S WREN	201
LONG-BILLED MARSH WREN	202
Key to Thrashers and Wrens	205
YELLOW-BELLIED WOODPECKER	208
RED-COCKADED WOODPECKER	210
RED-BELLIED WOODPECKER	211
PILEATED WOODPECKER	212
Key to Woodpeckers	216
CANADA JAY	217
Key to Crows and Jays	220
JUNCO	221
SNOWFLAKE	223
DICKCISSEL	224
SAVANNA SPARROW	225
GRASSHOPPER SPARROW	226
TREE SPARROW	227
SWAMP SPARROW	229
FOX SPARROW	230
PINE GROSBEAK	231
PINE FINCH	233
AMERICAN CROSSBILL	234
WHITE-WINGED CROSSBILL	235
REDPOLL	236
LARK SPARROW	237
SHARP-TAILED SPARROW	239
SEASIDE SPARROW	240
CLAY-COLORED SPARROW	241

CONTENTS

BACHMAN'S SPARROW	242
Key to Finches and Sparrows	246
ACADIAN FLYCATCHER	254
GREAT-CRESTED FLYCATCHER	255
OLIVE-SIDED FLYCATCHER	257
ALDER FLYCATCHER	258
Key to Flycatchers	260
HORNED LARK	261
TURKEY VULTURE	263
BLACK VULTURE	265
Key to Vultures	266
GOSHAWK	266
SHARP-SHINNED HAWK	268
COOPER'S HAWK	269
RED-TAILED HAWK	271
RED-SHOULDERED HAWK	273
BROAD-WINGED HAWK	275
SPARROW HAWK	276
MARSH HAWK	278
FISH HAWK	280
BALD EAGLE	282
SWALLOW-TAILED KITE	283
Key to Falcons, Hawks, and Eagles	285
SCREECH OWL	287
LONG-EARED OWL	288
SHORT-EARED OWL	290
BARRED OWL	291
GREAT HORNED OWL	292
BARN OWL	293
SNOWY OWL	294
Key to Owls	296
LOGGERHEAD SHRIKE	298
BUTCHERBIRD	300
Key to Shrikes	300
YELLOW-THROATED VIREO	301
WHITE-EYED VIREO	302
Key to Vireos	304
YELLOW WARBLER	307
REDSTART	309

CONTENTS

YELLOW-RUMPED WARBLER	310
BLACK-THROATED GREEN WARBLER	311
BLACK-THROATED BLUE WARBLER	312
BLACK AND WHITE CREEPING WARBLER	314
MARYLAND YELLOW-THROAT	315
RED-POLL WARBLER	316
PARULA WARBLER	317
CHESTNUT-SIDED WARBLER	318
BLACK-POLL WARBLER	321
CANADIAN WARBLER	322
NASHVILLE WARBLER	322
BLACK AND YELLOW WARBLER	324
PRAIRIE WARBLER	325
BLACKBURNIAN WARBLER	326
HOODED WARBLER	327
KENTUCKY WARBLER	329
YELLOW-BREASTED CHAT	331
OVEN-BIRD	333
NORTHERN WATER-THRUSH	335
LOUISIANA WATER-THRUSH	336
WORM-EATING WARBLER	337
WILSON'S WARBLER	339
Key to Warblers	342
PIPIT OR TITLARK	348
BROWN CREEPER	349
RUBY-CROWNED KINGLET	354
GOLDEN-CROWNED KINGLET	356
BLUE-GRAY GNATCATCHER	357
Key to Kinglets and Gnatcatchers	357
VEERY THRUSH	358
OLIVE-BACKED THRUSH	359
HERMIT THRUSH	360
Key to Thrushes	360
APPENDIX.	
Migration	367
Winter Birds	376
Field Observations	380
Observing in Towns and Villages	388
Books of Reference	390
Index to Illustrations	395
Index	399

INTRODUCTION

How to find a Bird's Name. — As this book is intended for beginners, scientific classification has been disregarded, and the birds which readers are most likely to know and see are placed first, the rarer ones left until later. For the benefit of those who have a definite bird to name, a color key based on markings visible in the field has been made to all the birds taken up (see pp. xxix–xlix); this, when run down, will lead by page reference to the description and picture of the bird in the body of the book. If the family to which the bird belongs is known, the species will be found more quickly by turning to the key of the family, referred to in the index.

If no definite bird is to be looked up, and one goes to the field unembarrassed by knowledge, with the whole bird world freshly opening for conquest, the matter of naming the birds and learning their ways is not a difficult one. Four things only are necessary — a scrupulous conscience, unlimited patience, a notebook, and an opera-glass. The notebook enables one to put down the points which the opera-glass has brought within sight, and by means of which the bird may be found in the key; patience leads to trained ears and eyes, and conscience prevents hasty conclusions and doubtful records. Two notebooks should be kept, one for permanent records and a pocket one for field use, as elaborations from memory are of little value to one's self, and still less to posterity. One of the best forms of permanent notebook is a pad, punched and fastened in an adjustable cover. The notes on each bird should be written on separate pages, and as they accumulate, the pages slipped out of the cover and arranged alphabetically for easy reference. Suggestions for field notes will be found in the observation outline, Appendix, p. 380.

WHERE TO FIND BIRDS. — Shrubby village door-yards, the trees of village streets and orchards, roadside fences, overgrown pastures, and the borders of brooks and rivers are among the best places to look for birds. Such places afford food and protection, for there are more insects and fewer enemies in villages and about country houses than in forests; while brooks and river banks, though without the protection afforded by man, give water and abundant insect life. Very few birds care for deep woods. The heart of the dark, coniferous Adirondack forest is silent — hardly a bird is to be found there. It is along the edges of sunny, open woodland that most of the wood-loving species go to nest.

How to Watch Birds. — In looking for birds be careful not to frighten them away. As shyer kinds are almost sure to fly before you in any case, the best way is to go quietly to a good spot and sit down and wait for them to return and proceed with their business unconscious of spectators. Do not look toward the sun, as colors will not show against the light.

In nesting time, birds may be found at home at any hour, as the nestling's meal-time comes without regard for callers; but during migration, birds are moving, and best seen from 4.30 to 8.30 a. m. and 4 to 8 p. m.

If you begin watching birds in the spring, when they are coming back from a winter in the south, you will be kept busy looking up the names of the new arrivals; but even when intent on the distinguishing marks of the birds, you may make a great many interesting discoveries as to their ways of life. It is one of the pleasures of the season to keep a dated list of the migrants as they come north. The first year this will be exciting from the daily surprises of new arrivals; and as the years go by it will be of increasing interest from anticipations based on old dates, and the changes that occur with variations of season. (See Appendix, p. 367.)

How Birds affect Village Trees, Gardens, and Farms. — Village improvement societies are doing a great deal to better and beautify our towns; but in their attempts to preserve the trees against the plagues of insects that in late years have descended upon them, they sometimes seem to be baffled by the magnitude of their task. Their best allies in this work have hardly been recognized, and it is most important to understand the nature and extent of the help that may be obtained. The relation of birds to insects is only just becoming known.

It is said that two hundred millions of dollars that should go to the farmer, the gardener, and the fruit-grower in the United States are lost every year by the ravages of insects — that is to say, one tenth of our agricultural products is actually destroyed by them. The ravages of the gypsy moth in sections of three counties in Massachusetts for several years cost the State, annually, $100,000. Now, as rain is the natural check to drought, so birds are the natural check to insects, for what are pests to the farmer are necessities of life to the bird. It is calculated that an average insectivorous bird destroys 100,000 insects in a year; and when it is remembered that there are over 100,000 kinds of insects in the United States, the majority of which are injurious, and that in some cases a single individual in a year may become the progenitor of several billion descendants, it is seen how much good birds do ordinarily by simple prevention.

The good they do in cases of insect plagues, like that of the grasshopper scourge in Nebraska and Kansas, is still more marked. Then, as self-constituted militia, they fly to the scene of action and make way with the rioters. An interesting case of this kind was seen in an old orchard in Illinois. The cankerworm had so taken possession that the orchard looked almost as if burned over. Forty different kinds of birds assembled in the place to feed upon the worms. One hundred and forty-one of the birds were shot and the contents of their stomachs examined, and more than one third of their food was found to be cankerworms; the feathered army was simply wiping out the horde of worms. A similar case occurred in Massachusetts, and after the visit of the birds a good crop of apples was raised in the orchard which had been devastated.

It is well known that, of the various groups of birds, the majority live upon insects; and while most insectivorous birds probably take some useful insects, as far as they have been studied but few eat enough to weigh against the large number of harmful insects they live on throughout the year. Among the insect-eaters are the Flycatchers, Warblers, Woodpeckers, Nuthatches, Orioles, Goatsuckers, Hummingbirds, Tanagers, Waxwings, Gnatcatchers, Kinglets, Vireos, Thrushes, Wrens, Titmice, Cuckoos, Swallows, Shrikes, Thrashers, Creepers, and Bluebirds.

It is not generally known, however, that the so-called seed-eaters both feed their young largely upon insects and eat many themselves; nor is it realized how much good they do by eating weed seeds. Prof. F. E. L. Beal has calculated that the little Tree Sparrow in Iowa alone destroys 1,720,000 lbs. of noxious weed seeds every year. Moreover, in summer seed-eaters eat blueberries, huckleberries, strawberries, and raspberries, and distribute their seeds unharmed over thousands of acres which would not otherwise support such growth.

These facts show how important it is that the birds should be protected and encouraged, except in the exceedingly few cases where for a short time they eat some one cultivated crop to such excess that the loss is not compensated by the good they do in destroying pests the rest of the year. The Department of Agriculture, realizing the losses that often result from the ignorant sacrifice of useful birds, constituted the Division of Ornithology, now a part of the Biological Survey, a court of appeal where accusations against the birds could be received and investigated.

The method used by the division is the final one — the examination of stomach contents to prove the actual food of the birds. A reference collection of 800 kinds of seeds and 1,000 species of insects has been brought together for comparison in determining the character of food-remains found.

After the examination of about eighty birds, the only one actually sentenced to death is the English Sparrow. Of all the accused Hawks, only three have been found guilty of the charges made against them, — the Goshawk, Cooper's, and the Sharp-shinned, — while the rest are numbered among the best friends of the fruit-grower and farmer. Of the Woodpeckers, the Sapsucker and Red-head may be beneficial or injurious, according to circumstances, as is the Crow Blackbird, but the rest of the family are highly beneficial. The Crow probably does more good than harm in thickly settled parts of the country.

To most of the remaining birds tried, the evidence is decidedly creditable. The Cherry Bird or Cedar-bird is acquitted as doing more good than harm; and it is proved that agriculturists owe especial protection and friendship to the Robin, Bluebird, Phœbe, Kingbird, Catbird, Swallow, Brown Thrasher, Rose-breasted Grosbeak, House Wren, Vireos, Cuckoos, Orioles, Shore Lark, Loggerhead Shrike, Wood Thrush, Redwing, and Meadowlark.

So far as it has gone, the examination of the stomach contents of birds has proved that, except in rare cases where individuals attack cultivated fruits and grains, our native birds preserve the balance of nature by destroying weeds that plague the farmer, and by checking the insects that destroy the produce of the agriculturist. The great value of birds is demonstrated. The questions are, how to attract them where they have disappeared, and then how to protect the crops from their occasional depredations. Mr. Forbush, who has experimented in the matter in Massachusetts, both fed the birds and planted bushes to attract them. He says: "It is evident that a diversity of plants, which encourages diversified insect life and assures an abundance of fruits and seeds as an attraction to birds, will insure their presence."

The cultivated crops can be protected in two ways — either by mechanical devices that frighten the birds away from the fruit or grain fields, or by the substitution of wild or cultivated foods. To frighten the birds away, white twine can be strung across berry beds; string, hung with bits of glittering waste tin, over fields; while stuffed Hawks and cats can be kept in orchards. To attract the birds from cultivated fruit, it is well to plant some wild fruit that will bear during the weeks when the birds eat the garden or orchard crops. In this connection Mr. Forbush says: "I wish particularly to note the fact that the mulberry-trees, which ripen their berries in June, proved to be a protection to the cultivated cherries, as the fruit-eating birds seem to prefer them to the cultivated cherries, perhaps because they ripen somewhat earlier;" and he adds: "I believe it would be wise for the farmer to plant rows of these trees near his orchard, and it is possible that the early June berry or shadberry might also be useful in this respect."

Professor Beal, who has charge of the stomach examinations in the Biological Survey, suggests planting berry bushes along the roads and fences and between grain fields.

To protect strawberries and cherries (May and June), plant Russian mulberry and June berry or shadberry.

To protect raspberries and blackberries (July and August), plant mulberry, buckthorn, elder, and choke-cherry.

To protect apples, peaches, grapes (September and October), plant choke-cherries, elder, wild black cherry, and Virginia creeper.

To protect winter fruits, plant Virginia creeper, dogwood, mountain ash, bittersweet, viburnum, hackberry, bayberry, and pokeberry.

Mulberries are eaten by the Flycatchers, Warblers, Vireos, Cuckoos, Blackbirds, Orioles, Finches, Sparrows, Tanagers, Waxwings, Catbirds, Bluebirds, and Thrushes.

Potato beetles are eaten by the Rose-breasted Grosbeak, Cuckoo, Quail, Hairy Woodpecker, Chewink, and Whip-poor-will.

Tent-caterpillars (which do most harm to apple and cherry trees) are eaten by the Crow,

Chickadee, Oriole, Red-eyed Vireo, Yellow-billed Cuckoo, Black-billed Cuckoo, Chipping Sparrow, and Yellow Warbler.

Cutworms (which cut off corn, etc., before it is fairly started in the spring, and are very destructive to grass) are eaten by the Robin, Crow, Catbird, Loggerhead Shrike, House Wren, Meadowlark, Cowbird, Baltimore Oriole, Brown Thrasher, and Red-winged Blackbird.

Ants (which spread plant-lice, destroy timber, and infest houses) are the favorite food of the Catbird, Thrasher, House Wren, and Woodpeckers, and are eaten by almost all land birds except birds of prey.

Scale insects (which are a fruit-tree pest, injuring oranges, olives, etc.) are eaten by the Bushtit, Woodpeckers, and Cedar-bird.

The May beetle (which ravages forest trees, and also injures grain and grass lands) is eaten by the Hermit Thrush, Wood Thrush, Robin, Meadowlark, Brown Thrasher, Bluebird, Catbird, Blue Jay, Crow Blackbird, Crow, Loggerhead Shrike, Mockingbird, and Gray-cheeked Thrush.

Weevils (which injure grain, forage, and market gardens) are eaten by the Crow, Crow Blackbird, Red-winged Blackbird, Baltimore Oriole, Catbird, Brown Thrasher, House Wren, Meadowlark, Cowbird, Bluebird, Robin, Swallows, Flycatchers, Mockingbird, Woodpeckers, Wood Thrush, Alice's Thrush, and Scarlet Tanager.

The chinch bug (which eats grain and wheat) is eaten by the Brown Thrasher, Meadowlark, Catbird, Red-eyed Vireo, Robin, and Bob-white.

The wire worm (which causes heavy losses in the cornfield) is eaten by the Red-winged Blackbird, Crow Blackbird, Crow, Woodpeckers, Brown Thrasher, Scarlet Tanager, Robin, Catbird, Baltimore Oriole, Meadowlark, and Cowbird.

Crane flies (which eat grass roots in the hay fields) are eaten by the Robin, Catbird, Wood Thrush, Gray-cheeked Thrush, Olive-backed Thrush, Crow, Crow Blackbird, and Red-winged Blackbird.

Cotton worms are eaten by the Bluebird, Blue Jay, Red-winged Blackbird, Thrushes, Prairie Chicken, Quail, Kildeer, Bobolink, Mockingbird, Cardinal, Cuckoos, and Swallow-tailed Kite.

Gypsy Moth. — Mr. Forbush, ornithologist of the Massachusetts State Board of Agriculture, gives the following list of birds seen to feed on the gypsy moth: Yellow-billed Cuckoo, Black-billed Cuckoo, Hairy Woodpecker, Downy Woodpecker, Pigeon Woodpecker, Kingbird, Great-crested Flycatcher, Phœbe, Wood Pewee, Least Flycatcher, Blue Jay, Crow, Baltimore Oriole, Purple Grackle or Crow Blackbird, Chipping Sparrow, Chewink, Rose-breasted Grosbeak, Indigo-bird, Scarlet Tanager, Red-eyed Vireo, Yellow-throated Vireo, White-eyed Vireo, Black-and-white Warbler, Yellow Warbler, Chestnut-sided Warbler, Black-throated Green Warbler, Oven-bird, Maryland Yellow-throated Warbler, American Redstart, Catbird, Brown Thrasher, House Wren, White-breasted Nuthatch, Chickadee, Wood Thrush, American Robin, Bluebird, and English Sparrow.

Grasshoppers and crickets are eaten by the Mockingbird, Thrasher, Bluebird, Wrens, Shore Lark, Goldfinch, Longspur, Grasshopper Sparrow, Song Sparrow, Junco, Lark Sparrow, Dickcissel, Rose-breasted Grosbeak, Blue Grosbeak, Indigo Bunting, Cardinal, Chewink, Bobolink, Cowbird, Red-winged Blackbird, Meadowlark, Baltimore Oriole, Orchard Oriole, Rusty Blackbird, Crow, Blue Jay, Kingbird, Crow Blackbird, Whip-poor-will, Nighthawk, Swift, Cuckoo, Red-headed Woodpecker, Flicker, Barn Owl, Great Horned Owl, Marsh Hawk, Sparrow Hawk, Gulls, Swainson's Hawk, Quail, Shrikes, Swallows, Vireos, Robin, Catbird, Screech Owl, Red-shouldered Hawk, Ruffed Grouse, Wild Turkey, and Prairie Hen.

Army Worm. — In the Massachusetts Crop Report for July, 1896, Mr. William R. Sessions gives a list of the birds he has seen feeding on the army worm during the summer: Kingbird, Phœbe, Bobolink, Cowbird, Red-winged Blackbird, Baltimore Oriole, Crow Blackbird, Chipping Sparrow, and Robin.

How to keep Birds about our Houses. — Protection from enemies, food to live on, and suitable nesting sites are the three considerations that determine a bird's place of residence. As insects are most numerous on cultivated land, about houses, gardens, and fields where crops are grown, most birds, if not molested, prefer to live where man does. Their worst enemies are gunners and cats. Gunners may be kept away by posting one's woods with signs forbidding shooting, and one's yard may be kept free from cats by fencing. Mr. William Brewster, president of the American Ornithologists' Union, has found after many experiments that the best fence for the purpose is tarred fish net or seine, six feet high, attached at the top to flexible poles; at the bottom threaded by rods pinned to the ground by tent pegs. When a cat jumps against this fence, the poles bend toward her so that she falls backwards unable to recover herself or spring over.

When we have protected our birds from their enemies, the next thing is to provide them with suitable nesting places. They are particularly fond of tangles of shrubbery; and by planting a corner of the yard with sunflowers and wild berry-bearing bushes we can at once supply them with food and with good shelter for their nests. Pans of water add greatly to the comfort of birds and attract them to drink and bathe. Birds like Martins, Bluebirds, Wrens, and Chickadees will usually occupy artificial nesting places provided for them — such as cans, gourds, and bird houses.

In the summer it is a very simple matter to keep the birds about us by supplying the necessary conditions; but people who live in the country can get more pleasure from the companionship of birds in winter than summer, and the question is how to draw the winter ones from the woods. It can be done very easily by taking a little pains to feed them.

Bones and a few pieces of suet or the fat of fresh pork nailed to a tree are enough to attract Chickadees, Nuthatches, Woodpeckers, and Blue Jays; and a rind of salt pork will draw the salt-eating Crossbills when they are in the neighborhood. For food that can be blown away or snowed under — such as grain, or crumbs from the table — it is well to nail up boxes with open fronts, placing them with the back to the prevailing wind. As some birds prefer to feed on the ground, it is a good thing to keep a space clear of snow under a window, from which food can be thrown without disturbing them: shy birds like Grouse will come more freely to corn or buckwheat scattered on a barrel under the cover of an evergreen. A window shelf protected by awning is also an admirable thing.

Most of these devices have been employed with great success by Mrs. Davenport, in Brattleboro', Vermont. She has fed the birds hemp seed, sunflower seed, nuts, fine-cracked corn, and bread. As wheat bread freezes quickly, in very cold weather she uses bread made from one third wheat and two thirds Indian meal.

Her flock, during the winter of 1895-96, included, as daily visitors, seven to ten Blue Jays, more than twenty Chickadees, three Downy Woodpeckers, one Hairy Woodpecker, three Nuthatches, more than forty Tree Sparrows, and one Junco. After the first of February new recruits joined her band — more Juncos, Song Sparrows, Fox Sparrows, a Redpoll Linnet, and two Red-breasted Nuthatches; and in March a Swamp Sparrow came. A flock of Siskins were so tame that when the seed she threw to them rattled on their backs, they merely shook themselves. In March a flock of Tree Sparrows sang so cheerfully their chorus 'made the March morning like June.' Before the snow had gone, Purple Finches came, and they remained all summer. On June 15, 1896, the birds that came were Purple Finches, Downy Woodpeckers, Nuthatches, Robins, Orioles, Blue Jays, Chipping Sparrows, and sometimes a Scarlet Tanager or a Thrush. Then followed the interest of the nesting season, when the old birds brought their broods to the house to drink and bathe. Altogether the response to the hospitality offered the birds was so eager that throughout the year the family almost never had a meal by daylight without the presence of birds on the window shelf.

The pleasure Mrs. Davenport gets from her flock is particularly worthy of record, because it is open to such a large number of bird-lovers at the cost of a little trouble, and, as she herself tells us, "however much one may do for the birds, that which comes in the doing is a revelation of sources of happiness not before suspected."

FIELD COLOR KEY

TO ADULT SPRING MALES MENTIONED IN THIS BOOK.

I. BRIGHT OR STRIKINGLY-COLORED BIRDS.

PAGE
- **A.** BLUE CONSPICUOUS IN PLUMAGE . . . xxix
- **B.** RED CONSPICUOUS IN PLUMAGE . . . xxxi
- **C.** YELLOW OR ORANGE CONSPICUOUS IN PLUMAGE xxxiii
- **D.** BLACK OR BLACK AND WHITE CONSPICUOUS IN PLUMAGE xxxviii

II. DULL-COLORED BIRDS.

- **A.** OLIVE-GREEN OR OLIVE-BROWN . . . xlii
- **B.** GRAY OR BLUISH. xliii
- **C.** BROWN OR BROWNISH xlv

[For special keys to Hawks and Owls, see pp. 285, 296.]

I. BRIGHT OR STRIKINGLY-COLORED BIRDS.

A. BLUE CONSPICUOUS IN PLUMAGE.

1. LARGE; HEAD CRESTED.
    2. Upper parts and band across the white under parts bluish gray; white ring around head and neck. Found by water. Call, a loud rattle. Plunges into water for fish.

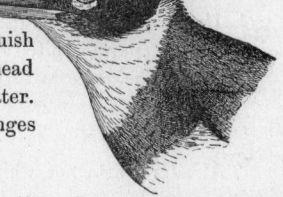

p. 157. BELTED KINGFISHER.

2'. Upper parts purplish blue, black ring around head and neck; wings and tail bright blue, barred with black and marked with white. Imitates cries of Hawks.

p. 154.   BLUE JAY.

1'. SMALL; HEAD NOT CRESTED.
3. *Body wholly blue or blue-black.*
 4. Shining blue-black . . . p. 48.   PURPLE MARTIN.

 4'. Ultramarine to cerulean blue and green.
p. 149.   INDIGO BUNTING.

3'. *Body not wholly blue or blue-black.*
 5. Under parts reddish brown.
  6. Upper parts steel-blue; tail deeply forked; forehead chestnut. Often seen skimming low over meadows for insects.

p. 49.   BARN SWALLOW.

 6'. Upper parts intense blue; tail not forked; forehead blue like back.   p. 41.   BLUEBIRD.

 5'. Under parts not reddish brown.
  7. Under parts white throughout; back steel-blue. Nests in trees or in bird-boxes.

p. 194.   TREE SWALLOW.

 7'. Under parts not white throughout; back grayish blue.

FIELD COLOR KEY

8. Throat and sides of breast black; back uniform, or with black markings in middle; small white spot on wing, which also identifies the dull, buffy olive female.

        p. 312.   BLACK-THROATED BLUE WARBLER.

8'. Throat and breast yellow, dark band on breast; back with yellowish patch; two white wing bars.

        p. 317.   PARULA WARBLER.

B. RED CONSPICUOUS IN PLUMAGE.

1. *Body mainly brownish.*

   Cap, rump, and under parts pinkish red. Seen in flocks in winter . . . . p. 236.   REDPOLL.

1'. *Body not mainly brownish.*
 2. GENERAL COLOR GREEN OR RED.
  3. *Body mainly green or greenish.*
   4. Scarlet crown patch. Migrant.

        p. 354.   RUBY-CROWNED KINGLET.

   4'. No crown patch; throat glancing ruby-red.

        p. 1.   RUBY-THROATED HUMMINGBIRD.

3'. *Body mainly red.*
 5. Bill crossed. Winter visitors that come in flocks with yellowish green females. Generally seen on coniferous trees. p. 234.   CROSSBILLS.

5'. Bill not crossed.
 6. *Wings and tail red.*
  7. Head with high crest; bill thick and red; black ring around base of bill. Female brownish; wings and tail dull red . . . . p. 65.   CARDINAL.

7'. Head without crest ; bill not thick or red ; no black around base of bill. Female olive-green and yellowish . . . . . p. 173. SUMMER TANAGER.

6'. *Wings and tail not red.*
 8. Wings and tail black, body scarlet. Female yellowish green. Found in northern woods . . p. 170. SCARLET TANAGER.

8'. Wings and tail brownish, body pinkish red ; bill short and thick.
 9. Large ; winter visitors.
   p. 231. PINE GROSBEAK.

9'. Small ; summer residents.
   p. 148. PURPLE FINCH.

2'. GENERAL COLOR BLACK OR BLACK AND WHITE.
 10. *Body black.*
  11. With red epaulettes. Bill long and pointed like an Oriole's. Song, *o-ka-lee.* Found in marshes.
   p. 96. RED-WINGED BLACKBIRD.

 11'. Without red epaulettes. Whole top of head red and crested ; nearly as large as Crow. Found in forests.
   p. 212. PILEATED WOODPECKER.

10'. *Body black and white.*
 12. Head wholly black or red.
  13. Head wholly red ; throat red ; belly white ; back and wings black and white in large patches. Often seen on fence posts.
   p. 131. RED-HEADED WOODPECKER.

13'. Head wholly black.
  14. Rose patch on breast; back black; rump and belly white; tail marked with white. Female sparrow-like.

  p. 166.   ROSE-BREASTED GROSBEAK.

  14'. Salmon-red patches on breast; tail marked with salmon . . . . p. 309.   REDSTART.

12'. Head not wholly black or red.
  15. Top of head red; throat red or reddish.
    16. Breast black, belly yellow. Found from Massachusetts northward in summer.

  p. 208.   YELLOW-BELLIED WOODPECKER.

    16'. No black on breast; under parts whitish, washed with red. Common in southern states.

  p. 211.   RED-BELLIED WOODPECKER.

  15'. Top of head not wholly red; throat white.
    17. Crown of head black; a small red spot on each side of back of head; back *barred* with white.

  p. 210.   RED-COCKADED WOODPECKER.

    17'. Crown of head with scarlet band behind; back *streaked* with white.
      18. Length 9 to 10 inches.

  p. 135.   HAIRY WOODPECKER.

      18'. Length 6 to 7 inches.

  p. 137.   DOWNY WOODPECKER.

C. YELLOW OR ORANGE CONSPICUOUS IN PLUMAGE.

1. *Whole head, throat, and most of back black.*
  2. Large; under parts orange; no salmon on wings or tail. Builds gray hanging nest, preferably in elms . . . . p. 56.   BALTIMORE ORIOLE.

xxxiv *FIELD COLOR KEY*

2′. Small; under parts white, with salmon-red patches on sides of breast, wings, and tail. Tail, when open, fan-shaped, showing salmon patches.

p. 309. REDSTART.

1′. *Whole head not black.*
3. CROWN BLACK.
    4. Throat and breast black; forehead and cheeks yellow.

p. 327. HOODED WARBLER.

4′. Throat and breast yellow.
    5. Back and under parts yellow.
        6. Wings and tail black ('Wild Canary').

p. 145. GOLDFINCH.

6′. Wings and tail not black. Migrant.

p. 339. WILSON'S WARBLER.

5′. Back olive; sides of throat black. Hunts near ground. Song, a loud ringing *klur-wee, klur-wee, klur-wee.*

p. 329. KENTUCKY WARBLER.

3′. CROWN NOT BLACK.
    7. Crown and throat red, breast black, belly yellow.

p. 208. YELLOW-BELLIED WOODPECKER.

7′. Crown and throat not red.
    8. *Rump conspicuously white or yellow.*
        9. Rump white, breast with black crescent. Large.

p. 127. FLICKER.

FIELD COLOR KEY XXXV

9'. Rump yellow. Small.

10. Crown with yellow patch; under parts black, yellow, and white; white wing bars and white on ends of tail feathers. First Warbler seen in spring and last in fall.

p. 310. YELLOW-RUMPED WARBLER.

10'. Crown bluish gray; under parts yellow, heavily streaked with black; large blotches of white on wings and middle of tail.

p. 324. BLACK AND YELLOW WARBLER.

8'. *Rump not white or yellow.*

11. Throat and sides of breast black; back olive-green, sometimes spotted with black; cheeks bright yellow; tail showing white.

p. 311. BLACK-THROATED GREEN WARBLER.

11'. Throat yellow or white.

12. Breast with solid black crescent; upper parts brown, streaked. White outer tail feathers seen in flight.

p. 106. MEADOWLARK.

12'. Breast without solid black crescent.

13. Throat with black spots or blotches forming necklace; sides not streaked; back, wings, and tail grayish, without white patches. Song, *rup-it-che, rup-it-che, rup-it-chitt-it-lit.*

p. 322. CANADIAN WARBLER.

13'. Throat without necklace.
  14. Sides of face and throat black, forming mask. Song, *witch-ery, witch-ery, witch-ery.*

        p. 315. MARYLAND YELLOW-THROAT.

14'. Sides of face and throat without black mask.
  15. Entire bird yellow; under parts streaked with reddish brown. Common in gardens, orchards, and shrubbery and along streams.

        p. 307. YELLOW WARBLER.

15'. Entire bird not yellow.
  16. *Back olive-green.*
    17. Crown with patch of different color.
      18. Crown patch orange and yellow, bordered by black.

        p. 356. GOLDEN-CROWNED KINGLET.

      18'. Crown patch chestnut; under parts bright yellow.
        19. Head bluish gray; under parts unstreaked.

        p. 322. NASHVILLE WARBLER.

        19'. Head not bluish gray; sides of throat and breast streaked.

        p. 316. YELLOW RED-POLL.

  17'. Crown without color patch.
    20. Throat and breast yellow; belly white or whitish.
      21. Wing crossed by two white bars; eye-ring yellow.

        p. 301. YELLOW-THROATED VIREO.

FIELD COLOR KEY

21'. Wing without bars; eye-ring and line to bill white; size large; song loud and varied.

p. 331.   YELLOW-BREASTED CHAT.

16'. *Back not olive-green.*

22. Back marked by distinct color patch between wings.

23. Back patch chestnut; cheeks marked with black; bird mainly yellow. Found in juniper thickets and bushy fields.

p. 325.   PRAIRIE WARBLER.

23'. Back patch yellow; bird mainly bluish; throat yellow; a bluish black or rufous band across breast; belly white. Nests in gray moss.

p. 317.   PARULA WARBLER.

22'. Back without color patch.

24. Throat with black patch; chin white; breast yellow; back brownish. Common in Mississippi valley. Sings in clover and grain fields.

p. 224.   DICKCISSEL.

24'. Throat without black patch; crown with patch of yellow or orange.

25. Crown patch orange; back mainly black; throat rich orange.

p. 326.   BLACKBURNIAN WARBLER.

25'. Crown patch yellow; sides chestnut. Back streaked with black; throat white.

p. 318. CHESTNUT-SIDED WARBLER.

D. BLACK OR BLACK AND WHITE CONSPICUOUS IN PLUMAGE.

1. MAINLY OR WHOLLY BLACK OR BLACKISH.
  2. *Wholly black or blackish.*
    3. Head and neck naked.
      4. Skin of head and neck red. Tips of wing feathers conspicuously separated in flight.

p. 263. TURKEY VULTURE.

   4'. Skin of head and neck black.

p. 265. BLACK VULTURE.

   3'. Head and neck not naked.
     5. Large; plumage always black. pp. 11, 16. CROWS.

     5'. Small; plumage rusty in fall.

p. 101. RUSTY BLACKBIRD.

  2'. *Not wholly black or blackish.*
    6. Head and neck brown or purplish.
      7. Head and neck brown . . . . p. 98. COWBIRD.

      7'. Head and neck purplish.

p. 93. CROW BLACKBIRDS.

    6'. Head and neck not brown or purplish.
      8. Red patches on shoulders.

p. 96. RED-WINGED BLACKBIRD.

      8'. No red patches on shoulders.
        9. *Back marked with white.*
          10. Under parts and top of head wholly black; back of neck with creambuff patch; back largely whitish.

p. 103. BOBOLINK.

FIELD COLOR KEY xxxix

10'. Under parts not wholly black; throat black; rose patch on breast; belly and rump white.

    p. 166. ROSE-BREASTED GROSBEAK.

9'. *Back not marked with white.*
  11. Throat black, belly white.
    12. Sides brown; tail showing white. Seen scratching among dead leaves on ground.

    p. 181. CHEWINK.

    12'. Sides salmon; tail showing salmon blotches. Seen flitting about undergrowth.

    p. 309. REDSTART.

1'. NOT MAINLY OR WHOLLY BLACK.
 2. *Wholly black and white.*
  3. Striped; head and under parts *not* clear white.
   4. Cap solid black.

    p. 321. BLACK-POLL WARBLER.

   4'. Cap striped black and white. Seen on tree trunks.

    p. 314. BLACK AND WHITE CREEPING WARBLER.

  3'. Not striped; head and under parts clear white.
   5. Size large; tail deeply forked. A southern bird of the air. Casual in Massachusetts.

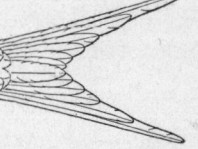

    p. 283. SWALLOW-TAILED KITE.

   5'. Size small; tail not forked; seen in flocks in winter, at which season its back is brownish.

    p. 223. SNOWFLAKE.

2'. *Not wholly black and white.*
  6. UNDER PARTS MAINLY YELLOW OR ORANGE.
    7. *Throat black.*
      8. Rest of under parts orange ; upper parts black and orange . . . . . p. 56. BALTIMORE ORIOLE.

      8'. Rest of under parts yellow ; head yellow and black, back olive . . . . p. 327. HOODED WARBLER.

    7'. *Throat not black.*
      9. Under parts without markings.
        10. Head with black cap.
          11. Wings and tail black . . p. 145. GOLDFINCH.

          11'. Wings and tail olive-green.
            12. No black on throat.
                    p. 339. WILSON'S WARBLER.

            12'. Black lines on sides of throat.
                    p. 329. KENTUCKY WARBLER.

        10'. Head without black cap ; a black band across forehead and cheeks.
                  p. 315. MARYLAND YELLOW-THROAT.

      9'. Under parts with markings ; head without black cap.
        13. Throat and crown red ; breast black, belly yellow . . p. 208. YELLOW-BELLIED WOODPECKER.

        13'. Throat and crown not red.
          14. *Back black;* wings and tail showing white.
            15. Throat and crown-patch orange.
                    p. 326. BLACKBURNIAN WARBLER.

            15'. Throat yellow ; crown bluish gray.
                    p. 324. BLACK AND YELLOW WARBLER.

          14'. *Back not black.*
            16. Size large ; black crescent on breast ; upper parts brownish . . . p. 106. MEADOWLARK.

16′. Size small; breast with necklace of black spots; upper parts gray.

p. 322.   CANADIAN WARBLER.

6′. UNDER PARTS NOT MAINLY YELLOW OR ORANGE.
17. *Top of head red.*
18. Back uniformly barred with black and white; under parts whitish, washed with red.

p. 211.   RED-BELLIED WOODPECKER.

18′. Back divided into black and white areas; whole head and throat red; belly white.

p. 131.   RED-HEADED WOODPECKER.

17′. *Top of head not red.*
19. Breast and belly chestnut; whole head, throat, and most of back black . . p. 61. ORCHARD ORIOLE.

19′. Breast and belly not chestnut; whole head not black.
20. Front of head and throat white; back of head and neck blackish; rest of body mainly grayish; plumage soft and fluffy. Northern birds.

p. 217.   CANADA JAY.

20′. Front of head and throat not white; back of head and neck not blackish.
21. *Upper parts blue.*
22. Head crested; throat gray with black collar.

p. 154.   BLUE JAY.

22′. Head not crested; throat and sides black.

p. 312.   BLACK-THROATED BLUE WARBLER.

21′. *Upper parts not blue.*
23. Throat white, sides of breast and rump yellow; breast black.

p. 310.   YELLOW-RUMPED WARBLER.

23'. Throat and sides of breast black; sides of head yellow.
p. 311. BLACK-THROATED GREEN WARBLER.

II. DULL-COLORED BIRDS.

                                      PAGE
    A. OLIVE-GREEN OR OLIVE-BROWN xlii
    B. GRAY OR BLUISH xliii
    C. BROWN OR BROWNISH xlv

A. OLIVE-GREEN OR OLIVE-BROWN.

1. UNDER PARTS SPOTTED.
 2. Crown with cap of different color.
  Crown golden, bordered by black lines. Common in dry woodlands. Song, a crescendo *teach*, or *teacher, teacher, teacher, teacher*.
  p. 333. OVEN-BIRD.

 2'. Crown without cap of different color.
  3. White line over eye; under parts streaked with black, *except on throat and middle of belly*. Wild, shy bird, difficult to approach.
  p. 336. LOUISIANA WATER-THRUSH.

  3'. Buffy line over eye; under parts — *including throat* — streaked with black. Comparatively tame and unsuspicious.
  p. 335. WATER-THRUSH.

1'. UNDER PARTS NOT SPOTTED.
 4. Head striped; top of head with four black lines alternating with yellowish lines. Found in dry, open woodland, near the ground . . . . p. 337. WORM-EATING WARBLER.

 4'. Head not striped.
  5. *Crown with red or orange patch.* p. 357. KINGLETS.

FIELD COLOR KEY

5′. *Crown without red or orange patch*.
  6. With wing bars.
    7. Conspicuous yellow ring around eye; eye white. Found in undergrowth. Song emphatic: "*Who are you, eh?*". . . . p. 302. WHITE-EYED VIREO.

    7′. No yellow ring around eye; eye dark. Found by streams in woods. Call, *pe-ah-yuk′*.
        p. 254. ACADIAN FLYCATCHER.

  6′. Without wing bars.
    8. White line over eye.
      Cap gray, bordered by blackish. Song broken and in triplets. Common everywhere in trees.
        p. 120. RED-EYED VIREO.

    8′. No white line over eye.
      Head and back uniform olive-gray. Song a sweet flowing warble. Found high in village elms.
        p. 126. WARBLING VIREO.

B. GRAY OR BLUISH GRAY.

1. PLUMAGE DISTINCTLY MARKED WITH BLACK.
  2. Throat black.
    Cap black, back gray. Call, *chick-a-dee*.
        pp. 67, 71. CHICKADEES.

2′. Throat not black.
  3. *Back bluish*.
    4. Top of head black; seen on tree trunks.
      5. Under parts white; no line on side of head. Common resident from Gulf states to Canada.
        p. 73. WHITE-BREASTED NUTHATCH.

5'. Under parts brown ; black line on side of head. Winter visitor ; nests mainly in mountains, or north of United States.

p. 76. RED-BREASTED NUTHATCH.

4'. Top of head bluish ; not seen on tree trunks. Tail black ; outer feathers white. Flits about actively, catching insects.

p. 357. BLUE-GRAY GNATCATCHER.

3'. *Back gray or slate.*
6. Crown gray like back ; black bar on side of face ; sides of tail white. Perches in exposed positions.

p. 300. SHRIKES.

6'. Crown black ; no black on face ; no white on tail ; under parts slate ; under tail patch reddish brown. Frequents thickets.

p. 6. CATBIRD.

1.' PLUMAGE NOT DISTINCTLY MARKED WITH BLACK.
7. Outer tail feathers white ; head not crested.
 8. Back and breast slate gray ; belly abruptly white. Common, familiar Snowbird.

p. 221. JUNCO.

8'. Back lighter gray ; breast and belly white ; size large. A well-known bird of the southern states.

p. 63. MOCKINGBIRD.

7'. Outer tail feathers not white ; head with high crest ; size small. Song, *pe-to, pe-to, pe-to.*

p. 151. TUFTED TITMOUSE.

FIELD COLOR KEY

xlv

C. BROWN OR BROWNISH.

1. SIZE RATHER LARGE.
 2. *Conspicuous white patches on wings, tail, or rump.*
  3. Wings long and pointed.
   4. Wings marked with white bar; no white on rump; tail forked; throat white; no bristles at base of bill. Call, *peent*, heard as bird flies high in air.

p. 188.   NIGHTHAWK.

   4'. Wings not marked with white bar; rump white; tail not forked . . . . p. 278.   MARSH HAWK.

  3'. Wings rather short and rounded, not marked with white; tail not forked.
   5. Rump white; under side of wings and tail yellow; black crescent on breast . . . p. 127.   FLICKER.

   5'. Rump not white; under side of wings and tail not yellow.
    6. Throat blackish, bordered by white bar; whole outer side of tail white; conspicuous bristles at base of bill.

p. 185.   WHIP-POOR-WILL.

    6'. Throat *not* blackish; white of tail limited.
     7. *Top of head not same color as back.* Forehead brownish; back of head bluish slate; tail graduated and showing white bordering in flight.

p. 29.   MOURNING DOVE.

FIELD COLOR KEY

7'. *Top of head same color as back.*
  8. Head and back bluish slate; breast pinkish. Outer tail feathers, only, showing grayish white in flight . . . . p. 78. PASSENGER PIGEON.

8'. *Head and back brownish; under parts whitish.*
  9. Lower half of bill yellow; outer tail feathers black, broadly tipped with white; wings largely rufous; ring around eye yellow.
         p. 160. YELLOW-BILLED CUCKOO.

  9'. Lower half of bill black; outer tail feathers brown, very narrowly tipped with white; wings without rufous; ring around eye red. p. 163. BLACK-BILLED CUCKOO.

2'. *No white patches on wings, tail, or rump.*
  10. Form slender; tail long; upper parts rich reddish brown; under parts white, heavily streaked with black. Song long and varied . . . . . . p. 177. BROWN THRASHER.

  10'. Form stout, hen-like; tail not long; body covered with markings.

      11. Neck with conspicuous black ruff; end of tail barred.
             p. 32. RUFFED GROUSE.

      11'. Neck without ruff; end of tail not barred.
             p. 37. BOB-WHITE; QUAIL.

RUFFED GROUSE.

FIELD COLOR KEY

1'. SIZE MEDIUM OR SMALL.
 2. Breast reddish brown or pinkish.
  3. Breast reddish brown ; top of head blackish.
     p. 17.   ROBIN.

  3'. Breast and forehead pinkish.   p. 31.   GROUND DOVE.

 2'. Breast not reddish brown or pinkish.
  4. Tail ending in needle-like spines ; wings long, narrow, and curved.
     p. 23.   CHIMNEY SWIFT.

  4'. Tail not ending in needle-like spines.
   5. Head with high crest ; end of tail with yellow band.
      p. 141.   WAXWING.

   5'. Head without high crest ; end of tail without yellow band.
    6. Forehead and throat yellow ; a slender tuft of black feathers over each eye ; a black bar across front of head, and black crescent on breast.
       p. 261.   HORNED LARK.

    6'. Forehead and throat not yellow ; no tuft of feathers over eyes ; no black bar across head.
     7. Tail with white bar across end ; crown with concealed orange patch ; under parts whitish.
        p. 83.   KINGBIRD.

     7'. Tail without white bar; crown without color patch.
      8. Tail showing reddish in flight ; throat pearl gray ; belly yellow ; head moderately crested.
         p. 255.   GREAT-CRESTED FLYCATCHER.

8'. Tail not showing reddish in flight; throat not gray; belly not yellow.

9. Upper parts uniform brownish or olive-brown; no spots, streaks, or bars above or below; usually seen making short sallies into the air for insects, returning to the same perch or another convenient one.

p. 260. FLYCATCHERS.

9'. Upper parts not uniform brownish or brownish olive; body more or less marked.

10. Wings long and powerful; feet small and weak; usually seen on the wing.

p. 196. SWALLOWS.

10'. Wings not long and powerful; feet not small and weak; not usually seen on the wing.

11. Tail stiff and pointed, used as a prop in climbing. Seen on tree trunks . . p. 349. BROWN CREEPER.

11'. Tail not stiff and pointed, and not used as a prop in climbing.

12. Bill conical for cracking seeds; color variable; mostly ground and bush-haunting birds.

p. 246. FINCHES AND SPARROWS.

12'. Bill slender for catching insects.

13. Wagtails; tails constantly wagged; usually seen in flocks on ground. Hind toe-nail elongated . . . . . . p. 348. PIPIT.

13'. Not Wagtails.
 14. Size relatively large; upper parts and tail not barred or streaked; breast spotted . . . . . p. 360. THRUSHES.

 14'. Size relatively small; upper parts or tail barred or streaked; breast not spotted . . . . p. 205. WRENS.

BIRDS OF VILLAGE AND FIELD

Fig. 1.

Ruby-throated Hummingbird: *Trochilus colubris.*

Adult male, upper parts, bright green; throat, metallic ruby red. *Female and young*, similar, but without red on throat. Length, about 3¾ inches.

GEOGRAPHIC DISTRIBUTION. — Eastern North America; breeds from Florida to Labrador; winters from southern Florida to Central America.

What tantalizing little sprites these airy darters are! Quietly feeding before the trumpet-vine over the piazza one moment, gone with a whirr the next, where, how far, who can say? As the mother bird vanishes and reappears, reappears and vanishes, it becomes plain that she is carrying food to her young. Her nest is the most exquisite of all the beautiful structures of winged architects, her domestic life and ways of caring for her young among the most original and curious. Surely the patience of the bird-lover should be equal to the task of discovering her home. When found, it proves to be, like its builder, the smallest of its kind, a thimble of plant-down coated with delicate green lichen, formed and decorated with wonderful skill, and saddled so dextrously to a bough that it would seem but a part of the tree itself. When the eggs are first laid, their white shells are so thin as to be almost transparent, and when the young come out of the little white pearls it seems a seven days' marvel that such mites can ever become birds.

It takes three full weeks for them to reach man's estate and leave the nest. During that time the care of the mother is most interesting. She is certainly kept busy, for sixteen young spiders have been found in the stomach of a nestling only two days old. The Hummer feeds the young by regurgitation, plunging her needle-like bill into their tiny throats — 'a frightful-looking act,' as Mr. Torrey says. When she finds the brood ready to leave the nest, her anxiety becomes so great that her nerves quite get the better of her. One mother bird Mr. Torrey was watching at such a time went so far as to leave her tree and fly tempestuously at an innocent Sparrow, driving him well out of the tomato patch.

When her young were fairly launched upon the world, her happiness was shown by a most remarkable exhibition of 'maternal ecstasy.' She came intending to feed a nestling perched on a branch, but then, as a human mother unexpectedly stops to caress her little one, she opened her wings and circled around her little bird's head. Lighting beside him, her feelings again overcame her, and she rose and flew around him once more. As Mr. Torrey writes, "It was a beautiful act, . . . beautiful beyond the power of any words of mine to set forth; . . . the sight repaid all my watchings thrice over, and even now I feel my heart growing warm at the recollection of it." "Strange thoughtlessness, is it not," he asks pertinently, "which allows mothers capable of such passionate devotion — tiny, defenseless things — to be slaughtered by the million for the enhancement of woman's charms!"

While the mother is so devotedly caring for her little ones, what is the father doing? That seems to be the question. Mr. Torrey has been looking up the matter, and in 'The Footpath Way' tells us that out of fifty nests of which he has had reports, only two were favored by the presence of the male, as far as the evidence went. On the other hand, Mr. Torrey himself watched one male who, whether a householder or a bachelor, devoted himself most assiduously to doing nothing. Hour after hour, day after day, and week after week, he was found perching in the same tree, apparently scarcely allowing himself time for three meals a day. Here certainly are mysteries worth clearing up. Such conduct must not pass unchallenged. Let each field student hie forth with glass and book, and wrest from these unnatural Benedicts full accounts of themselves.

It is not in its home life alone that the Hummingbird is interesting. We can hardly see one without being filled with wonder. While standing in the garden watching the 'burly dozing humblebee' wandering in 'waving lines' from flower to flower, who has not been startled by the sudden vision of a whizzing Hummer darting past straight to some favorite blossom? How do these little flower-lovers work together — does the world hold blooms enough for bee and bird, or can the bee glean when the Hummingbird has done? This much we know: while, as Emerson says, the bee is 'sipping only what is sweet,' the Hummer is probing for tiny gauzy wings hidden in the sweet.

And, whatever their own wants, both little creatures are at work helping to carry out the marvelous ends of the great mother Nature; for while the plants supply them with food, they in turn leave the flowers laden with rich pollen, carrying it on their rounds, and leaving it where it will give new life to other blossoms.

How perfectly the little feathered messenger is fitted for his task! See the long bill that enables him to probe the flower tubes. Watch him as he feeds before a honeysuckle. There he stands as steadily as though perched on a branch, held up by the whirring mill fan-wings whose rapid motion renders them almost invisible. What power is lodged in those inch-long feathers! In autumn they will bear him away over rivers, over mountains, far from the snow-covered north, to the land of the orange and palm.

In nature the race is to the swift, and surely these little Hummingbirds are well fitted to compete with their fellows. Even their dress is perfectly adapted to the conditions of their lives. To attract the favor of his lady, the Hummingbird wooer has a throat of flaming ruby; while she, to whom a flashing gorget would bring danger at the nest, is clad in quiet green; and the young, untaught in the ways and dangers of the great world, are dressed in the inconspicuous tints of their mother.

Fig. 2.

Catbird: *Galeoscoptes carolinensis.*

Body, slate gray; cap and tail, black; patch under base of tail, reddish brown. *Length*, about 9 inches.

GEOGRAPHIC DISTRIBUTION. — Breeds from the northern portion of the Gulf states to New Brunswick; west to the Rocky Mountains and Saskatchewan; winters from Florida southward to Panama.

To any one who really knows him, it seems almost incredible that this much loved bird of our gardens and homes, this Mockingbird of the north, should be the subject of persecution, but so it often is; for however much the birds trust us, and whatever pleasure they give us, if they chance to help themselves to ever so little of our fruit — material creatures that we are — all the rest is forgotten, and they are at once doomed. Ordinarily the Catbirds take such a small fraction of the growing fruit that we should be glad to share with them, and even when they take more, a third of their diet for the year is still made up of injurious insects. Putting aside all sentiment, however, as a simple matter of economics it is bad policy to destroy any bird, except as a last resort. As has been said by Mr. Judd, one of the government examiners of their food, "by killing the birds their services as insect-destroyers would be lost, so the problem is to keep both the birds and the fruit." The study of this problem has led to a most important discovery, that some birds, the Catbird among the number, actually prefer wild fruit to cultivated. Most of the complaints of depredations come from parts of the country where there is little wild fruit. From this it will be seen that by planting berry-bearing bushes and trees it may be possible to prevent losses to cultivated fruits, and at the same time attract more birds, and so secure their much-needed help in destroying insect pests. A slight idea of the good the Catbird does in destroying pests may be had from the fact that 30 grasshoppers have been found in each of 5 Catbird stomachs, while one third of the bird's food is made up of insects. Experiments have shown that he prefers the red mulberry to cherries and strawberries; and stomach examinations show that he eats twice as much wild fruit as cultivated. He is reported to do much more harm in the central United States, where wild fruits are scarce, than near the coast, where they are abundant. Mr. Judd suggests that where he does damage to cherries and strawberries, such crops can be protected by planting the prolific Russian mulberry, which also affords good food for domestic fowls. In speaking of the Catbird's diet, Mr. Nehrling, who has made a special study of the food of birds, assures us that the Catbird's " usefulness as a destroyer of innumerable noxious insects cannot be estimated too highly," that " it is a service compared with which the small allowance of fruit it steals is of little importance;" for "from early morning to sunset it watches over the fruit-trees and kills the insects that would destroy them or their fruit." " Of course it takes its share, especially of cherries, but for every one it takes, it eats thousands of insects;" and the economist concludes wisely, " Where there are no small birds there will be little fruit." When feeding their young, the Catbirds are continually bringing them numbers of caterpillars, grasshoppers, moths, beetles, spiders, and other insects, and in the south the numbers are doubled, as the birds raise two broods.

The old birds often begin preparing for the second family a few days after the first has left the nest; but, while the female is engaged, the male takes care of the first brood, warning, feeding, and guiding them till, by the time the second brood claim the father's attention, the first know how to care for themselves. "That the parents love their young exceedingly," as Mr. Nehrling says, "is evident on approaching the nest. With anxious cries, with ruffled plumage, and drooping wings they flutter about the intruder." If reassured by kindness, though, they become very trustful, and discriminate only against those they do not know. One pair which the ornithologist watched "would allow even the children to look at their eggs and young without becoming in the least uneasy and frightened. They certainly knew that they were protected and that the children too loved them. But as soon as a stranger approached the structure they screamed so loudly and evinced such noisy distress that the chickens in the barnyard cackled, and old hens hurried to get their broods in safety." In protecting their young against cats and snakes in the woods and thickets, the birds make such a commotion they warn other birds and even quadrupeds of impending danger. The nest which the Catbird defends with so much courage is a bulky mass of twigs, grasses, and dead leaves, and is lined with rootlets; a very different type from the compact, delicate little cup of the Hummingbird. But if there is any lack of beauty in the nest itself, it is made up by the eggs, which are a rich greenish blue, and might well excite the pride of any mother bird.

While the Catbird's reputed power of mimicry is very great, some consider its song almost entirely original. Besides the song, and the mewing call that has given the bird its name, Mr. Bicknell, in his valuable paper on 'The Singing of our Birds,' calls attention to another "characteristic vocal accomplishment — a short, sharp, crackling sound, like the snapping of small fagots" — which, he adds, is heard in the dog days, and is generally given hurriedly as the bird seeks the security of some bushy patch, or darts into the thick cover along the road.

For several summers one of these friendly birds was the chorister and companion of a gentle old lady, a lover of birds and flowers, who lived alone in a cottage hidden behind an old-fashioned garden, whose rose-covered trellises and rich masses of fragrant blooming lilacs, flowering shrubs, and encircling trees made a favorite resting-place for feathered travelers in spring and fall, and the chosen home of many birds in summer. Of all those that built in the garden, the Catbird was the pet and comrade of the garden's hospitable owner. When she threw open her blinds in the morning, he would fly up and call till she came out and answered him; then he would seat himself contentedly and pour out his morning song. During the day he would often call her to the window or door in the same way, never resting till she whistled back to him. His nest was in a tangle beside the garden fence, which ran under a cover of bushes; and after he had promenaded back and forth on it all day, attending to his domestic duties, at sunset he would fly to his favorite branch in the garden to sing before his sympathetic friend. And so, through the soft twilight, as she sat alone looking out upon the flaming poppies, opening yellow primroses, and tall stately lilies, cheered and enraptured she would listen to his impassioned sunset song. That the friendly bird was really attracted to the garden by his love of human companionship was shown presumably one spring, for his gentle mistress was away from home when he came north, and though the garden was blooming, it apparently seemed deserted to him, for he went elsewhere to build his nest. When the old lady returned she missed him sadly, but later she was satisfied that it was he who sometimes appeared in the garden at sunset and sang to her in the home trees.

American Crow: *Corvus americanus*.

Entirely black, with steel-blue or purplish reflections. *Length*, about 19¼ inches.

GEOGRAPHIC DISTRIBUTION. — North America, from the fur countries to Mexico; winters from the northern United States southward.

Crows are known to every one, and most of us have seen long lines of them straggling across the sky at sunset, and have watched the black processions, more scattered and flying low, as the birds returned looking for food the following morning. The country people tell us they are going to a Crow caucus, and perhaps that is as near the truth as we can guess; for, if they do not gather to talk things over, it is surely the social instinct that moves them. In some places, as many as 300,000 gather at these nightly roosts, scattering to their feeding grounds when morning comes. One of the winter roosts is on historic ground at Arlington, the old home of General Lee. This roost covers fifteen acres of land, and all winter, from the middle of the afternoon till twilight, the birds may be seen from Washington crossing over the Potomac to the heights beyond. Some years ago Staten Island was visited by birds from three New Jersey roosts in winter, and in summer there were two roosts on the island itself.

When the Crows scatter to nest, scarecrows appear in the country, for the farmers are much troubled by the sight of the birds in the cornfields. Professor Beal acknowledges that when Crows and Blackbirds gather in great numbers about cornfields, or Woodpeckers are noticed at work in an orchard, it is perhaps not surprising that they are accused of doing harm. But he adds that careful investigation will often show that they are actually destroying noxious insects, and that even those which do harm at one season may compensate for it by eating noxious species at another. When the Crows are actually eating corn, however, the dangling, dejected-looking effigies put out to scare them have little effect; but cords strung across a field, and hung with bits of tin that swing and glitter in the sun, seem to suggest a trap, and so keep the wary birds away. A still surer method of crop protection is to soak some corn in tar and scatter it on the borders of the field subject to their attacks. A few quarts of corn used in this way will protect a field of eight to ten acres.

Professor Beal's conclusions regarding this much-discussed bird are, that "in the more thickly settled parts of the country the Crow probably does more good than harm, at least when ordinary precautions are taken to protect newly planted corn and young poultry against his depredations. If, however, corn is planted with no provision against possible marauders, if hens and turkeys are allowed to nest and to roam with their broods at a distance from farm buildings, losses must be expected." It certainly seems worth while to take a little trouble to make the Crows harmless, for they eat so many

Fig. 3.
Grasshopper, eaten extensively by Crows.

grasshoppers, tent-caterpillars, May beetles, and other pests that their service in destroying injurious insects can hardly be overestimated. When gypsy moths are stripping the woods of their foliage, the old Crows often take their young to feed on them; besides this, they kill so many field-mice, rabbits, and other harmful rodents that, apart from their good offices as scavengers, they prove themselves most valuable farm hands.

Some farmers appreciate this, and, when not tarring the corn, take the trouble to feed the birds old corn during the time when they would be pulling up the young sprouts, for they realize that the workman is worthy of his hire, and would no more think of shooting Crows than horses and cows because they demand grain in in return for their work.

Though the Crow is of especial interest to the farmer, he is of still greater interest to the bird student; for he is one of the drollest, most intelligent, and individual of birds. His sedate walk, his gestures and conversation, proclaim him a bird of originality and reflection, who will repay our closest study. He is sure to be discovered in peculiar pursuits. Doctor Mearns found him

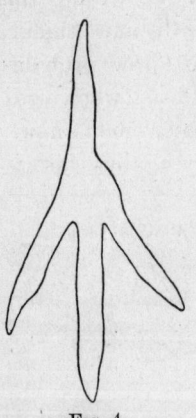

Fig. 4.
Footprint of Crow.

fishing through the ice on the Hudson, watching at the fissures in the ice alongshore, at low tide, pulling out whatever fish were passing. And we are told by Mr. A. M. Frazer of an original pet Crow who had a way of his own to rid himself of parasites. He would "deliberately take his stand upon an ant mound and permit the ants to crawl over him and carry away the troublesome vermin."

The intelligence of the Crow is also seen at the nest, where his domestic virtues shine out brightly. To cradle his heavy young, he picks out strong twigs and carries them high up in a treetop, and, when the nest is done, stands guard over his handsome green eggs, and later his young, by keenly scrutinizing all passing gunners and boys of evil intent. Nuttall ascribes strong family affection to the Crows. He thinks they remain mated through life, and says that, not only does the male feed his mate on the nest and brood the eggs in her absence, but when the young have left the nest, both old birds "continue the whole succeeding summer to succor and accompany their offspring in all their undertakings and excursions."

Fish Crow: *Corvus ossifragus*.

Entirely black, more glossy than the common Crow, and usually much smaller. *Length*, 16 inches.

GEOGRAPHIC DISTRIBUTION. — Gulf and Atlantic coast as far north as southern Connecticut; resident except at the extreme northern part of its range.

In Washington the Fish Crows are very common, and the black figures may often be seen on the towers of the Smithsonian, when their raven-like croak may be plainly heard and interpreted as a solemn 'never more' by jocose ornithologists discussing their stuffed brothers inside. In the National Zoölogical Park they are more common than the ordinary Crow, and may be seen wading in the shallows of Rock Creek. When the other Crows are with them, they may still be readily known, if not by their smaller size, by their hoarse, guttural *car*, which Mr. Burroughs describes as less masculine than the clear, strong *caw* of the American Crow.

Fig. 5.

Robin: *Merula migratoria.*

Adults, upper parts blackish brown; under parts bright reddish brown; throat striped black and white; corners of tail white. *Young in nesting plumage,* spotted with black. *Length,* 10 inches.

GEOGRAPHIC DISTRIBUTION. — Breeds from the mountains of the Carolinas and Virginia westward to the Great Plains, and northward to the arctic coast; winters from southern Canada and the northern states (irregularly) southward.

Though the Robin is a common bird, he is uncommonly interesting, because he is an old friend, and so secure of our friendship that he lets us share his home life as few birds will. Great intelligence was shown by a Robin family of my acquaintance, not only in the construction of the strong adobe frame for their nest, but — after the hatching of the blue eggs — in methods of family government and parental care; in disciplining the greedy, carefully feeding the weak; and finally, when the tremulous nestlings were launched on their own wings, in teaching them caution, and driving off their enemies sometimes, in cases of extraordinary danger, by rousing the neighborhood against the threatening monsters. What human tenderness the old birds show in their family relations, not only in caring for their little ones, but in the small offices of daily happy companionship! how grateful is the gentle song, how tender the watchful solicitude of the male, and how trustful the quiet home affection of his mate as they work together for their brood!

Other delights of discovery await the patient, unobtrusive observer as he listens to the song of the Robin, with its individual variations — the cries of warning, anxiety, and simple good cheer; the joyous daybreak chorus; the tender carol at the nest, and the low, meditative evening song rising from the dewy lawn.

But, beside the sympathy and affection which the Robin rouses by his love and song, the bird has a habit which in recent years has called the attention of the ornithological world to him with renewed interest. Mr. William Brewster has announced that, as the Crow resorts to roosts in winter and after the nesting season, the Robin betakes him to similar roosts before and during the nesting season, sometimes as many as 25,000 birds being found together.[1] Most commonly, the male Robin seems to go to the nightly roosts with his first brood of big spotted young while his mate is on the nest with her second set of eggs or young. At first this seems too much like the club habit which affects family men of larger growth, but on closer examination it proves very harmless. Mr. Walter Faxon, a close observer of a roosting father bird, found him a most exemplary Robin. He did not leave home till nearly sunset, after he had fed his little family of young for the night. Then he flew to the top of a spruce-tree, and, "after singing a good-night to his wife and babies, took a direct flight for the roost." Then next morning the "model husband and father returned to his family at 3.40 (sunrise, 4.29), his arrival being announced by his glad call and morning song." Indeed, far from interfering with family life, the summer Robin roosts have an important office to fulfill, for in going to them the young birds are taught to follow the lead of their parents, and so prepared for the migration that is before them.

On their way south, near St. Louis, Mr. Otto Widmann has found the Robins roosting in winter

[1] *The Auk*, vol. vii. No. iv. p. 360; *The Footpath Way*, p. 153.

in a tract of reeds.[1] In ordinary winters they probably remain till spring, he thinks, but when severe weather comes presumably go on to roosts still farther south.

As the Robin is particularly fond of wild fruit, he can winter comfortably wherever wild berries still cling to the bushes. This diet seems to agree with him, though nearly half his food for the year is animal. He not only eats wasps, bugs, spiders, angle-worms, and a large number of grasshoppers, crickets, and caterpillars, but destroys the March fly larvæ that injure the grass in the hayfield. He also ate the army worm that invaded the country in 1896 (Fig. 6). The Robin has been accused of taking cultivated fruit, but examinations show that less than 5 per cent. of his food is grown by man. As Professor Bruner, the author of 'Birds of Nebraska,' and one of the close students of bird economy, pertinently remarks: "He is a poor business man who pays ten dollars for that which he knows must later be sold for fifteen cents or even less. Yet I have known of instances where a Robin that had saved from ten to fif-

Fig. 6. Army Worm, eaten by Robin.

[1] *The Auk*, vol. xii. No. i. p. 1.

teen bushels of apples that were worth a dollar per bushel, by clearing the trees from cankerworms in the spring, was shot when he simply pecked one of the apples that he had saved for the grateful or ungrateful fruit-grower." Professor Beal, who has made a study of the Robin question, suggests that as the Russian mulberry ripens at the same time as the cherry, if those who complain that the Robin eats their cherries will only plant a few mulberry bushes around their gardens or orchards, they will probably protect the more valuable fruit. The wild fruits the Robin eats are of interest to most bird-lovers as showing what can be planted not only to prevent the bird from doing harm, but to attract him about our homes. The wild fruits found in his stomach are dogwood, wild grapes, wild black cherry, choke-cherry, bird cherry, mulberry, greenbrier berry, cranberry, blueberry, huckleberry, holly berry, elderberry, hackberry, service berry, spice berry, hawthorn, bittersweet, Virginia creeper, moonseed, mountain ash, black haw, barberry, pokeberry, strawberry bush, juniper, persimmon, saw palmetto, California mistletoe, and bayberry.

Many of these berries remain on the bushes till winter, and so keep the birds from going south for food, for the Robin will linger if he can find anything to live on. Doubtless it was imagination, for others report differently, but the Robins I saw in Florida sat around in the orange groves with a homesick air, as if they were only waiting till time to start home again. When they do come back, what good cheer they bring with them! I remember one long winter spent in the country when it seemed that spring would never come. At last one day the call of a Robin rang out, and on one of the few bare spots made by the melting snow there stood the first redbreasts! It was a sight I can never forget, for the intense delight of such moments make bright spots in a lifetime.

Wood Thrush : *Turdus mustelinus.*

(See Fig. 220, p. 361.)

Upper parts warm brown, *brightest on head;* under parts white, heavily spotted with black. *Length*, about 8¼ inches.

GEOGRAPHIC DISTRIBUTION. — Eastern United States; breeds as far north as Minnesota, Massachusetts, and Ontario; winters in Central America.

The Wood Thrush is probably the best known and the most familiar of the thrushes. In Norwich, Connecticut, I have seen it nesting close by the sidewalk of a village street.

Its large size, heavily spotted breast, and the rich golden brown of its back, brightest on its head, distinguish it from the other thrushes.

Its nest is sometimes near the ground, but usually fifteen to twenty-five feet above it. The nest is made largely of leaves, and has an inner wall of mud, like that of its cousin the Robin, and its eggs are similar to the Robin's.

The call note of the Wood Thrush is a rapid *pit-pit;* his song a calm, rich melody which, heard beside the chorus of spring songs, chattering Wrens, loquacious Vireos, and jovial Catbirds, Thrashers and Chats, sets vibrating chords that none of the others touch. As a young woman told me once, after first hearing the Thrush: "I don't know what it is, but," putting her hand on her heart, "it makes me feel queer." Indeed, the song is so distinct one does not need to build up associations in order to appreciate it, as is the case with so many songs, but can at once feel the quieting touch of its hymn-like melody.

Chimney Swift: *Chætura pelagica.*

(Plate II. p. 24.)

GEOGRAPHIC DISTRIBUTION. — Breeds from Florida to Labrador; west to the Great Plains; winters in Mexico and Central America.

Among the commonest birds seen in the sky over a New England village are the Swifts. They are dark little birds, who row through the air like racers, twittering socially as they go. Sometimes as you watch them on a village street you will see them suddenly stop short and pitch down the black mouth of a chimney, for it is now only the most old-fashioned ones who nest in hollow trees.

In many inland towns, attention is attracted to the Swifts by their habit of roosting at night in the large chimneys of church or court-house. In Wooster, Ohio, Mr. Oberholser has seen as many as a thousand about the court-house, and large numbers have been noted in Norwich, Conn. It is interesting to watch their movements. As Nuttall says, when the birds go to roost, "before descending, they fly in large flocks, making many ample and circuitous sweeps in the air; and as the point of the vortex falls, individuals drop into the chimney by degrees, until the whole have descended."

However much we believe in change of scene, it seems odd for a balloonist to live in a cellar, to be coursing about among the stars one moment, hung up on the wall of a dark sooty flue the next; but the Swifts are quite put to it, for it would be very bad form, in fact do outrage to all the traditions of the race, if one of them were to perch on a tree for a moment. There is actually no record of their alighting anywhere except in a hollow tree or chimney. They even gather their nesting materials on the wing, breaking off bits of twig in their feet and, it is said, with their bills, literally, in passing. Accordingly, as by our deeds the world knows us, their wings are developed till they look like strips of cardboard more than bunches of feathers, outdoing those of their Hummingbird connections, who transact their business as they go. On the other hand, their feet, like those of Chinese ladies,

PLATE II. — CHIMNEY SWIFT

Sooty, throat whitish; wings long and slender; tail tipped with spines. *Length*, about 5½ inches.

CHIMNEY SWIFT 25

are so little used that they are small and weak (Fig. 7). They serve mainly as picture-hooks, for the birds hook them over the edge of the nest or into a crack in the chimney, and proceed to go to sleep hanging like pictures on a wall. Even when thus employed, the feet do not have to do the 'whole duty of man'; for the tail comes in to act as a prop, being bent under the bird to brace against the wall. Doubtless, by this habit, the end of the tail has gradually lost its feathery character, the webbing being worn off, till now only the stiff, bone-like quills of the feathers remain. These he uses like little awls, to stick into the bricks (Fig. 8).

FIG. 7.
Weak foot of Chimney Swift.

FIG. 8.
Tail feather of Chimney Swift, used to brace against wall.

As the Swifts get their meals on the wing — they are exclusively insectivorous, and are good enough to eat mainly what are to us either disagreeable or positively injurious insects — they have wide gaping mouths and tiny bills, in marked contrast to the Hummingbirds, which, though in the same order, have with different food habits developed in the opposite direction, and have long probe-like bills to suit their needs (Figs. 9 and 10).

Another phase of this wonderful adaptation of form to habit is shown when the Swift comes to build its nest. It would be quite impossible for an ordinary bird to fasten a wall-pocket of twigs to a perpendicular chimney, but the Swift is provided with a salivary glue that defies anything but heavy rain, actually having been known to hold firm when the brick to which it had glued the nest was broken away. Nature selects beneficial qualities rigorously, or rather the struggle for life is so intense that only the best fitted survive to hand down their characters to their race; but Nature makes no meaningless display. Eggs are colored because they are exposed to enemies, and those whose colors best disguise them are most likely to escape the eyes of enemies; but let the eggs be laid in a tree trunk, a hole in the ground, or otherwise out of sight, and as a general rule they will be white. There is no force at work to eliminate the white ones. So we see this negative adaptation in the eggs which the Swift secretes in a chimney, — they are pure white.

Fig. 9. Short, widely gaping bill of Swift.

Fig. 10. Long, probe-like bill of Hummingbird.

It would be exceedingly interesting to watch the Swifts at the nest; and while their habits ordinarily render this impracticable, Mr. Otto Widmann, the original and philosophical student of birds, has shown how it may be done. He accomplished it by building a miniature chimney, a wooden shaft eighteen inches square and six feet high, on top of a flat tower where he could look down on the birds at will. It is encouraging to read that it was occupied the day after it was completed. In studying his tenants, Mr. Widmann found that the birds cannot build in damp weather, as the glue must have dry air to harden in. As only a small amount of this glue is secreted daily, nest-building, with the interruptions of rainy days, sometimes takes nearly three weeks. One pair of Mr. Widmann's birds spent two days in laying their foundation, besmearing the wall and fastening the first sticks to it. When the first egg was laid, ten days later, the nest was only half done, and from that time, curiously enough, building and laying went on together. When the young were two weeks old, Mr. Widmann could not find them when he went to the chimney; but while wondering what had become of them, one of the parents came with food, and he discovered that "all four were huddling side by side, hanging on the wall immediately below the nest and entirely hidden from view above." The next week, Mr. Widmann says, "I was still more surprised when, bending my head over the shaft, the youngsters jumped right against my face with a strong, hissing noise, which I believe must be a very effective means of frightening unsuspecting visitors." When the brood actually left the chimney for several nights they were brought back by the parents.

Doctor Brewer notes that Swifts often feed their young quite late into the night, and this can readily be believed by those who have heard the rumbling and roaring in chimneys where they live.

Mr. Chamberlain, in his notes on Canadian birds, tells us that the first flight of the Swifts is most interesting to witness. "The solicitude of the parents and their coaxing ways; the timid hesitation of the young birds, and their evident desire to emulate their seniors; the final plunge into mid air, and the first few awkward efforts to master the wingstroke, make this one of the episodes of bird life which bring these children of the air very close to the hearts of their human brethren."

Major Bendire, in his monumental work, 'Life Histories of North American Birds,' says that few birds are more devoted to their young than the Chimney Swift, cases being recorded where the parent was seen to enter a chimney in a burning house, even after the entire roof was a mass of flames, preferring to perish with its offspring rather than forsake them. A most remarkable case of devotion is cited in the Life Histories from Forest and Stream. A full month after the other Swifts had gone south for the winter, an old bird was discovered bringing food to one of its young which had fallen from the nest, and had become so entangled in a hair that it could not get out of the chimney. The note says: "His anxious mother who had cast in her lot with him, to remain and to die with him, for the time of insects was about gone, came into the chimney and actually waited beside me while I snipped the strong hair and released him." As Major Bendire comments, from his sympathetic knowledge of bird life: "This instance certainly shows a tender side of bird nature, and such instances are far more common than they appear to be, if we could only see them."

Mourning Dove: *Zenaidura macroura*.

General coloring fawn; under parts pinkish; sides of the neck with metallic pink reflections; *a small black mark below the ear;* tail showing a bordering of black and white in flight. *Young*, feathers tipped with whitish. *Length*, about 12 inches.

GEOGRAPHIC DISTRIBUTION. — North America, breeding from Cuba north to southern Canada and New England, and wintering from southern Illinois and New York to the Greater Antilles and Panama.

It is pleasant to know that this beautiful Dove is a familiar resident of most of the United States, for it is one of our most attractive birds. Sometimes we see the soft fawn-colored creature look-

FIG. 11.
Mourning Dove.

ing out at us from the foliage of a tree, turning its head from side to side to inspect us, while its mate calls solicitously, "*coo-o-o, ah-coo-o-o—coo-o-o—coo-o-o;*" again, we see it walking along the ground, moving its head back and forth with the peculiar motion of the Doves; then we hear a musical whirr as it passes swiftly through the air beside us, and on looking up catch sight of the

FIG. 12.
Tail of Mourning Dove.

white circlet of its long vanishing tail (Fig. 12); or perhaps watch it soar low over the bushes with wings stiffly spread till it gets near the nest, when it alights with a wabbling motion of wings and tail.

But the pleasantest part of this acquaintance comes when we visit the bird at its nest. To be sure it does not always build where there are people. In the dry part of Arizona, Major Bendire found it nesting a long distance from water, so far that it could only go to drink twice a day, but its habit was so well known that old mountaineers followed it when in search of water. In the east, however, when sure of protection the Dove will make its home in our gardens.

In southern California one gentle brooding bird let me come close under her loose twig nest to talk to her, though her mate was troubled at first, for he is a watchful and devoted guardian. Major Bendire thinks the pairs remain mated through the year, as they are seen together summer and winter. Indeed, the name 'Turtle Dove' which has become synonymous with tenderness and affection is more appropriate than the name Mourning Dove, for with long familiarity the low cooing, which at first seems mournful, sounds more tender and soothing than sad. At times the bird seems almost to speak its own Latin name, *ma-crou-ra;* but at all events its sweet musical call bespeaks the gentle nature of the Dove.

Ground Dove : *Columbigallina passerina terrestris.*

Adult male, forehead and under parts pinkish; top of head gray; back brownish; wings showing reddish brown in flight; tail blackish. *Adult female*, similar, but forehead and under parts almost without pink. *Length*, 6¾ inches.

GEOGRAPHIC DISTRIBUTION. — South Atlantic and Gulf states; north to North Carolina; west to Texas; more common near the coast than inland.

In the south, this little Dove makes a pretty picture of trustfulness as it walks down the streets of the towns. But the tourists, who should be most anxious to preserve the beautiful objects of the countries they visit, have done their best to destroy it; and as the friendly birds are also victims of the millinery craze, they are fast being killed off.

In Florida they are particularly fond of the orange groves, but in Bermuda they may be found almost anywhere. Near the shore one day I stopped under a small red cedar, when to my astonishment one of the Doves came tumbling down almost upon my head. When it fluttered off trailing, I looked up in the cedar and was delighted to discover a nest among the branches. The birds are noted for their devotion to their young, and this was only another touching instance of the way they will endanger their own lives to save those of their little ones.

In feeding their nestlings, these as well as other Doves regurgitate the food they have taken into their crops, and when it is mixed with the milky fluid which softens it give it to the tender young in a form that makes appropriate the fabled name of 'Pigeon's milk.'

Ruffed Grouse: *Bonasa umbellus* and races.

GEOGRAPHIC DISTRIBUTION. — Northern North America; north in the eastern states to British Provinces; south to middle states, and in the mountains to northern Georgia; resident.

Walk through the market and you will recognize pathetic strings of game hanging by their

RUFFED GROUSE

necks in the shambles. The beauty and life of the poor birds being gone, they seem without interest. But walk through a Partridge woods and the presence of the living birds in the shadowy forest lends it charm and new delight. You are startled by a loud whirr, and a covey of birds, before invisible, rises from almost under your feet, whirling away through the bushes so fast your eye can scarcely follow their flight. As they disappear you berate your dullness, for they look so large it seems inexcusable that you have not discovered them. They are almost the size of the domestic fowls, to which they are related; but though they walk about on the ground like hens, their soft wood-colors tone in with the colors of the sunlit brown leaves, and neutralize the light so perfectly that it is a difficult matter to see them. They are protectively colored, we have been accustomed to say, meaning that they approach the colors of their surround-

FIG. 13.
Ruffed Grouse.

ings, being ground-color to match the ground, as the Hummingbird is green to match the green leaves on the trees he frequents, and as the desert birds are sand-color and the arctic ones white to match the snow. But Mr. Abbott H. Thayer, the artist, has shown that there is something more than mere color likeness in protective coloration, a marvelous gradation of tint to counteract the effects of light and shade. As he states the law: "*Animals are painted by nature, darkest on those parts which tend to be most lighted by the sky's light, and vice versa,*"[1] that is, darker above and lighter below. He demonstrates this most conclusively by means of pictures of birds as they are in nature, in contrast to those in which he has painted the under parts uniform with the dark upper parts, or, as he says, "extended the protective coloration all over them." As we look at the pictures, the natural birds are almost invisible, seem scarcely to exist; while the painted ones stand out boldly, unmasked, before us (Plate III.).

The Grouse is one of the best examples of this wonderful law of adaptation, of the gradation of tints; and it is also a wonderful example of pure color correspondence to surroundings, and the use of color pattern to disguise form. When the brooding bird sits on her buffy eggs at the foot of a tree, the white that is mixed with the dark brown of her back matches the effect of sunlight

[1] *The Auk*, vol. xiii. No. ii. p. 125.

PLATE III. — RUFFED GROUSE AS IN NATURE

RUFFED GROUSE WITH UNDER PARTS MADE UNIFORM WITH UPPER PARTS

Upper parts warm brown, streaked with white and black; tail transversely barred with brown and black; under parts whitish, barred with brownish; ruffs on shoulders brown or black. Ruffs smaller in the female. *Length*, 17 inches. (By courtesy of *The Auk*.)

on the brown leaves so well that it is hard to tell where the leaves end and the bird begins. Then the dark band crossing the end of her tail breaks the tail form.

The Grouse is well adapted to the needs of its life in matters of form as well as coloration. As it spends its time on the ground, it has a strong foot, like that of the hen and pheasant, its congeners, in contrast to the weak perching foot of the air-dwelling Swift. (See Fig. 7, p. 25.) In winter this is still more remarkably modified to suit its habits. The bird does not go south in winter, but has to wade through the snow for its food; and to meet this necessity its toes, which in summer are bare and slender, in winter are fringed so that they serve admirably for snowshoes.

The short, rounded, hen-like wings of the Grouse also suit its short, rapid flights; for the bird does not migrate, and when startled in the woods does little more than shoot out like a bomb and then gradually curve back to earth again, contrasting markedly both in form and habit with the long, slender-winged Swift (see Fig. 19, p. 45), who lives in air and winters in Central America. Though the wings of the Grouse are not suited to long flights, they are admirably formed for musical instruments. The domestic rooster claps his as he crows; but the Grouse when moved to song instead of crowing beats the air with his wings till it resounds with his resonant drumming. He often does this at night in spring and fall, and has been known to drum by moonlight when the snow was on the ground and the mercury near zero. He usually has one special drumming log, and the roll of his tattoo coming through the woods is one of the best-loved sounds in nature, calling one's thoughts to the quiet shaded depths of the forest.

As the Grouse is a shy woods bird, it is a rare pleasure to have him live on your preserves; but it can easily be accomplished. Protect your woods with signs forbidding hunting, and in winter when he can no longer find maple-leaf worms, and the buds of the trees are small, scatter corn and buckwheat between the house and the woods, and soon you will find his pretty footprints in the snow beside the tracks of the squirrels. Then some winter morning, as you look through your blinds, perchance you will be rewarded by the sight of the handsome bird himself, with ruffs and tail spread out, strutting turkey-cock fashion before his mate. In summer you may have the added pleasure of coming on a brood of young Partridges, soft and downy as little chickens, strolling along the wooded edge of a meadow, daintily picking wild strawberries under the eye of their mother. She clucks to them, and when they have had their fill squats on the ground and takes them under her protecting wings like a devoted hen. The Partridge is an anxious parent, decoying the observer away from her young with signs of great distress. Wilson, of the classic triumvirate, Audubon, Wilson, and Nuttall, gives a most interesting experience of his with a Partridge who had only one young bird, and on being overtaken, after fluttering before him for a moment, "suddenly darting toward the young one, seized it in her bill and flew off."

Bob-white: *Colinus virginianus.*

Adult male, upper parts wood-brown; throat and line from bill to neck white; black patch on breast; rest of under parts whitish barred with black. *Adult female,* similar, but throat buffy, and black of breast less or absent. *Length,* 10 inches.

GEOGRAPHIC DISTRIBUTION. — Eastern United States from southern Maine and the Dakotas southward to the Gulf of Mexico; resident wherever found.

This beautiful bird is known mainly as 'Quail on toast,' but in usefulness and interest of habit it holds a high place among our birds. As a weed-seed and insect destroyer it is of such economic importance that in Wisconsin, where it has been practically exterminated, attempts have recently been made to reëstablish it.

FIG. 14.
Bob-white.

It eats the potato beetle — seventy-five potato bugs were found in one Quail stomach — and it is particularly fond of the moth that lays the egg that produces the injurious, omnivorous cutworm. As each moth lays multitudes of eggs, the destruction of a few thousands of moths at the right time

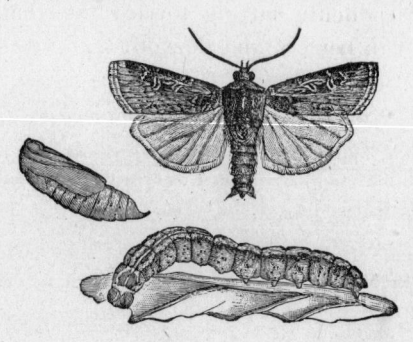

Fig. 15.
Cutworm, eaten by Quail.

would prevent the hatching of an army of worms able to destroy large fields of corn and grain; so that in a field where there were a few old Quail, as the birds raise two to three broods of from ten to thirty young each, but few moths would lay their eggs. It would be wise for other states to follow the example of Wisconsin and introduce fresh Quail in the old haunts where they have been thoughtlessly exterminated. Aside from the use of the Quails as game birds, their numbers suffer great loss by winter snows; for like their relatives the Grouse they do not migrate, and in severe storms often huddle together and are buried, when, if a crust forms over them, they are unable to get out, and die in large numbers.

Those who know the Quail in the field are familiar with his delightful call of *Bob-white*, a loud clear whistle that locates him at a long distance. It is such a striking note that once, when a single Quail strayed beyond his usual limits in northern New York, he was fairly driven back by the excited dogs of the neighborhood, for at sound of his whistle they would go bounding over the fields toward him, as if in answer to the call of their masters. The result of this reception of the stranger was a sore disappointment to the observers of the locality, for Bob-white is one of the most delightful birds to study.

There are few prettier sights than a family of old Quail with their young walking about fearlessly in a woodland meadow. The bird's domestic life is particularly interesting from the part the male plays in the family, helping to build the nest, feeding his mate on the eggs, and, in case of her death, brooding in her place. Doctor Brewer, in his biographies of North American birds, gives a graphic account of meeting with a male engaged in the care of his brood. "They did not see me until I was close upon them," he says, "when the old bird, a fine old male, flew directly towards me, and tumbled at my feet as if in a dying condition, giving at the same time a shrill whistle, expressive of intense alarm. I stooped and put my hand upon his extended wings, and could easily have caught him. The young birds, at the cry of the parent, flew in all directions, and their devoted father soon followed them, and began calling to them in a low cluck."

The Bob-white like the Partridge readily responds to protection, and when not shot at will become very tame, even nesting about houses and gardens. For three successive years Mrs. Mabel Osgood Wright had broods raised in a tangle in her garden, old and young ranging in the neighborhood during the summer, but in the shooting season returning to hide under a protecting hemlock hedge.

The Ruffed Grouse and Bob-white are the only members of their family we are likely to meet, and there is no question of confusing such hen-like birds with those of any other family, while there is little danger of mistaking one for the other.

Key to Male Grouse and Quail.

Common Characters. — Hen-like birds that live on the ground.

1. Large (length about 17 inches). Ruffs on shoulders ; dark bands on tail . . p. 32. RUFFED GROUSE.

1'. Small (length about 10 inches). No ruffs on shoulders or bands on tail. p. 37. BOB-WHITE.

BLUEBIRD 41

Fig. 16.

Bluebird: *Sialia sialis*.

Adult male, upper parts deep blue; throat and breast reddish brown; belly white. *Adult female*, upper parts grayish blue; under parts duller. *Young*, in nestling plumage, spotted with whitish. *Length*, about 7 inches.

GEOGRAPHIC DISTRIBUTION. — Eastern United States; breeds from the Gulf states to Manitoba and Nova Scotia; winters from southern Illinois and southern New York southward.

Although the Bluebird did not come over in the Mayflower, it is said that when the Pilgrim Fathers came to New England this bird was one of the first whose gentle warblings attracted their notice, and, from its resemblance to the beloved Robin Redbreast of their native land, they called it the Blue Robin. From that time on, this beautiful bird has shown itself so responsive to friendly treatment that it has won a deep place in the affections of the people. The bird houses that were put up for it insured its presence in villages and city parks until the introduction of the House Sparrow, but since that time the old familiar friend has had to give way before the quarrelsome stranger. Mr. Nehrling, however, gives us the grateful information that by a simple device the Bluebird boxes may be protected from the Sparrow. It seems that the Sparrow, being no aeronaut, — not to say of earthly mind, — finds difficulty in entering a hole unless there is a perch beside it where, as it were, he can have his feet on the ground. The Bluebird, on the contrary, aside from his mental cast, is so used to building in old Woodpecker holes, none of which are blessed with piazzas or front-door steps, that he has no trouble in flying directly into a nest hole. So, by making the Bluebird houses without perches, the Sparrows may be kept away. Mr. Nehrling urges that cigar boxes should never be used for bird houses, which is surely wise, for we would neither offend the nostrils of feathered parents nor contaminate the feathered youth. In the south, he tells us, the cypress knees furnish excellent materials for them. He suggests, moreover, that sections of hollow branches and hollow tree trunks can be used in addition to the usual board houses. When this is done, the section of the branch should be sawed in two, bored out for the nest cavity, and then nailed or glued together and capped at each end to keep out the rain. It should then be fastened securely to a branch or tree trunk with strong wire. Bird houses of some sort are especially necessary on the prairie and in other regions where few natural nesting sites are to be found.

One of the most effective ways to attract the Bluebird, however, is by planting wild berry-bearing bushes, particularly in the west, where such bushes do not grow naturally. For while three quarters of the Bluebird's food consists of grasshoppers, crickets, caterpillars, and similar insects, and it is " exceedingly useful to the horticulturist and farmer, destroying myriads of larvæ and insects which would otherwise increase and multiply to the great injury of vegetation," the Bluebird is not a bird of one idea, but extends his dietary to wild fruits, and by means of them may be brought about our houses. A variety of bushes can be planted, for he has been found to eat bird cherry, chokeberry, dogwood, bush cranberry, huckleberry, greenbrier, Virginia creeper, strawberry-bush, juniperberry, bittersweet, pokeberry, false spikenard, partridgeberry, holly, rose haws, sumac, and wild sarsaparilla.

Wilson, in speaking of the Bluebird engaged in courting his mate, says in his delightful way: "If a rival makes his appearance, . . . he quits her in a moment, attacks and pursues the intruder as he shifts from place to place, in tones that bespeak the jealousy of his affection, conducts him, with many reproofs, beyond the extremities of his territory, and returns to warble out his transports of triumph beside his beloved mate."

As we watch the Bluebird, one of the most noticeable things about him, in spite of his familiar friendliness, is a certain untamable spirit of the woods and fields. As he sits on a branch lifting his wings, there is an elusive charm about his sad quavering *tru-al-ly, tru-al-ly*. Ignoring our presence, he seems preoccupied with unfathomable thoughts of field and sky.

House Wren: *Troglodytes aëdon.*

Upper parts, wings, and tail brown, finely barred with black; under parts whitish. *Length*, 5 inches.

GEOGRAPHIC DISTRIBUTION. — Eastern North America; breeds as far north as Manitoba and Maine; and winters from South Carolina southward.

Crows, Doves, Hummingbirds, Swifts, and Quail are all birds of strongly marked family characters, but Wrens are no less so. They are small brown birds that match the color of the earth, and creep about in odd nooks and crannies searching diligently for insects. As their daily round is not disturbed by soaring ambition, the Wrens have short, round wings like

FIG. 17.
House Wren.

HOUSE WREN

the modest Grouse and Quail, very different from the long ones of the more aspiring Doves, Hummingbirds and Swifts (see Fig. 19 and Fig. 100, p. 190). They are jolly little tots, always full of business, but still more full of song. The Crow, the Quail, and the Dove talk, and the Hummingbird and Swift sing according to their light and vocal anatomy, but

FIG. 18.
Short, round wing of Wren.

the Wrens and Catbirds are the only birds we have mentioned thus far who are on the list of noted

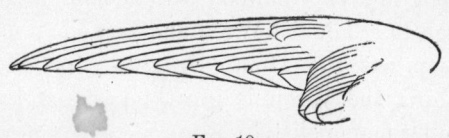

FIG. 19.
Long, slender wing of Swift.

songsters. The House Wren is one of the most tireless of his family, fairly bubbling over with happiness and music all the day long. In northern New York he is not often seen, but on a visit to Vassar I remember coming face to face with a preoccupied bit of a Wren perched on a fence post, singing away with more gusto than if delivering an oration. At Farmington, Connecticut, the Wren is an established villager, so used to worldly amusements he will make love and discuss nesting materials with his mate while the tennis balls of Miss Porter's girls are flying through the air.

In building, Wrens abhor a vacuum. One pair were so possessed to fill a space they had chosen that their eggs actually addled while they were stuffing in twigs! The eggs are rather novel in color, being uniformly marked with fine pinkish spots.

Tin fruit cans, though not highly decorative, make good nests for the wrenkins, who also like olive jars and other structures not wholly modern in matters of plumbing and ventilation. When a tin can is used, it is well to turn back the lid and put in a cap of wood with a hole just large enough to admit the Wren and just small enough to keep out the House Sparrow; for, like the Bluebird, the Wren is greatly pestered by this grasping monopolist.

One little bird who lived at Sing Sing, New York, was fairly besieged by the Sparrows. Fortunately it built near the house of a special champion of birds, Dr. A. K. Fisher, and whenever the doctor heard a commotion he would go to its assistance, shooting down the Sparrows that were tormenting it. One day, when the familiar note of alarm came and he hurried to the window, the Sparrow was so near the Wren that the doctor had to shoot with great care not to hit his little friend. The Wren was not at all disturbed, however, but sat on his branch unmoved while the

HOUSE WREN

shot was fired, and as the Sparrow fell turned his head over and watched his neighbor go to the ground with unconcealed satisfaction. Wrens nest in all sorts of odd nooks and corners. A pair of Washingtonians one year started to build in Mr. Gardiner Hubbard's greenhouse, in the pocket of the gardener's coat. At night, when the man came for his coat, he would find sticks in his pocket, but it was not for some days that he realized who was playing this very practical joke upon him. Then the kind-hearted attendant was greatly perplexed, for he could not spare his coat. He compromised, however, by substituting an old one which suited the Wrens just as well, and in a short time there was a set of little brown eggs snugly ensconced in the bottom of his pocket. When showing them to me, the gardener got down a tall glass jar from a shelf in which was another Wren's nest, and told me that a pair had also built on the knot of a loop of rope that had hung in the greenhouse.

Mr. Nehrling speaks of a pair of Wrens which built their nest in an old wooden shoe in which a gardener kept his strings, the orthodox couple calmly accepting the strings as a special gift of Providence. Another practical pair actually crept inside a human skull Doctor Fisher was bleaching in an apple-tree, and raised their brood there, untroubled by ghosts. The doctor was so impressed by their adaptability that he waived all claim to his skull, and the Wrens' nest is now on exhibition in the National Museum.

Original and entertaining as the wrenkins are, they are worthy of respectful consideration for another reason: they bring up their large families — sometimes they raise from twelve to sixteen young in a season — on a diet of worms; so, whether they appropriate our shoes or our skulls, they should be welcomed to our gardens, because they reduce the insects and increase the family spirits.

Purple Martin: *Progne subis.*

Adult male, shining blue black. *Female and young*, upper parts duller; under parts grayish. *Length*, 8 inches.

GEOGRAPHIC DISTRIBUTION. — North America; breeds from Florida and the table lands of Mexico north to Newfoundland and the Saskatchewan; winters in Central and South America.

As long ago as when Audubon was traveling through the middle states, he reported that "almost every country tavern had a Martin-box on the upper part of its signboard," and commented characteristically: "I have observed that the handsomer the box, the better does the inn generally prove to be." He also found that the Indians hung up calabashes for the Martins, so they would keep the vultures from the deerskins and venison that were drying.

Calabashes are used extensively in the south, and Mr. Nehrling assures us "that the Martin is as well satisfied with the simple hollow gourd attached to a pole near a negro hut, as with the most ornamental and best arranged Martin-house in the beautiful gardens and parks of rich planters and opulent merchants. Where no nesting-boxes are provided," he says, " our Martin will not breed, and it hardly ever accepts nesting-boxes attached to trees, preferring locations where the chance is given to dart in and out uninterrupted by any obstacle."

The struggle between the Martins and Sparrows is so bitter that one pair of Martins Mr. Widmann watched, intelligently adopted the strategical plan of never leaving the nest alone, taking turns in going for food, because as he explains, "it is comparatively easy to keep a Sparrow out of a box, but it is impossible for a Martin to dislodge him after he has built a nest."

Barn Swallow: *Chelidon erythrogaster.*

(Plate IV. p. 50.)

GEOGRAPHIC DISTRIBUTION. — North America, north to Greenland and Alaska; breeds throughout the greater part of its range; winters as far south as southern Brazil.

Next to the Martin, the Barn Swallow is the most easily known of his family. He is usually found beating low over a meadow for insects. As he sweeps near us, the rich metallic sheen of his back is well seen; and as he flies up to a telegraph wire, his long forked tail and deep chocolate breast identify him beyond question. Like the Swift (see Fig. 7, p. 25) and Hummingbird, the Swallows live in air and feed when flying, and so have undeveloped perching feet (compare Figs. 20, 21), unfitted for walking; nevertheless they sometimes condescend to visit the earth for nesting materials and the lime which they need to harden their eggshells. Their eggs, like those of the Eave Swallow, are white, heavily spotted with brown.

Fig. 20. Weak foot of Barn Swallow.

If you watch a row of Swallows perched on a telegraph wire, you will hear the bright, happy warble which adds so much to their attractiveness. In addition to this twittering song, their call note is said to be a "soft and affectionate *witt, witt*, and the cry given in time of danger a harsh *trrrr, trrrr*."

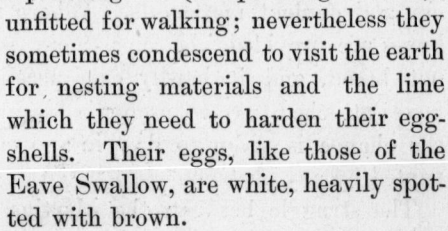

Fig. 21. Strong foot of Song Sparrow.

The homely old proverb, "One Swallow does not make a summer," shows how intimately these birds are associated with the close of winter. As Mr. Nehrling puts it, in his enthusiastic way: "We welcome their first appearance with delight, as the faithful harbingers of flowery spring and ruddy summer; and when, after a long frost-bound and boisterous winter, we hear it announced that 'the Swallows have come,' what a train of charming ideas are associated with the simple tidings!"

PLATE IV. — BARN SWALLOW

Upper parts steel-blue; tail deeply forked, with white spots on outer feathers; throat chocolate. *Length*, about 7 inches.

But as it is a pleasure to have the birds come back in spring, it is always with a feeling of regret that we see them gather for their southward flight in fall; for the silence of the deserted barns and telegraph wires suggests the coming winter.

Before beginning their southward journey, the Swallows gather in large flocks. Sometimes they can be followed from farm to farm. They go so slowly and stop so often on the way that the young birds gradually get used to following the old ones. Then they make prolonged stops at definite roosts, sometimes in trees and sometimes in marshes along river banks. It is a most interesting sight to watch them then. In an article in 'The Auk,' Mrs. Bates gives a graphic account of a roost in the willows along the Kennebec River, in Maine, at which the movements of the birds are most remarkable. At sunset, she says, they begin pouring in, and " at intervals *clouds* of Swallows will evolve something like order out of their numbers and perform *en masse* . . . fantastic curves, spirals, counter-marches, snake-like twists and turns, with the sky for a background." [1]

Mr. Chamberlain once happened on a curious meeting-place of the Swallows. A flock several thousand strong actually flew down the chimney of a deserted house and settled themselves for the night on the floors of the rooms, like so many wayfaring tramps.[2]

[1] *The Auk*, vol. xii. No. i. p. 48.
[2] *Some Canadian Birds*, p. 5.

Eave Swallow; Cliff Swallow: *Petrochelidon lunifrons.*

Forehead whitish; crown steel-blue; throat brown; steel-blue patch on brown breast; tail almost square, with a *light spot on rump. Length*, about 6 inches.

GEOGRAPHIC DISTRIBUTION. — North America, north to the limit of trees; breeds throughout its range in the United States and Canada, except the south Atlantic and Gulf states; winters from Central to South America.

If the number and variety of Swallows seem confusing, go to an old barn around which the birds are flying, and examine their adobe domiciles. Under the eaves you will find a row of queer gourd-shaped mud nests, hanging mouth down; and as you watch you may see one of the house-owners disappear in a nest, disclosing as he does so the light rump which distinguishes the Eave from all other Swallows.

FIG. 22.
Eave Swallow.

The nest is interesting in itself, for it is made of pellets of mud, rolled till they are almost round; but the most surprising thing about it is the way its retort form is changed by the intelligent builders according to the slant of the rafter against which it is supported, the weight of the bulge being adjusted with marvelous skill.

If, while you are watching Eave Swallows, a fork-tailed Barn (see Plate IV. p. 50) disappears through the barn-door and you follow it to its nest, you will be surprised at the difference in the two structures. At first sight, the nest of the Barn seems a simple cup lined with hay and feathers. On close inspection it proves less simple than it looks; for, Doctor Brewer says, it is made up of ten or twelve distinct layers of rolled pellets separated by layers of fine grass, possibly glued together with saliva. Sometimes the ingenious birds build out an extra platform beside the nest that they may rest on the doorstep at night, and when the young fill the house in the daytime. Audubon says that when building they often stop at intervals to let the mud dry and harden.

As Mr. Nehrling suggests, Swallows prefer barns with openings in the gables, so that they can fly freely in and out; and he gives us a valuable hint, telling us that as the nests will not adhere to smooth boards, he has often helped the birds by nailing pieces of rough board across the rafters of the peak.

Some countrymen are prejudiced against Swallows or Phœbes building in their barns, as they think the parasites of the birds will infest the cattle; but it should be remembered that bird parasites will not live on animals, and that, on the other hand, Swallows, especially the Barn, live largely upon the flies that torment stock. The

Eave Swallow, which builds about houses as well as barns, is a blessing to man in another way, for it eats enormous quantities of winged ants, mosquitoes, injurious wheat midgets, spotted squash

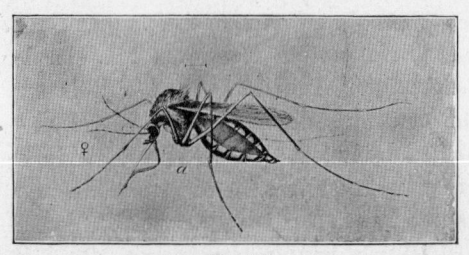

Fig. 23.
Mosquito, eaten by Eave Swallow.

beetles, and beetles that work under the bark of trees. As Doctor Brewer says of the Barn Swallows: "There is no evil blended with the many benefits they confer on man; they destroy the insects that annoy his cattle, injure his fruit-trees, sting his fruit, or molest his person."

Bank Swallow: *Clivicola riparia.*

Adults, dark above, light below, with a *dark band across the breast*. Length, about 5¼ inches.

GEOGRAPHIC DISTRIBUTION. — North America, north to Labrador and Alaska; breeds locally from the middle United States northward throughout its range; winters as far south as Brazil.

In going through carriage or railroad cuts in sandy banks, one is often struck by the number of elliptical holes in the cliffs. If you go up to them and rap on the walls the startled cliff-dwellers responsible for these mural decorations will often fly out in a whirl about your head. The excavations vary in depth from twelve inches to four feet, and are made with a careful avoidance of stones that might fall from the roof upon the helpless heads of the babes in the bank. The eggs, being concealed, are white.

Fig. 24.
Bank Swallow.

The Swallow's habit of nesting in colonies is an interesting example of the 'sociability of birds,' which Mr. Widmann says can best be indulged by long-winged birds like Swallows, as they can more easily spread over the extent of territory necessary for commissary reasons.

Fig. 25.

Baltimore Oriole: *Icterus galbula.*

Adult male, entire head and neck black; most of the body bright orange; wings and tail mainly black. *Adult female*, upper parts brown and black; under parts dull orange; throat sometimes spotted with black. *Length*, about 7½ inches.

Geographic Distribution. — Eastern United States, north to New Brunswick and Manitoba, west to the Great Plains; breeds from the Potomac and Ohio valleys northward; winters in Mexico and Central America.

In the temperate regions of the United States there are few brilliantly colored birds, as gaudy coats are found mostly in tropical regions, where they match the brilliancy of the flowering treetops. We can best appreciate how rich the tints of the Orioles are when we compare them with the gray Catbird, the sooty Chimney Swift, the fawn-colored Doves, and the brown Wrens and Grouse. It would seem that the Oriole race was endangered by the striking orange and black, but the mothers who brood the nests and protect the little ones are well concealed by a dull orange dress, and the color pattern of the males must disguise their form at a distance. Then, perhaps, as Mr. Fuertes has suggested, it is well that attention be called from the female and young by the gaudy plumage of the male. However that may be, the Orioles are strong and swift of wing, and in time of danger seek safety in flight; while the Wrens and Quail with short wings (see Fig 18, p. 45) find their greatest safety in standing motionless against their natural background.

Besides having strong wings, the Oriole has a sharp-pointed bill, which makes a good weapon and a good fork; being especially adapted to holding the long worms and large insects on which the bird feeds. While eating a great many bugs, grasshoppers, and beetles that injure the locust, apple, and elm trees, the Oriole has a weakness for caterpillars, and, most fortunately for the farmers, for the click beetles (Fig. 26), the adults of the wire worm, among the most insidious of pests, mining at the roots of turnips, potatoes, and corn. Few birds like the hairy caterpillars, but Doctor

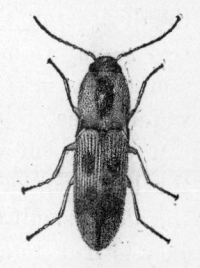

FIG. 26.
Click Beetle (adult of wire worm), eaten by Oriole.

Fisher has seen the Oriole go up before a caterpillar's nest and, after puncturing it with his bill, stand and wait for the caterpillars to come out. As each one appeared he seized it and after sucking the juices of its body threw away the hairy skin covering. The doctor also reports that the young Orioles are very fond of mulberries, and says he has seen "a whole brood camping in a mulberry-tree." As a relish in lieu of olives, the Oriole sometimes takes a few grapes and peas, though peas have been found in only 2 out of the 113 stomachs examined. As for the grapes, Mr. Lawrence Bruner suggests in his 'Notes on Nebraska Birds,' if "especially in dry sections we take pains to water our birds during the dry season, they will be much less apt to seek this supply from the juices of fruits that are so temptingly near at hand. Place little pans of water in the orchard and vineyard where the birds can visit them without fear of being seized by the house cat or knocked over by a missile from the alert 'small boy,' and I am sure that the injury to fruit to a great extent at least will cease." Speaking of the Baltimore Oriole, he adds: "As insect destroyers, both this bird and the Orchard Oriole have had an undisputed reputation for many years; and the kind of insects destroyed by both are of such a class as count in their favor." One far-sighted man, who reports that the Oriole eats his grapes, nevertheless adds that the bird is worth its weight in gold as an insect destroyer. New Englanders are to be congratulated that in the towns where they are having such a serious time with the insect pests the Orioles are common enough to give them material help. In Farmington, Connecticut, with a very incomplete census of the village, I once found nine or ten pairs of nesting Orioles.

When the birds are such common villagers one has a good opportunity to watch them make their nests, and it is then that the full perfection of their long, slender bill is seen (see Fig. 112, p. 192), for they are weavers with ready-made weaving needles for sewing the hairs and delicate fibres in and out. The Oriole bill is as efficient an instrument for weaving as the short bill of the Swallow (see Fig. 120, p. 193) is for rolling mud pellets. The taste of the Oriole leads it to hang its nest to the most flexible swaying branch it can find, while the Swallow's taste leads it to build against an immovable rafter, and the Bluebird's to hide away inside a wooden house; for individuality and adaptability are almost as strong in birds as in men. Though the long pocket of the Oriole, moving with every breeze, seems a frail cradle for a brood of heavy nestlings, in reality it is so skillfully attached to its supporting branches that it has been known to hold firm during a cyclone which swept down most of the other nests in a neighborhood. Oriole eggs like others hidden in cavities are white, but singularly scrawled and spotted. The males usually reach the nesting ground two or three days before the females. The same nest is sometimes used for several seasons, Orioles like many other aristocrats being somewhat conservative as to building-sites and becoming particularly attached to localities. Major Bendire thinks few birds are more devoted to each other than these, and believes that they remain mated through life. The young are very active, and for a day or two before they leave the nest, Audubon says, creep in and out of it like young Woodpeckers. Since the Oriole likes to hang his cradle to our elm-trees, he accepts our friendly advances, and as he is bound by no prejudices is quite ready to take the bright-colored worsteds put out for his nest, weaving them in with as much complacency as the sober grays of his own providing.

The Oriole is one of the most companionable of birds, for his bright coat is seen constantly flashing back and forth around our houses; and when he is at work his cheery, exuberant song comes back to us with such a joyful ring it must raise the most lugubrious spirits. Until too much engrossed with family duties, the beautiful birds sing a great deal, and the variations in the song make it always grateful. There is a bright vivacious song, an equally hearty scold, a high shrill whistle, and a richly modulated love song, one of the most exquisitely finished and tender of bird songs. Indeed, the Oriole is a prince among birds, with character as positive as his dress and with such winning ways and so melodious a voice that he is sure of the affection of all who study him.

Orchard Oriole: *Icterus spurius.*

Adult male, entire head and neck black; wings, tail, and back mainly black; rest of body chestnut. *Adult female*, upper parts olive-green; under parts dull yellow. *Young male in second year*, similar to the female, but with the throat black, and patches of chestnut on the under parts. *Length*, about 7¼ inches.

GEOGRAPHIC DISTRIBUTION. — Eastern North America; breeds from the Gulf states to Massachusetts, Ontario, and North Dakota, and winters in Central and northern South America.

"The Orchard Oriole, though far less brilliantly colored than its eastern congener the Baltimore Oriole, is equally well known though not quite as conspicuous. It is a restless, impulsive, but well-disposed bird, and, though not particularly shy, it is nevertheless difficult to observe closely, as it generally conceals itself in the densest foliage while at rest, or else flits quickly about from twig to twig in search of insects, on which it lives almost exclusively throughout the summer months. . . .

"Few birds do more good and less harm than our Orchard Oriole, especially to the fruit-grower. The bulk of its food consists of small beetles, plant lice, flies, hairless caterpillars, cabbage worms, grasshoppers, rose bugs, and larvæ of all kinds, while the few berries it may help itself to during the short time they last are many times paid for by the great number of noxious insects destroyed, and it certainly deserves the fullest protection." (Bendire.) Locust leaf-mining beetles are also on the Oriole's list, and it is interesting to note that, in a case where it had a choice between cherries and mulberries, it took mulberries.

Major Bendire notes: "The Orchard Oriole is a very sociable bird, and does not object to other species nesting in the same tree with it; it seems to be on especially good terms with the Kingbird." Its nest is cup-shaped and less pensile than the Baltimore's, not so deep, and usually made of grasses plucked green, which gives the structure the fragrance of new hay. The eggs are bluish white and spotted, but less irregularly streaked than those of the Baltimore.

Fig. 27.

Mockingbird : *Mimus polyglottos.*

Body gray, lighter below; wings and tail blackish, marked with white. *Length*, 10½ inches.

GEOGRAPHIC DISTRIBUTION. — Breeds from the Bahamas, Mexico, and southern California to southern Illinois and northern New Jersey, and rarely to Massachusetts; winters from Virginia southward.

The Mockingbird is a more accomplished cousin of the Catbird. His song has more finish, his technique is better, and when moved by love his lay becomes a wonder of ecstatic melody. "During the solemn stillness of the night," Wilson tells us, "as soon as the moon rises in silent majesty, he begins his delightful solo; and serenades us the livelong night with a full display of his vocal powers, making the whole neighborhood ring with his inimitable medley."

Southerners feel about the Mocker as northerners do about the Robin, and the bird becomes very tame when kindly treated. Nevertheless, though it is so responsive to man's companionship, destroys so many noxious insects, and has a voice of such famous quality, it is being gradually exterminated. Mr. Nehrling quotes from Mr. Carl Dänzer: "We hear complaints from Louisiana of the disappearance of the Mockingbird. There as elsewhere the birds are shot, year in and year out, by villainous boys, both old and young, and as the bird loves to settle near human dwellings, its very trustfulness leads to its own destruction. Then there is the unfortunate circumstance that the bird is adapted to cage-life and brings a high price; this is the cause of the nests being eagerly sought and robbed of their half-fledged occupants. Carloads of Mockingbirds are sent annually from the south to the north. . . . Should matters continue as heretofore, all the American birds of attractive plumage or voice will be exterminated, at least in the neighborhood of our larger cities. Only the most severe laws, enforced by the most vigilant public sentiment, can be of any service. . . . The transportation of birds'-skins, hundreds of thousands of which are sent even to foreign countries for millinery purposes, should be forbidden under penalty of heavy punishment. Only the severest laws, enforced without compunction, can effectually stop the demoralizing, shameful love of destruction, which threatens to rob our landscapes of their most charming bird-life." To this Mr. Nehrling adds a plea for the schools and press to take up the work of bird protection, concluding: " Parents and teachers, divines and newspapers can do infinite good in this matter. . . . Cruelty must vanish and yield to a nobler, kinder mode of thinking."

Cardinal: *Cardinalis cardinalis.*

Adult male, entire body, wings, and tail red; chin and ring round base of bill black; head with high crest. *Adult female*, bill, wings, and tail red; body brownish. *Length*, 8¼ inches.

GEOGRAPHIC DISTRIBUTION. — Eastern United States; breeds from Florida and Texas to Iowa and southern New York; resident throughout its range.

Like the Mockingbird, the Cardinal is known to most northerners as a cage bird, but in Central Park visitors are sometimes surprised by its familiar whistle, and on looking up are delighted by a glimpse of one of these high-crested red beauties, as he flies to cover, giving a flash of rich color to the landscape. In Ohio, Mr. H. C. Oberholser says it is found along the shaded streets of the towns and

FIG. 28.
Cardinal.

in door-yards where it can indulge its fondness for rose bugs. In the Washington Zoo Cardinals are common, and after February their song often rings through the bare woods. When spring comes they may be heard there every day, and they are so used to park visitors that you can stand almost under the tree in which one is singing and watch him as, with head thrown back and tail hanging, he brings out his long-drawn liquid note — *cue, cue, cue*. Even when you do not hear the song or see the bird, you may guess its presence from the thin '*chip*' which resembles that of its relative the Rose-breasted Grosbeak.

In the matter of food, it is said that the Cardinal eats the seeds of rank weeds. Though these birds usually live only in pairs, Nuttall, when in South Carolina during severe weather, once saw a flock passing to a roost at sunset. The flock was so large that it took twenty minutes to pass over. The naturalist exclaims: "The beautiful procession, illumined by the last rays of the setting sun, was incomparably splendid as the shifting shadowy light at quick intervals flashed upon their brilliant livery."

Chickadee: *Parus atricapillus*.

Top of head, nape, and throat black; rest of body gray; under parts lighter; wing and tail feathers edged with white. *Length*, about 5¼ inches.

GEOGRAPHIC DISTRIBUTION. — Eastern North America; breeds from southern Illinois and Pennsylvania northward to Labrador, and southward along the Alleghanies to North Carolina; in winter migrates a short distance below the southern limit of its breeding range.

He who knows the Chickadee only by name is an enviable person, for he has still before him the initial pleasures of one of the choicest of all bird friendships. When seen in a clearing as the pretty bird flits from one tree to another, his short wings and long tail give him a bobby flight by which we can recognize him at a distance. But when he clings to the gray branches, his soft grayish suit with its black cap and the trimmings that cut the bird form hide him as well as the brown suit of the little Wren protects him when hunting in the dark crevices of the brown earth. In many respects the Wren and Chickadee are as unlike as their livery. This is especially true of their songs, for while the Wren lives up to his family connections — being related to the Catbird and Mocker — the Chickadee is no musician. Still every note he utters is dear to his friends, and he has a varied

FIG. 29.
Chickadee.

repertoire. There are the sweet Chickadee call which gives him his name, the soft sunny *day-day-day* he cons over to himself, the sweet sad *phœ-be* whistle of spring and summer, and the pleasant conversational *chick-a-day-ah-day-day-day-day-day-day*. Both Wren and Chickadee are cheering, trustful little tots, eminently good for the blues, evoking every bird-lover's gratitude and affection.

In the spring, when the feathered tourists are coming back and the excitement of nest-building is absorbing our attention, we do not think much about the Chickadee except to notice its clearly whistled *phœ-be* occasionally coming from the woods; but some day we are given a thrill of pleasure by the appearance of a pair of the fluffy Black-caps leading around a family of young, grown almost as big as themselves, quite unbeknown to us.

From that time on until the following spring we can have the society of the friendly Chickadees if we but offer them a little food when cold weather comes, and their good cheer is so grateful that we are glad to do anything to keep them about us. A piece of suet nailed to a tree pleases them very well, but they also like the fat of fresh pork; and it is a good idea to fasten bits of pork at intervals along a clothes-line, for the cord is strong enough to make a steady perch for the birds as they peck at the meat. In northern New York a

Chickadee who came to us for food used to get so preoccupied eating that he would let me walk close under him on snowshoes.

But though the birds are glad of the dainties we may offer them, they are quite capable of finding food for themselves, even in the bleakest winter weather, for they live on grubs, and on the eggs of moths hidden under the bark of trees. They are particularly fond of the eggs of the cankerworm moth (Fig. 30). Mr. Forbush of the Massachusetts State Board of Agriculture calculated that one Chickadee in one day would destroy 5,550 eggs, and in the twenty-five days in which the cankerworm moths run or crawl up the trees, 138,750

Fig. 30.

Cankerworm moth, much eaten by Chickadee.

eggs. He was so impressed with the value of the birds' services that he attracted them to an infested orchard by feeding them there during the winter; and the following summer "it was noticed that while trees in neighboring orchards were seriously infested with cankerworms and to a less degree with tent-caterpillars (Fig. 84, p. 162), those in the orchard which had been frequented by the Chickadees during the winter and spring were not seriously infested, and that comparatively few of the worms and caterpillars were to be found there." Mr. Forbush concludes that birds that eat insect eggs are most valuable to the farmer, as they feed almost entirely on injurious insects and their eggs, and are present all winter when other birds are absent. The bill of the Chickadee — a sharply pointed little pick — is admirably suited to this work of excavating for eggs and grubs hidden under the bark. It also makes a good carpenter's tool, and one that is much needed; for when the Chickadee cannot find an old Woodpecker's hole to rent, he has to go to work to tunnel out a nest for himself. Maynard says that in excavating the birds carry the pieces of wood some distance away before dropping them, and that when they build in decayed wood "they are often obliged to abandon a nearly finished domicile on account of dampness which is caused by the water that is absorbed by the punky wood during wet weather." On the Hudson, Doctor Mearns has found them lining their nests with cottony fuzz from the stems of tall ferns in a swamp. He says they began at the bottom of the fern stems and climbed up, "gleaning to the very tops, which often bent down under their weight until they touched the water, when they flew to another plant." In this way they gleaned among the ferns until they had accumulated bundles of fern-down as large as hickory nuts.

FIG. 31.
Bill of Chickadee.

Doctor Brewer gives a remarkable instance of the maternal devotion shown by the Chickadees: "A Black-cap was seen to fly into a rotten stump near the roadside in Brookline. The stump was so much decayed that its top was readily broken off and the nest exposed. The mother refused to leave until forcibly taken off by the hand, and twice returned to the nest when thus removed, and it was only by holding her in the hand that an opportunity was given to ascertain that there were seven young birds in her nest. She made no complaints, uttered no outcries, but resolutely and devotedly thrust herself between her nestlings and the seeming danger. When released she immediately flew back to them, covered them under her sheltering wings, and looked up in the faces of her tormentors with a quiet and resolute courage that could not be surpassed."

Carolina Chickadee: *Parus carolinensis*.

Similar to the northern Chickadee, but smaller; wings and tail feathers not edged with white. *Length*, about 4½ inches.

GEOGRAPHIC DISTRIBUTION. — Southeastern United States; north to southern New Jersey and Illinois; west to Missouri and Texas; resident from southern New Jersey southward.

One spring day, on first coming to Washington, when out in the Zoölogical Park with a field class, I heard a song that was new to me. Creeping up cautiously, we were able to get under the very tree on which the bird was hunting, and the class stood with notebooks raised, taking down his song as solemnly as if the unconscious songster had been discoursing to them in the lecture-room. He was a Carolina Chickadee, and his notes resembled *whee-dle-lah'*, *whee-dle-lee'*, and seemed a very definite as well as pretty woodland tune.

In Missouri, Mr. Nehrling put up nesting-boxes for these little southerners, and was rewarded by having several pairs build about his house. He became much interested in watching them feed their young. " Without interruption from early morning till late in the afternoon," he observes, " the parents keep bringing minute insects, worms, larvæ and insect eggs, which they collect from the boughs, bark, and leaves of the trees and shrubs ; " and he concludes, " like all our Titmice, and the rest of our small birds, the Carolina Chickadee is a very useful creature, and should enjoy to its fullest extent man's friendship and protection."

Mr. Nehrling calls attention to the Chickadees' timidity and flight. They are terrified by the sudden passage of any bird that may be mistaken for a Hawk, he says, " for they know only too well that their powers of flight are sadly deficient, and that escape from an enemy in the open air is almost impossible." He adds that when a flock is about to start across a treeless space, they can be stopped by making a buzzing sound and throwing a hat in the air, they are so much in fear of enemies.

White-breasted Nuthatch: *Sitta carolinensis*.

(Fig. 32, p. 74; and Fig. 34, p. 77.)

Males, top of head black; back bluish gray; wings and tail marked with black and white; under parts white. *Females*, similar, but black of head duller. *Length*, about 6 inches.

GEOGRAPHIC DISTRIBUTION. — Eastern North America; breeds from the Gulf states to Minnesota and New Brunswick; generally resident throughout its range.

In the north a special debt of gratitude is due the birds that accept our winter hospitality, and the Nuthatch is one of our main dependences, coming with the Chickadees, Woodpeckers, and Blue Jays to visit our suet. In the south it is also found during cold weather in company with the Tufted Titmice and Kinglets, and in spring and fall with flocks of migrating Warblers; but the Chickadee and Nuthatch are most frequently seen together, and in summer both retire to the woods and build their nests in tree trunks. The Nuthatch is as quaint and droll as the Black-cap is plump and friendly, but the two agree in being very much preoccupied with their own matters. The Nuthatch spends most of his time moving about, head down, on tree trunks, or suspended under a branch like a fly on the ceiling, and it is said that he even sleeps hanging head down. Once, when watching a family of youngsters, I fell to wondering whether they were born with acrobatic skill or whether age steadied their heads, and just at that moment one of the brood started

Fig. 32.
Nuthatch and Chickadee.

over the edge of a limb. It hesitated an instant, but then circled around the branch as naturally and easily as a boy would run down hill.

The family of six to which this adventuresome youngster belonged was constantly on the move. The old ones hunted over the rosettes of lichen on the tree trunks in a business-like way, when they had finished one tree starting briskly for the next 'great bole,' calling *yak, yak, yak, yak-ah, ak-ah, ak-ah*, for the little ones to follow; and the youngsters, although they had been running around hither and yon hunting with most independent airs, seemed quite ready to go where meals were sure, so all six went trailing off together in pretty family fashion.

While watching them, I saw some quaint per-

WHITE-BREASTED NUTHATCH

formances. Once a little chap standing looking up at a tree trunk made a coquettish, bobby bow and scrape to his mate(?) hanging head down facing him, and she(?), with a superior air, promptly flew around to the back of the tree. But just at that moment a chipmunk, 'a rival nutter,' appeared at the foot of the tree below the coquetting Nuthatch, whereupon he in turn gave a quick spread of wings and tail and beat a retreat. They were playful, jolly little birds, and when alone would often go chasséing up the trees, chirruping softly to themselves.

In spite of the ingenuous ways of these charming foresters, there is a prejudice against them, arising from their being confused with the Sapsuckers, and they are persecuted by those who owe them the most gratitude, for, as a matter of fact, insects most destructive to the fruit-grower's crops are among their favorite foods. The Nuthatch is, as Doctor Mearns denominates him, "an eminently useful and industrious bird," for " he devotes his entire existence to the occupation of scrambling about upon the tree trunks, grubbing out insects from their hiding-places under the bark. At this commendable employment . . . he spends his days; and when night comes, he betakes himself to a hole in some tree, where, weary with his day's toil, he sleeps the sleep of the just till daybreak." Audubon observes that he sleeps hanging head down. In describing the nesting habits of the Nuthatches he notes that both birds work together, "all the time congratulating each other in the tenderest manner. The male, ever conspicuous on such occasions, works some, and carries off the slender chips chiseled by the female. He struts around her, peeps into the hole, cherups at intervals, or hovers about her on the wing. While she is sitting on her eggs, he seldom absents himself many moments; now with a full bill he feeds her, now returns to be assured that her time is pleasantly spent."

The Nuthatches nest as they mainly live, in the woods, and their notes are among the softest, most pleasing sounds in nature. They have a peculiar woodland quality which, like the drumming of the Grouse, has the power of transporting one to the quiet, leafy forest.

Red-breasted Nuthatch: *Sitta canadensis.*

(Fig. 33, p. 77.)

Male, top of head and *line through the eye* black; line over eye white; upper parts bluish gray; under parts reddish brown. *Female*, similar, but black replaced by bluish gray. *Length*, about 4½ inches.

GEOGRAPHIC DISTRIBUTION. — North America; breeds from Manitoba and Maine northward, and southward along the Alleghanies to the mountains of North Carolina; winters from about the southern limit of its breeding range to the Gulf states.

The Nuthatch is a bird who always seems self-possessed and full of business. Even the one that

RED-BREASTED NUTHATCH

Audubon saw blown on shipboard in a gale three hundred miles from shore was no exception, for the instant it lit on the rigging it set to work to look for food as calmly as if it had been on the side of a tree trunk in the woods.

Except in the north, the Red-breasted Nuthatch is not often seen in the nesting season, so when it appears on its migrations the day is distinguished. The bird is

FIG. 33.
Red-breasted Nuthatch.

smaller than the White-breast, and can be recognized at a glance by the stripes on its head and the reddish brown of its breast. Its voice also is quite different from that of the common Nuthatch. The Adirondack forest is a good place to see this bird. One day, when rocking in a boat under the overhanging trees of Lake Placid, I was given a thrill of pleasure by the sight of one of the beautiful little creatures creeping down a branch almost to my very paddle.

FIG. 34.
White-breasted Nuthatch.

Passenger Pigeon: *Ectopistes migratorius.*

Upper parts bluish; back and sides of neck with metallic reflections; under parts deep pink. *Length,* about 16¼ inches.

GEOGRAPHIC DISTRIBUTION. — Eastern North America, northward in the interior to Hudson Bay, breeding locally throughout the more northern part of its range.

Old inhabitants still recount the great flights of the wild Pigeon in the days when the sun used to be darkened by their multitudes, and Wilson tells of a flock that was four hours in passing, its line covering two hundred and forty miles and the movement of its column being like the "windings of a vast and majestic river." At that time the birds nested in roosts sometimes forty miles long, and the people would come from all parts of the country, with "wagons, axes, beds, and cooking utensils," camping on the ground with their families for days where they could plunder the roosts. "The noise in the woods was so great as to terrify their horses," Wilson says, "and . . . it was difficult for one person to hear another speak without bawling in his ear. The ground was strewed with broken limbs of trees, eggs, and young squab Pigeons . . . on which herds of hogs were fattening . . . the woods presented a perpetual tumult of crowding and fluttering multitudes of Pigeons, their wings roaring like thunder, mingled with the frequent crash of falling timber."

Now, like the buffalo, hardly any Pigeons are

left to bear testimony to the destruction which American thoughtlessness has wrought, and the sight of a single migrant stopping in one's woods is cause for much congratulation!

The Passenger Pigeon, the Mourning Dove, and the Ground Dove are the three best known of the family, and stand by themselves distinct from all other eastern birds. As a family, the Doves are not gifted with song, but their soft voices, delicate tints, and gentle ways render them among the most attractive of our birds. They are encouraging to the beginner, for they help him realize that birds are not all alike, and really may be easily classified. As the Doves belong to the family of the domestic Pigeons, the Quails and Grouse to the family of the domestic fowls, other birds may be quickly separated off from the number of confusing, unknown songsters. The Crow and Hummingbird stand apart, and the Chimney Swift and Swallows are easily distinguished, while the brilliantly colored Cardinal and Oriole are not to be confounded with the little brown Wrens of the ground or the gray-blue Chickadees and Nuthatches of the trees. The Bluebird and Robin every one recognizes; and the two melodious cousins, the Catbird and Mockingbird, speak for themselves. By grouping the birds you know and then eliminating them from those you do not know, identification of the unknown ones becomes much simplified. If you know that a bird is neither a Wren, Nuthatch,

Chickadee, Hummingbird, Crow, Swallow, Quail, or Dove, you will not have to hunt through those families for it, when looking for its name. *Elimination* is the short cut to *identification*. If you know what a bird is *not*, you will soon know what it *is*.

Key to Adult Male Doves.

1. Small (length about 7 inches); tail almost square; wings showing reddish brown in flight. Southern.

    p. 31.   GROUND DOVE.

1'. Large (length 12 to 16 inches); tail long and pointed.
2. Top of head same color as back — bluish slate; no black spot on side of neck. p. 78. PASSENGER PIGEON.

2'. Top of head not same color as back; forehead brownish; back of head bluish slate; back brownish; a small black spot on side of neck below eye.

    p. 29.   MOURNING DOVE.

Least Flycatcher; Chebec: *Empidonax minimus*.

(Plate V.)

GEOGRAPHIC DISTRIBUTION. — Eastern United States, west to the Great Plains; breeds from Pennsylvania and Nebraska northward; winters in Central America.

Through the open windows in a New England village come many bird songs, but none strike the ear with more distinctness than the frequently reiterated call of *che-beck'*. It has no poetic suggestions, but after one has traced it to the fluffy little white-breasted Flycatcher up in the trees,

PLATE V. — LEAST FLYCATCHER

Upper parts brownish olive; under parts grayish, darker on breast and sides; wing bars ashy white; lower mandible horn-color. *Length*, about 5½ inches.

the voice will recall a pleasant picture. Besides its regular call of *che-beck'*, the Least has several conversational notes, a call that Major Bendire gives as ' s'-lick, s'-lick,' and a low, twittering warble, ' whit-we-we.' If you watch the pretty bird in nesting time you will see it fly to its nest, sometimes on a horizontal limb, but more often high up in a crotch where you can just see its owner's tail beyond the edge of the compact round cup. Like all its family, it snaps its bill when it catches a fly, and shakes its wings and tail to emphasize its remarks.

The Least is a most friendly little bird who quickly responds to kindness. Doctor Brewer tells of a pair that began by coming to a house for cotton for their nest, and finally drew nearer and nearer till they built in a clump of honeysuckles in a corner of the piazza. Mr. Manly Hardy also gives an interesting instance of the friendliness of these attractive little folks. A pair built regularly near or in his garden, and seemed to remember him from year to year. When he was hoeing, they would perch near by and fly down beside him to catch the insects that he disturbed.

A still more remarkable case of confident friendship came to my knowledge in Farmington, Connecticut. The Chebec was the pet of a lady whose shrubby yard had many nesting birds. Almost every day through the summer, when she would go out to water her garden at five o'clock the Chebec would come flying in to have her give him a shower-bath. While waiting for her to get out the hose, he would "fly down on the fence and begin his talk;" then she would come up within five or six feet of him and turn the hose upon him gently. In describing it she said: "Of course he does n't like a very strong shower. He says *che-beck'* in between, and when he has had enough he flies into the bushes and preens himself beautifully. I wish you could see him shake himself!" On the days when the fountain spray was set on the grass, when it made an arch high enough, the little Flycatcher would dart through it back and forth almost in a circle, resting occasionally on the fence, as his friend interpreted it, "to think about it probably, and say *che-beck'*, thanks." At times, when he tired of these methods of bathing, he would drop down on the ground and shake himself in the wet grass blades, as a Canary does in a bath-tub. After telling about all the attractive ways of the friendly bird, the little lady concluded: "Now you do not wonder that I called him the darling little fellow, for I really have an affection for him;" and then she went on to say that, although she lived by herself in her cottage, she found so much companionship in her birds and flowers and trees that she could never be lonely.

FIG. 35.

Kingbird: *Tyrannus tyrannus*.

Upper parts blackish; under parts white, washed with gray on breast; head with a concealed red patch; *tail tipped with a white band*. Length, about 8½ inches.

GEOGRAPHIC DISTRIBUTION. — North America, north to New Brunswick and Manitoba; rare west of the Rocky Mountains; winters in Central and South America.

The sight of a Crow being chased by a bird

less than half its size is a very familiar one in the country, and an equally common one is that of a gray bird with a white breast sitting on a roadside fence, occasionally darting up with a loud, twittering cry. By watching him a little he will often be seen hovering over a weed in a meadow, his fluttering wings supporting him so well that he seems to be hanging in air. At other times we may see him start up from an apple-tree top and fly obliquely into the air as energetically as if bound for the zenith; then suddenly whirl and sail back on outspread wings, the white band on his fan-shaped tail showing to the best advantage.

Now what are we to infer from all these performances? That he is a doughty warrior, ready to cross lances with the black giants of the land, is plain to see; but what mean all his curious aerial evolutions? The answer is simple, — he is moved by no occult impulses, but is merely pursuing the prosaic occupation common to all mortal men, — getting his dinner! To be sure, he does it with many unnecessary flourishes and much superfluous show of enjoyment, exciting our admiration, not only by his grace of wing, but by his power of sight. Indeed, one careful observer has seen a Kingbird start from a telegraph pole one hundred and seventy-five feet away, and fly up to within twenty-five feet of him for an insect which was invisible to the man, though the bird had seen it one hundred and fifty feet away!

In fact, he has been so loudly accused of eating honey-bees that the examiners of bird stomachs in the Department of Agriculture have made a special study of his food. Of 218 stomachs examined, only 14 contained any trace of honey-bees, and nearly all those were drones; so, to say the least, the habit is much less prevalent than supposed. In addition to this negative evidence, it has been found that 90 per cent. of his food is insects, mostly injurious kinds. Among them are the gadfly, so terrifying to horses and cattle; the destructive clover-leaf weevil, rose chafer, ants, and grasshoppers. Several asparagus beetles were found in one stomach, and 40 rose chafers in another. The King is especially an orchard bird, though in addition to fruit beetles he eats many grain destroyers when he hunts in the meadows. Indeed, the conclusion reached by the ornithologists is that the Kingbird is one of the best helps the farmer has in the destruction of harmful insects. One correspondent exclaims fervently, "I honor and esteem

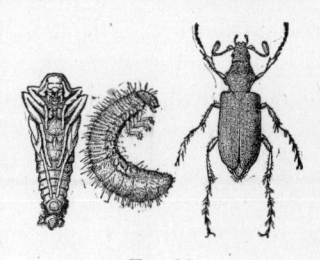

FIG. 36.

Rose Chafer, eaten by Kingbird.

this bird for the millions of ruinous vermin he rids us of!"

In the matter of fruit the Kingbird is most exemplary, eating only three or four kinds of cultivated fruit. If he were to harm any one kind, it would be a simple matter to attract his attention to some wild fruit, since he feeds on wild red and black cherries, choke-cherries, elderberries, mulberries, wild grapes, spice bush, sassafras, cornel, red and ground cedar, buckthorn, magnolia, and pokeberry. His vegetable foods are almost entirely wild fruits of no economic value. As a Flycatcher, the Kingbird is a good representative of the family, having the big head, large shoulders, and Quaker dress. The bill is also the typical Flycatcher bill — flat and broad, with a clasp at the end, and stiff, bristly hairs at the base, both of which help to hold the insects that have been seized. (See Fig. 38, p. 92.)

Besides being such an important citizen in his public capacity, the Kingbird is most interesting in his domestic life, as Mrs. Miller demonstrates in her valuable study of a nest in 'Little Brothers of the Air.' She shows that he is no tyrant, but merely a watchful guardian of the nest, and she calls attention to the little-known song with which he shows his domestic happiness. The Kingbird will amply repay close watching, and his large, low orchard nest offers one of the best opportunities for careful study of bird character. A curious case of nest guardianship is told me by Mrs. G. C. Maynard, whose son one day climbed a Kingbird's tree to look at the eggs. The old birds flew at his head so angrily that he had to get his hat to protect himself. When he appeared a second time, after the birds thought they had driven him off, and coming shielded by a hat which rendered their attacks futile, the Kingbirds were overwrought; and although the boy did nothing but look at their eggs, from that time on they could not bear the sight of that hat. Whenever the lad passed with it on, they would fly at him; and one day, when his mother snatched it up as she hurried to the orchard, although they were quite accustomed to her visits to their tree, they swooped down and actually struck the offending head-covering with their wings.

Phœbe: *Sayornis phœbe.*

Upper parts grayish brown; under parts white, washed with yellowish. *Length,* about 7 inches.

GEOGRAPHIC DISTRIBUTION. — Eastern North America; breeds from South Carolina to Newfoundland and Manitoba, and winters from North Carolina to Cuba and Mexico.

The Phœbe, like the Robin, is one of the homely, confiding birds for whom we have a peculiar affection. Like the Robin, she often comes about our houses and builds her nest in a crotch of the piazza, as if putting her brood under our protection. Though she may not be as neat a housekeeper as some, her presence is such a valuable nature-lesson for our children that she should be eagerly welcomed for that reason alone. Beautiful indeed is the sympathy that grows up between

Fig. 37.

the family in the big mossy nest in the piazza and the little folks that watch below. How fearless the old birds become as the days go by! And how anxiously all their enemies are driven off for them; how eagerly their nestlings are watched; and finally, with what mingled feelings of pride and regret the first flights of the departing brood are witnessed!

When the Phœbe does not nest under the sheltering roof of a house, it often builds on a rafter of an old shed or barn, where it may be seen perching on the ridgepole with crest raised and wings and tail hanging. It may also be found nesting under bridges and on rocks or cliffs. When seen, now and then it cries out *hip'*, *hip'*, or with a jerk of the tail calls *phœ'-be*, *phœ'-be*. It sits turning its head and looking over its shoulder this way and that till, spying an insect, it suddenly darts into the air, snaps its bill conclusively, and then settles back on a perch. In Florida the Phœbe is said to vary this practice by lighting on the backs of cattle, taking a ride with the laudable excuse of catching flies. For like the Kingbird it is a Flycatcher and makes its living from our insect pests. Few fish are rejected that visit the Phœbe's net. Not only does it help clear the air of the flies and wasps that annoy cattle, but it eats May beetles and click beetles, both of which injure the crops; and also helps free the trees of elm leaf-beetles, and the vegetable gardens of squash beetles, bugs, caterpillars, grasshoppers, and the bean and pea weevils. When it is seen perched on mullein stalks after its arrival in the spring, it is lying in wait for the moth of the cutworm. In fact, as Professor Beal says, " it is evident that a pair of Phœbes must materially reduce the number of insects near a garden or field, as the birds often, if not always, raise two broods a year, and each brood numbers from four to six young." He concludes: " There is hardly a more useful species about the farm and it should receive every encouragement and be protected from cats and other marauders, for it will repay such care a hundred fold."

Wood Pewee : *Contopus virens.*

Upper parts blackish brown ; under parts whitish, washed with olive ; wing bars whitish ; lower mandible pale brown or yellowish. *Length*, about 6½ inches.

GEOGRAPHIC DISTRIBUTION. — Eastern North America ; breeds from Florida to Newfoundland ; winters in Central and South America.

In Ohio it is almost exceptional to find an orchard without its pair of Wood Pewees, Mr. H. C. Oberholser says ; and in Farmington, Connecticut, on the grounds of Miss Porter's school and also on the village streets, one of the commonest bird notes is the clear, plaintive *pee'-ah-wee* of the sweet-voiced Flycatcher. Once heard and listened to, the note will never be forgotten. Some birds' songs, like the ordinary one of the Mockingbird, impress you as matters of execution and at times of gossip, but the minor call of the Wood Pewee seems the simple, sincere utterance of the heart. Of course the Pewee, being mortal, is not always in poetic mood, and in its commonplace moments it has a rapid, twittering *twit'-ter-rah*, given with quivering wings and tail. Mrs. Miller says it has also a low, pleasing song.

The voice of the Wood Pewee is recognized quickly, but the bird itself is a little hard to find in a treetop, and when not singing may be confused with the Phœbe. Two things help one, however, for to the patient observer the Pewee's habit of flying out after insects will betray his whereabouts; and his distinct whitish wing bars will separate him from his cousin, the Phœbe. Then, too, he is smaller and sits more upright than the plump, fluffy Phœbe.

When watching a Pewee in Farmington one day, I was much puzzled by her actions. Again and again she crossed a wide open space and flew against the side of a tree trunk. What food could she be finding there? Putting up my opera-glass, I was delighted to discover a round patch of light green lichen on the spot to which she went, and following her flight saw her go straight as an arrow to a crotch in a treetop, where she sat down and went to moulding a little knot in the crotch. She had been gathering lichen for her nest! It seems a simple matter, but after years of delight in the exquisite lichen-covered nest of the Wood Pewee — a nest excelled by none but the Hummingbird's — it is enough to start one's pulses to see the dainty builder actually putting on her decorations. To the true bird-lover life cannot be altogether blank while such pleasures are to be had for the looking.

Grouped together, the four commonest Flycatchers can easily be distinguished from each other. In size they grade down from the Kingbird to

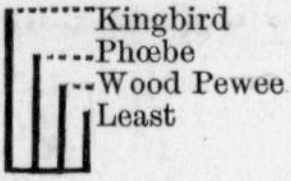

...Kingbird
...Phœbe
...Wood Pewee
...Least

the Least, and each one has distinctive characters. The Kingbird can be told at a glance by his large size and the white band on the end of his tail; the Wood Pewee may be distinguished from the Phœbe by its white wing bars; while the Least may be known by its small size, its wing bars, and call of *che-beck'*. (See Plate XIII. p. 258.) The Kingbird is the one seen chasing Crows and Hawks; the Phœbe, the house, barn, and bridge bird; and the Wood Pewee, the pensive, poetic architect of the lichen-covered nest.

Looked at as a group, all four birds have the prominent Flycatcher characters — the gray plumage, large heads and shoulders, and broad, flat, slightly hooked, bristling bills (Fig. 38).

Fig. 38.
Bill of Flycatcher.

As flycatching birds, the Flycatchers' methods of hunting differ markedly from those of the Swifts and Swallows, who simply go through the air devouring all they meet; for the Flycatchers lie in wait for passing insects, flying out from a perch and dropping back again to wait for more. Grouped by song, the Flycatchers rank with the songless Grouse and Doves, or the minor songsters, such as Swallows, Chickadees, Nuthatches, and Hummingbirds; rather than with the Mockingbirds, Catbirds, Wrens, and Orioles. Like some other birds, they have the useful power of regurgitating indigestible portions of their food.

Fig. 39.

Crow Blackbird: *Quiscalus quiscula* and allies.

Adult male, head, neck, and breast metallic iridescent purplish; rest of body bronzy, purple, or green. *Adult female*, duller, but back with traces of iridescence. *Length*, 12½ inches.

GEOGRAPHIC DISTRIBUTION. — United States east of the Rocky Mountains; north to Newfoundland and Great Slave Lake; breeds throughout most of its range; winters from North Carolina and southern Illinois to Texas.

Before the chill of melting snow is out of the air, while spring is still vacillating in her advance upon March, bustling troops of Crow Blackbirds appear on the brown grass and in the bare trees, making such a merry clatter and looking so big and positive that all uncertainty seems over, and we can no longer doubt that summer is on the way. Our spirits rise as we watch them walk about, gurgling and squeaking jovially to each other, and we welcome them as we do the Jack-in-the-pulpit and the Wake-robin, though later in the spring our thoughts may be filled by rarer, more delicate flowers and more tuneful birds.

How full of business the birds appear as they walk over the lawns and parks regardless of observers who stop to admire their glossy, iridescent coats, and who smile as they fly up on a branch with a squawk to scrape their bills and shake their tails! When they fly, lookers-on are still more interested, for they spread their long tails and turn them into rudders with which to steer their course. When the Crow Blackbirds go to nesting, they still keep in colonies. They build bulky nests of mud and grasses, and lay bluish eggs singularly scrawled. As their name suggests they have many mannerisms of the Crows, with whom, like other birds who get most of their food on the ground, they share the habit of sedately walking instead of hopping as tree-feeding birds do when they descend to earthly matters. It would indeed seem strange and unseemly for a dignified Grouse or Dove to hop, but on the other hand how greatly out of character would it appear for a merry Chickadee to walk!

The food the Blackbirds get on the ground varies. In some localities, at certain seasons of the year, they fall upon the grain fields in flocks of hundreds or thousands and do much harm. This is very exceptional, however, in the east. Ordinarily about one third of their food consists of insects, the greater part of which are injurious. One of their commonest occupations is following

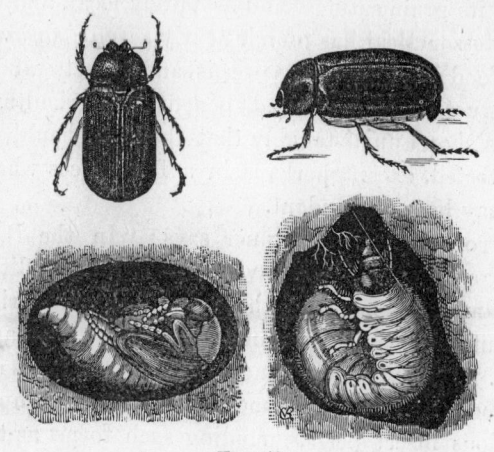

Fig. 40.
May Beetles and White Grubs, eaten by Crow Blackbird.

the plow, after which their stomachs are found 'crammed with grubs.' They also eat grasshoppers, crickets, locusts, adult grubs or May beetles (Fig. 40) and the destructive rose bug and curculio. In fact, Professor Beal concludes that "by destroying insects they do incalculable good."

Red-winged Blackbird: *Agelaius phœniceus*.

(Plate VI.)

GEOGRAPHIC DISTRIBUTION.—North America, from Costa Rica to Great Slave Lake and New Brunswick; breeds throughout most of the United States and its Canadian range, and winters from Virginia southward.

In Minnesota there is a bounty on the Red-wing, but its grain-eating habit is purely local, and, as Professor Beal has found, nearly seven eighths of its food is of injurious weeds and insects whose destruction is a decided benefit to agriculture. This shows unmistakably that the bird should be protected, except perhaps in a few places where it may be too abundant.

Prof. Lawrence Bruner says: "In the Red-winged Blackbird we have a friend that we little dream of when we see the large flocks gathering about our cornfields during late summer and early fall. During the balance of the year it is engaged most of the time in waging war upon various insect pests, including such forms as the grub worms, cutworms, grasshoppers, army worm, beet caterpillar, etc. Even when it visits our cornfields it more than pays for the corn it eats, by the destruction of the worms that lurk under the husks of the large per cent. of the ears in every field.

PLATE VI. — RED-WINGED BLACKBIRD

Adult male, epaulettes bright scarlet, edged with whitish; rest of plumage black. *Adult female*, upper parts dark brown, streaked; under parts buffy, streaked with brown; throat tinged with orange or yellow. *Length*, about 9½ inches.

"Several years ago the beet fields in the vicinity of Grand Island were threatened with great injury by a certain caterpillar that had nearly defoliated all the beets growing in many of them. At about this time large flocks of this bird appeared, and after a week's sojourn the caterpillar plague had vanished."

Throughout the summer the Red-wing feeds largely on insects, and even while grain is still to be had it begins to eat weed seed, and continues through the winter serving the farmer by destroying such pests as ragweed, foxtail grass and bindweed. In fact, statistics show that 57 per cent. of its total vegetable food is composed of noxious weeds, as against 13 per cent. of grain. In the ricefields of the south, Doctor Fisher tells us, the Red-wing does considerable good in winter by eating the volunteer rice, which is degenerate grain that has escaped from the cultivated squares of rice.

Fig. 41.
Clover Leaf-beetle.

Besides having an economic interest in the Redwing, every bird-lover must be personally attracted to him. Who is not conscious of a thrill of pleasure at sight of one of the handsome birds sailing down to a fence with scarlet epaulettes fairly standing out on his shoulders, and who can but respond to the sight of a flock swinging over the blades of a marsh? The birds of the lawn have their own place in our affections, but the *o-ka-lee* of the Red-wing stirs associations whose richness is all their own. Bolles speaks of the theory that all bird music is imitative of the sounds best known to the species, and this seems to be borne out by the notes of the Red-wings, for they have 'the sound of water running through their sweet measures.'

Cowbird: *Molothrus ater*.

Adult male, head and neck brown; rest of plumage glossy black with metallic reflections. *Adult female*, dark brownish gray, lighter below. *Length*, about 8 inches.

GEOGRAPHIC DISTRIBUTION. — Breeds from Texas to New Brunswick and Manitoba; rarer in the western United States; winters from southern Illinois and Virginia southward to Mexico.

'Buffalo Bird' used to be one of the names of the Cowbird on the plains, and Major Bendire says that in the prairie states now "one will rarely see a bunch of cattle without an attending flock of Cowbirds, who perch on their backs, searching for parasites." This occupation is not interrupted by the ordinary cares of family life, for the Cowbird builds no nest of its own, but foists its offspring upon its neighbors.

Probably the historic cause of this remarkable habit would give us more charity for the bird, but it does such violence to the one redeeming instinct of the lowest types of man and beast that it is hard not to regard the bird with unqualified aversion. Not only is it entirely lacking in the maternal but in the conjugal instincts, for it practices polyandry. On the other hand, the male Cowbird is polygamous, and Mr. Ridgway tells us "becomes quite amorous during the breeding season, parading before the females with spread wings and tails, now and then swelling up till he seems ready to burst; but the looked-for catastrophe is prevented by the emission of a ridiculous squeaking song, when he subsides to his original proportions." The only thing that can be said in favor of the female Cowbird is that she takes pains to place her eggs where they are most likely to be hatched. Major Bendire gives a list of ninety-one birds in whose nests she has been known to leave her eggs: but though this includes Woodpeckers, Flycatchers, Orioles, Thrushes, Sparrows, Vireos, Wrens, and Warblers, the birds most frequently imposed upon are so small that the Cowbird's big, crowding nestling will be the one to survive when it is a question of size and resisting power. It is said that as many as seven Cowbird eggs have been found in a single nest, but there is usually only one. The eggs generally hatch before those of the rightful owners of the nest, and the young grow so rapidly and to such size that they either smother or crowd out the smaller birds. Major Bendire exclaims indignantly: "A brood of insectivorous and useful birds is almost invariably sacrificed for every Cowbird raised." Mr. Ridgway, in his interesting book on the birds of Illinois, gives a vivid picture of the female Cowbird when she is searching for a nest in which to deposit her egg. "She hunts stealthily through the woods," he says, "usually among the undergrowth, and when a nest is discovered, patiently awaits from a convenient hiding-place the temporary absence of the parent, when the nest is stealthily and hastily inspected, and if found suitable she takes possession and deposits her egg, when she departs as quietly as she came." Some of the foster parents abandon their nests, or build a second nest over the eggs, but usually the milk of human kindness conquers, and the little bird does her best to bring up the foundling.

In the village of Farmington, Connecticut, we once saw a Song Sparrow on a lawn feeding a Cowbird bigger than she. When she handed it a worm, one of my field class exclaimed in astonishment, "I thought the big bird was the mother." And well she might, for when the fat nestling towered above its foster parent, insistently shaking its wings, the poor, hard-worked little Sparrow, with her own wings tight at her sides and a general harried air of hurry, looked thinner and smaller and meeker than ever before. It was pathetic. Close at her heels pressed the big, impatient Cowbird, whose existence had probably cost the lives of her own brood, not one of whom was left alive to follow the little mother.

Rusty Blackbird: *Scolecophagus carolinus*.

Adult male in nesting plumage, uniform glossy bluish black. *Adult female in spring*, slate color, glossy above, duller below. *Adults in fall and winter*, upper parts tipped with brown or rusty; under parts tipped with buffy. *Length*, about 9½ inches.
GEOGRAPHIC DISTRIBUTION. — Breeds from the Adirondacks and Northern Minnesota, northward to Labrador and Alaska; winters from Virginia southward.

In spring, when large flocks of Blackbirds are roaming over the country, one may perhaps be confused by them, but with a little care they will easily be distinguished. The Crow Blackbirds may be known by their large size and long tails. The male Cowbird may be told at a glance by his chocolate colored head, the Red-wing by his epaulettes, and the Rusty by his *uniform* glossiness. The female Red-wing, on the other hand, may be recognized by her streakedness; while the female Cowbird can be distinguished from the Rusty by the larger size of the Rusty, and the fact that it is slaty in spring and rust-color in fall and winter. The bill of the Cowbird (Fig. 42) is distinctive in all plumages, being short and thick, as is seen from comparison with that of the Meadowlark (Fig. 43), which the Red-wing's resembles in type. In the nesting season identification is simple, for the female Red-wings are with their gorgeously epauletted mates in the marshes; the Cowbirds are

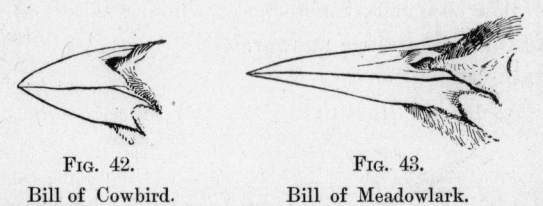

Fig. 42.
Bill of Cowbird.

Fig. 43.
Bill of Meadowlark.

wandering about the pastures with the cows; and the Rusty Blackbirds have disappeared to their northern homes.

Major Bendire says that the Rusty Grackle " is much more of a forest-loving species than the other Blackbirds, and during the breeding season it appears to be far less gregarious. Its favorite haunts in the Adirondacks are the swampy and heavily wooded shores of the many little mountain lakes and ponds found everywhere in this region, and here it spends the season of reproduction in comparative solitude."

In winter, the Major says, the Rusty Blackbirds may be seen occasionally about barns and stockyards, usually by themselves, but sometimes in company with other Blackbirds. He observes that their mode of flight resembles that of the Red-wing, and that " when feeding, while moving along, the rearmost fly over the others and alight again in the front ranks. Their notes are much more musical than those of the Grackles or other Blackbirds. The ordinary call note sounds like 'tchäck, tchäck,' several times repeated; another is like 'turulee, turulee, turulee,' uttered in a clear tone, and varied occasionally to 'trallahee, trallahee.'"

Fig. 44.

Bobolink: *Dolichonyx oryzivorus*.

(Plate VII. p. 104.)

GEOGRAPHIC DISTRIBUTION. — Breeds from southern New Jersey and central Illinois northward to Nova Scotia, and westward to Utah and Montana; leaves the United States by way of Florida, and winters in South America.

The return of the birds is a record of daily increasing pleasure, but it is only a quickening and a promise until the glad day in May when we go to the meadows and find that the Bobolinks have come. Then the cup of summer gladness seems full. The Bobolinks like a field adjoining an orchard, so that they can fly up and make a singing gallery of the apple-tree tops, but the high nodding weeds of a meadow also please them very well. Just on the edge of the beautiful old village of Farmington they keep the meadows ringing with their songs. I remember passing one field where the birds made black spots on the isolated weeds in the distance, and other black forms started up out of the deep grass nearer by and crossed and recrossed the meadow in intersecting lines singing, till my companions, some of them hearing the song for the first time, pressed to the meadow fence and stood in silent delight listening to the jubilant chorus. The joyous birds seemed to fly back and forth for the very purpose of freer song, the rapid, jumbled, tumbling medley needing the motion of the wings for its fullest outpouring. One day I saw a curious sight: a singing Bobolink when in mid air raised his wings over his back and held them there like set sails, and then threw up his head and throat as if to let the song bubble out. The flying birds often put down their wings and hold them stiff as they sail down to the ground.

When watching a field of Bobolinks, one is impressed by their originality of dress. While most other birds are lighter underneath than above, the Bobolink is just the opposite. But instead of being an exception to the law of protective coloration, this may be to protect him from the weasels and other nocturnal enemies that come on him when he sleeps on the ground. Then, too, the Bobolink's diurnal enemies see him from above; he lives without cover, in an open,

PLATE VII. — BOBOLINK

Adult male in spring, head, under parts, wings, and tail black; back of neck with buffy patch; back largely grayish white; tail feathers pointed. *Female, young, and adult male in fall*, upper parts brownish, streaked with black; under parts buffy. *Length*, about $7\frac{1}{4}$ inches.

exposed meadow. If he were black above, he would be a target for all passing Hawks and other gunners. At all events he is light above: his top colors approximate to the meadow tints, but his breast, invisible when he is on the ground by his nest, is a glossy, handsome black which may well please the eye of his lady. When he rises from the friendly cover of the meadow to wing his way to the south, he shows another wonderful example of nature's work in eliminating dangerous characters and fostering the beneficial ones. He moults, and the whole Lincoln family proceed on their travels, like so many demurely dressed Sparrows.

When the Bobolinks go south they stop on the way, first in the marshes, where they are known as 'Reed-birds,' and then in the ricefields of South Carolina and Georgia, where they are known as 'Rice-birds.' Here they do great harm, and are killed in such numbers that our northern meadows are fast losing their choruses; for it is a lamentable fact that the intelligence which leads a bird to adopt as food the crops which man has planted must in many cases prove its own destruction. Most of the devices that have been tried to protect the rice have failed, but in the neighborhood of St. Louis a number of planters have adopted a helpful measure. When feeding on the rice in its milky state, the birds need to wash their bills frequently to free them from the gummy matter that comes from the rice, so the planters draw off the water from the fields, obliging the birds to take time to go a long distance for water. In the north it is hard for us to realize how much harm the Bobolink does, and without a personal knowledge of the losses of our southern planters we must deplore the extermination of our northern favorite, for it is the bird which, since our childhood, has been the joy of our meadows.

Fig. 45.

Meadowlark: *Sturnella magna.*

Adults in summer, upper parts streaked brownish; under parts bright yellow, breast with black crescent. *In winter*, plumage duller. *Length*, 10¾ inches.

GEOGRAPHIC DISTRIBUTION. — Eastern North America; breeds from the Gulf of Mexico to New Brunswick and Minnesota; winters from Massachusetts and Illinois southward.

The Bobolink and Meadowlark are the two

songsters of our eastern meadows, but how they differ! One can scarcely listen to them in the same mood. Robert o' Lincoln's song is of June gladness, of strong sunshine making the daisies whiter and deepening the buttercup's gold; while the Meadowlark's, as he springs from the dew-laden grass and sails up into the blue sky, is so fresh and pure it seems to come on the wings of the morning, and gives the deeper beauty of that day in June when Heaven would try the earth if it be in tune. The Bobolink's mood is one of care-free happiness; the Meadowlark's suggests the fervent joy that is akin to pain.

In passing a Bobolink meadow one can hardly miss seeing the merry minstrels, but one may often look a field over in vain for the Lark, whose sad, clear voice is ascending to heaven. The musician is so nearly the color of the meadow that it takes a keen eye indeed to discover him. Like the Bobolink, he shows his beauty only to his mate. His back is dull, streaked brown and white, but his breast is a golden yellow hung with a necklace of richest jet. Ordinarily the bird knows very well how to make use of his dull coat, but sometimes life presents problems for bird as well as beast. A most perplexing moment once came to a Lark. He found himself on a fence between a Hawk and a collector! To which should he expose his brilliant breast? His brothers in the locality, at sight of this same collector, had promptly turned their backs to him, looking back at him only over their shoulders, but this bird kept his back to the Hawk and stood facing the man. As the collector was a *naturalist*, the bird's trust was not misplaced, and he lived to again sing his joy to his mate.

Incredible as it seems to the nature-lover, the Meadowlark is often shot for food, although on purely economic grounds, as Professor Beal pertinently remarks, it is "entitled to all possible protection, and to slaughter it for game is the least profitable way to utilize a valuable species."

It has been said that the Meadowlark eats clover-seed, but in looking for it in stomach contents it was found in only 6 out of 238 stomachs, and 99 per cent. of the food at clover time was found to be insects, mainly grasshoppers, insects whose ravages have been notorious from the earliest times. Professor Beal says: "The number eaten is so enormous as to entitle the Meadowlark to rank among the most efficient of our native birds as a grasshopper destroyer." It is estimated that the value of the grass crop saved by the Meadowlarks on a township of thirty-six square miles, each month during the grasshopper season,

Fig. 46.
Grasshopper.

is about twenty-four dollars. "Nor are the other components of the insect food less important except in quantity. Some of the most injurious beetles form a considerable percentage of the stomach contents." Among the other insects eaten by the Meadowlark are May beetles, ants, bugs, caterpillars, curculios, and leaf-beetles. In conclusion, Professor Beal says: "Far from being injurious, it is one of the most useful allies to agriculture, standing almost without a peer as a destroyer of noxious insects."

With the Meadowlark we come to the last of the Blackbird and Oriole family that we shall take up. As a group they are strongly marked birds, of striking colors, of good size — when compared with the smaller Chickadees, Wrens, and Hummingbirds — having strong bills and feet as compared with the Swallows and Swifts. (See Figs. 47, 48.) Among themselves they differ widely. The brilliant Orioles are birds of the treetops; the Blackbirds, Bobolink, and Meadowlark, largely birds of the ground.

Fig. 47. Weak foot of Swallow.

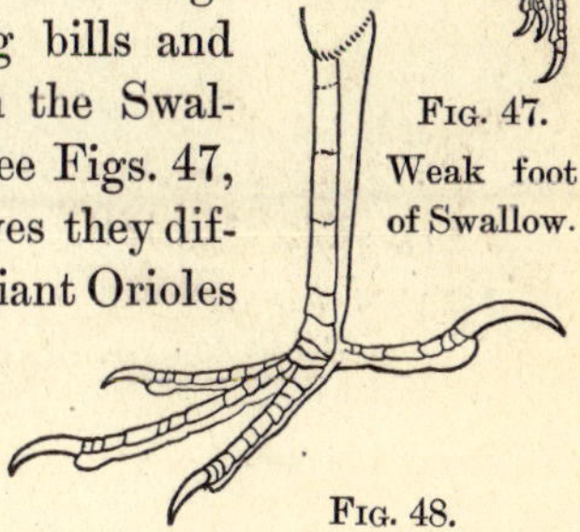

Fig. 48. Strong foot of Blackbird.

Of the two eastern Orioles, the male Baltimore is always more or less yellow and black, while the adult male Orchard Oriole is chestnut and black.

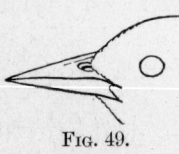

The Orchard Oriole is also smaller and builds a shallower nest of grass. The Blackbirds are alike in general characteristics. They all walk — the Orioles hop — and they get most of their food on the ground. The Crow Blackbird, Red-wing, and Rusty are most nearly alike, and as their food habits are similar, they have similar bills. (See Fig. 121, p. 193.) The Cowbird and Bobolink are less exclusively insectivorous, and so their bills approach more to the seed-eater conical type of bill (see Figs. 42, p. 102; 50, p. 110, and 119, p. 193), contrasting quite sharply with the long, pointed bills of the Orioles (Fig. 49), Meadowlark (see Fig. 43, p. 102), and Blackbirds (Fig. 121, p. 193). The Blackbird and Oriole types of bill contrast well with the flytraps of the Swallows, the probes of the Hummingbirds, and the bills of the Doves, Wrens, and Flycatchers. (See Figs. 120, 118, p. 193; 106, 107, p. 192.) In the same way, the tails of the Bobolink and Meadowlark, which live among the grasses, have become specialized, being quite sharp and pointed, as if worn by friction (see Fig. 51); while those of the treetop Orioles, or the Blackbirds that frequent short-cropped pasture land or mown fields, have theirs unmodified.

The Blackbirds and Bobolinks, like the Crows, Swifts, and Swallows, are eminently social birds, spending most of their time in flocks.

Key to Nesting Plumage of Adult Male Blackbirds and Orioles mentioned in this Book.

1. Small (length about 7 to 7½ inches).
 2. Plumage mainly black and white; under parts black; back black and white, with buffy patch on nape. Found in meadows . . . . p. 103. BOBOLINK.

 2'. Plumage mainly black and orange, or black and chestnut. Head and throat black.
  3. Rest of under parts yellow or orange.
   p. 56. BALTIMORE ORIOLE.
  3'. Rest of under parts chestnut.
   p. 61. ORCHARD ORIOLE.

1'. Large (length 8 to 13 inches).
 4. *Plumage mainly brown and yellow;* back brownish; under parts yellow, with black crescent on breast; outer tail feathers white. Lives in meadows.
   p. 106. MEADOWLARK.
 4'. *Plumage mainly black.*
  5. Shoulders with red epaulettes; rest of plumage black. Found in swamps and marshes.
   p. 96. RED-WINGED BLACKBIRD.
  5'. Shoulders without red epaulettes.
   6. Head and neck brown; rest of body glossy black. Found in pastures with cattle . p. 98. COWBIRD.

112 KEY TO BLACKBIRDS AND ORIOLES

6'. Head and neck not brown.

7. Tail normal; body *uniformly* glossy bluish black; migrant. Plumage rusty in fall migration.
p. 101. RUSTY BLACKBIRD.

7'. Tail long and fan-shaped; body not uniformly bluish black; head, neck, and breast metallic purple or bluish; rest of body metallic with iridescent bars . . . . p. 93. CROW BLACKBIRD.

FIG. 52. Meadowlark.

FIG. 53. Bobolink.   FIG. 54. Red-wing.

REPRESENTATIVES OF BLACKBIRD AND ORIOLE FAMILY.

Chipping Sparrow: *Spizella socialis.*

Top of head reddish brown; under parts plain gray; back brown streaked with black; bill black. *Length*, about 5¼ inches.

GEOGRAPHIC DISTRIBUTION. — Eastern North America; breeds from the Gulf states to Newfoundland and Great Slave Lake; winters in the Gulf states and Mexico.

Mr. Torrey says if he could have his way this little bird should be known as the 'door-step Sparrow,' and certainly no name could be more appropriate. Many delightful instances are on record concerning particularly tame Chipping Sparrows, but none is more interesting than that given by Mr. Robert B. Lawrence, a nephew

FIG. 55.
Chipping Sparrow.

of the distinguished ornithologist, George N. Lawrence, who tells how a 'Chippy' acquaintance of his father's became a confidential friend. Mr. Lawrence says in a note in 'Forest and Stream:' "For years at our place in Flushing, L. I., my father has fed some half dozen of these Chipping Sparrows, and the young birds have taken bread or seed from his hand when it was held near the ground, but the old birds would never allow any such familiarity. One of the adult birds, however, seemed more inclined to do so than his companions, and at last, in the summer of 1879, mustered courage enough to follow the example of the young birds, and, finding no ill effects, jumped onto my father's finger, and, sitting there, ate his breakfast. The ice once broken, 'Dick,' as we christened him, seemed to lose all fear, and from that time always ate his breakfast from my father's hand. . . . This continued all the summer, but when fall came, with the first cold blasts Dick took his departure for the summer regions of the south. The next April, however, he returned and without any hesitation came one morning to my father's call and in his old accustomed way ate his breakfast from my father's hand. Dick and his mate built their nest in the vines which clambered over our piazza and spent the summer with us. . . . This year he has gone farther, as he has several times, while sitting on my father's hand, ceased eating and poured forth his song of thanks. . . . It has long been known that birds would return to the same locality year after year, but that a wild bird should remember a person's voice and come back after his long wandering as

FIG. 56.
Crab Grass, eaten by Chipping Sparrow.

Fig. 57.

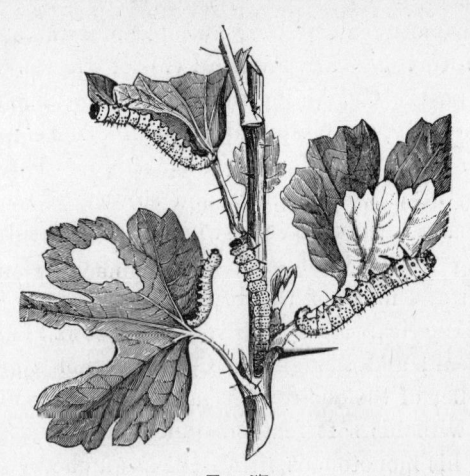

Currant Worm.

tame and confiding as when he went away is, I think, very remarkable."

Since the Chippy is the first of the Sparrows to be studied, it will be well to look at him closely in order to see what are his family traits. He has the cone-shaped, seed-cracking Finch bill, — the type we saw approached by those of the Cowbird and Bobolink, but like most Sparrows is not exclusively granivorous. As a seed-eater he destroys the foxtail and crab grass that disfigure our lawns, and he helps, too, to free our premises from pigweed, chickweed, and knotweed; while as an insect-eater he does us a good turn by eating cabbage-worms, tent-caterpillars, cankerworms, and gypsy-moth caterpillars, and particularly affects cutworms and army worms, two of our worst insect pests. Combining insect with vegetable food in this way, the Chippy does not find it necessary to go as far south for his winter supplies as exclusively insectivorous birds, and so we find him, in company with other short-winged seed-eaters, wintering in the Gulf states and Mexico, while the Swift and many of the Flycatchers go on to Central America. As a family, the Sparrows are very musical; and though the Chippy is not a gifted member of the choir, when he sits on a tree in the sun, with his soft feathers fluffed up about him, even his monotonous little trill has a cheery summer sound.

Song Sparrow: *Melospiza fasciata*.

Upper parts brown, streaked with black; under parts white, streaked with black, and with a dark central blotch on breast. *Length*, about $6\frac{1}{4}$ inches.

GEOGRAPHIC DISTRIBUTION. — Eastern North America; breeds from northern Illinois and Virginia north to Quebec and Manitoba; winters from southern Illinois and Massachusetts to the Gulf states. No considerable area of the United States is without one of the geographic races of the Song Sparrow.

The Song Sparrow is another of our commonest birds. It is larger than Chippy, and its clan instead of wearing red caps usually wear black buttons on their white-striped vests (Figs. 55, 58).

Being vegetarians in winter, they are able to abide in the north; and even in Illinois and Massachusetts, where the winds blow lustily over the snow, the cheering winter birds occasionally favor us with a summer song. Indeed, in many places the welcome voice of the Sparrow has been heard in every month of the year except December.

Fig. 58.
Song Sparrow.

Like the Chippy and other philosophers, the Song makes the most of the table that is spread for it, changing with good grace from the seeds that winter offers to the insects that summer brings. Mr. Nehrling considers it one of our most useful birds from the eagerness with which it sets upon injurious caterpillars, grasshoppers, and leaf-eating beetles, to say nothing about cabbage worms and moths; while the persistency of its search for rose bugs, cutworms, and all kinds of beetles rivals that of the most ardent entomologist. While we have need of every pair of these useful birds, Mr. Nehrling believes that many of their garden nests are destroyed

Fig. 59.
Pigweed, eaten by Song Sparrow.

by strolling cats, and many of the birds both young and old killed by the prowlers. "Cats should never be tolerated in garden or field," he exclaims emphatically. "They do more harm to our familiar garden birds than all other enemies combined." This testimony is borne out by Mr. Brewster, who says that stray grimalkins have even penetrated the forests of Maine, their tracks actually being commoner there than those of any wild animal. As a matter of humanity to the cats as well as to the birds, Mr. Brewster urges that all city and village cats should be licensed just as much as the dogs, and no unfed vagrants allowed at large, where to keep from starving they will prey upon our song-birds.

When not prematurely killed by feline marauders, in some localities the Song Sparrow is said to rear three broods in a season. It builds on or near the ground, and its eggs are bluish white heavily marked with brown.

The Song Sparrows are among the gentlest and most winning birds we are blessed with, and when they nest near the house may easily be induced to come to the doorstep for crumbs. Their song bears the test of every day; for while it is not brilliant, it has all the sweetness of the gentle bird's own simple nature, and heard far from home stirs chords that the more brilliant strangers do not touch. Even its chirp has a contented quality that it does one good to hear.

Furthermore, the student who is interested in noting bird songs will find the Song Sparrow's well worth study, for it varies remarkably. Fifteen varieties of its song have been noted in one week, and the same individual often has a number of tunes in his repertoire.

Vesper Sparrow; Grass Finch: *Poocœtes gramineus.*

Brownish gray, streaked; *patch on wings, reddish brown; outer tail feathers showing white in flight. Length,* about 6 inches.

GEOGRAPHIC DISTRIBUTION. — North America; breeds from Missouri, southern Illinois, and Virginia northward to Manitoba and Nova Scotia; winters on the Atlantic coast from Virginia southward.

When scared up from roadside fences, this Sparrow may be known by its color, which is lighter than the Song Sparrow's, in connection with the white feathers that flash from the sides of its tail as it goes. As its name indicates, its most interesting character is

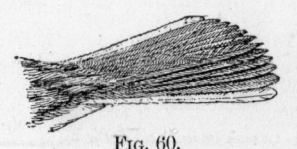

FIG. 60.
Tail of Vesper Sparrow.

its evening song. One of its twilight recitals is especially marked in my memory. The choral society was an Easthampton one, and some enthusiastic bird-lovers in the beautiful old Massachusetts town invited me to attend its vespers. A brilliant Bluebird led us from the long, shaded village street into 'Green Lane,' an old grassy way bordered by rail fences leading west to the golden sunset, and the bird's sweet, quavering call had hardly died away when we were greeted by the voice of one of the Sparrows we had come to hear. He was perched on a stake in the meadow beside the lane, and as we stopped to listen poured out his beautiful vesper hymn. It had scarcely ceased when it was taken up by another of the rich-voiced choristers, and soon was being sung by glad, sweet voices scattered far through the meadows. In the stillness of the hour, with the level fields reaching to the golden horizon, the peaceful evening song seemed full of new beauty, and we listened in silence to its calm, melodious notes till the sunset afterglow faded from the sky and the twilight shadows gathered around us.

Red-eyed Vireo : *Vireo olivaceus.*

(Fig. 63, p. 126.)

Crown gray, bordered by black ; a *conspicuous white line over the eye ;* upper parts olive-green ; under parts white. *Length*, about $6\frac{1}{4}$ inches.

GEOGRAPHIC DISTRIBUTION.—Eastern North America; westward to British Columbia ; breeds from the Gulf states to Labrador and Manitoba ; winters in Central and South America.

If you listen carefully to the bird songs in villages, about country houses, or even in open woodlands, it will not be long before you distinguish the voice of the Red-eye. His song is a monotonous but cheerful monologue made up of short

Fig. 61.
Red-eyed Vireo.

broken sentences, in triplets, given as he hunts over the branches for food. 'Where's a worm? Where's a caterpillar? Where's a worm?' he queries as he goes, answering his own question very comfortably to himself. There is nothing ecstatic about his song. It seems merely the accompaniment of his occupation. He sings as a contented man whistles at his work. His call note is quite a different matter. From it one would imagine him the most discontented of mortal birds, for it is a complaining, mewing *wheeough*. It is only fair to say, though, that often when he gives it he has cause for complaint, for at such times you frequently find some feathered bugaboo abroad in the land.

If it were not for the Vireo's song you would

easily pass him unnoticed, for as the Sparrows are brown to match the weeds and fields, the little greenlet is dressed to tone in with the green leaves and the light in the woods, being greenish above and white below. But if you once set eyes on him you can easily identify him, for over his eye he has a white border to his gray cap. A bird's cap is not usually easy to see, if he lives in the trees; but the Red-eye has a trick of turning his head over as he looks critically at the leaves, which is of great service to the inquisitive groundling below.

Like the Orioles, Vireos are public benefactors, practical foresters, working out their self-appointed commission to preserve our village and forest trees. They are, first and foremost, caterpillar-eaters, but they also do great good by their fondness for bugs and weevils, May beetles, inchworms, and leaf-eating beetles. Like other epicures, they understand that fruit sauce gives zest to a meat diet. Doctor Fisher says they are extravagantly fond of the aromatic fruits of the benzoin bush, sassafras, and magnolia. Indeed, when the Red-eyes are gathered along the Gulf coast in the fall, he says they feed almost exclusively on the berries of the magnolia, and become exceedingly fat. It is thought that the magnolia imparts a delicate flavor to the flesh, but however this may be, the sad fact remains that immense numbers of the little songsters are slaughtered and exposed for sale in the French markets of New Orleans under the name of '*petit grasset*.'

The question may arise as to what the Vireos and other little berry-eaters are doing with the botany of the land, whether they are laying low the wild fruits as they are the weeds. It is an interesting subject. The difference lies just here. The fruit-eaters want the soft pulp — the fruit, — and either eject the hard pits or swallow them whole, so merely acting as distributing agents for the fruit stones; but the weed destroyers eat the seeds themselves, crushing the cases, and so killing the germs of future weeds. Whatever proportion of the Vireo's food may be vegetable, it necessitates no modification of bill from the slender insectivorous type (see Fig. 109, p. 192), as it is only for cracking hard substances that the Sparrows need the conical seed-eater type of bill. (See Fig. 119, p. 193.) Neither does the berry-eating habit of the Vireo lessen the length of the journey which it makes in winter, together with other insect-eaters; for berries, it would seem, are not as reliable a harvest as weed seeds, and Central America, with its winter insects, seems to offer the fullest larder. Being subject to enemies, the birds migrate under cover of the night, and some morning give us a delightful surprise by filling with song a grove that was silent and untenanted the night before.

In the woods, the Vireos' nests are among the

commonest and most beautiful. They are exquisite little birch-bark hanging baskets, often with pieces of wasp nest and bits of paper tucked in.

Aside from their beauty, the Vireos' nests are particularly interesting to watch, as the confidence of the birds is easily won, and if it is not abused they will admit you to most intimate relations.

A delightful episode occurred one spring in Easthampton, Massachusetts. In an apple-tree close beside a house, a pretty Red-eye quietly hung her basket nest and had laid two eggs before she was observed by any of her human neighbors. Then the motherly owner of the house discovered her and was so pleased to find her there that, as she went and came at her work inside, she would talk to the little creature brooding her nest on the apple bough by the window. In this way the two became such good comrades that the woman soon thought she would like to feed her pet. First she offered her a large cracker, but this was so alarmingly big that the Vireo flew away at sight of it; when a small piece was handed up to her at the end of a stick, however, she took it gladly, and from that time on her friend fed her every day.

As the food would slip off the stick, the woman nailed a mucilage-bottle cover to the end of it for a cup, and in this way was able to serve boiled egg and other dainties in the apple-tree. A glass cup was hung up beside the nest, but the bird was never seen to drink from it, although when water was put in her own tin she would sit on the nest and 'drink like a chicken,' which is interesting, as it is said that Vireos usually quench their thirst daintily with dew or rain-drops on the leaves.

The people of the village flocked to see their trustful little neighbor, and when the good woman of the house wanted to show her friends the Vireo's eggs she had only to hold the food-cup far enough from the nest to tempt her away from the eggs, or else give her an unusually large piece of cracker, when she would quietly fly off with it. If, when she was being fed, the wind blew her branch away from the cup, the friendly Vireo would crane her neck to reach after the food.

The little creature was so kindly treated she lost all fear of her neighbors, and actually let one of them stroke her feathers while she sat on the nest. But just as her friend was thinking of the pleasure she would have watching the brood when they hatched, suddenly all the eggs disappeared, leaving the Vireo cradle hanging empty on its branch. It was a sorry ending of the pleasure of the spring, and the villagers came to condole with the good woman who was so suddenly bereft. "I felt as if there had been a funeral," she said sadly, in telling me of it.

Warbling Vireo: *Vireo gilvus.*

Upper parts grayish green; under parts slightly washed with yellowish; no wing bars. *Length*, about 5¾ inches.

GEOGRAPHIC DISTRIBUTION. — North America; breeds as far north as the Hudson Bay region; winters in the tropics.

FIG. 62.
Warbling Vireo.

FIG. 63.
Red-eyed Vireo.

The Warbling Vireo is peculiarly a village bird, and when the Red-eye lives in town the two will be heard at the same time. The song of the Warbling can easily be distinguished, for the broken utterances of the Red-eye are totally different from the smoothly flowing warble of the smaller bird. When seen, the absence of the gray cap will mark off the Warbling from his larger cousin, though one does not often get sight of the little olive bird, he is so busy in the elm-tops where his mate builds her nest and lays her eggs — smaller counterparts of those of the Red-eye. Doctor Brewer says the Warbling is particularly abundant among the elms of Boston Common, and Mr. Torrey also reports it there.

FIG. 64.

Flicker; High-hole; Yellow-hammer: *Colaptes auratus*.

Adult male, back brownish, barred with black; throat pinkish fawn and rest of under parts lighter, spotted with black; red band on back of neck; *rump white;* black stripe on sides of throat and black crescent on breast; under side of wings and tail yellow. *Adult female*, similar, but without black streaks on sides of throat. *Length*, 12 inches.

GEOGRAPHIC DISTRIBUTION. — North America west to Alaska and the eastern slope of the Rocky Mountains; breeds throughout its range, and winters from Illinois and Massachusetts southward.

Though the Flicker is to be found with us during the winter, his loud ringing *if-if-if-if-if-if-if* is especially associated with the spring smell of the damp woods-earth, and the first glad awakening. Sometimes it is only a single note, a loud, far-reaching *clape*, that makes our pulses leap with the assurance that the cold silence of winter is broken and spring has come. At the sound of the familiar voice we hurry toward it, but may have a long distance to hunt, for it carries far through the woods. The first glimpse of the splendid great bird repays us for our tramp. High up on a tree trunk he may be clinging, Woodpecker fashion, with his back to us, the scarlet patch on the back of his neck showing to good advantage. How strong and powerful he seems! To the beginner who has puzzled his brains and strained his ears and eyes over the faint notes and the confusing forms of small migrants vanishing through the treetops, the sight of such a big, strikingly marked bird at rest is a double satisfaction. There is no mistaking his call, there is no mistaking his person. Even when he flies — with undulating motion — the big, round white spot at the base of his tail marks him as far as he can be seen.

Once placed in the woods, the Flicker should be kept track of. Soon his companions will come, and with the soft spring days his 'thoughts will turn to love,' and then he will merit the closest attention, for he is a gallant wooer, full of original ways. "It is an exceedingly interesting and amusing sight," Major Bendire tells us, " to see a couple of males paying their addresses to a coy and coquettish female; the apparent shyness of the suitors as they sidle up to her and as quickly retreat again, the sly glances given as one peeps from behind a limb watching the other — playing bo-peep — seems very human. . . . The defeated suitor takes his rejection quite philosophically, and retreats in a dignified manner." To this Mr. Burroughs adds of the Flicker wooer: "He spreads his tail, he puffs out his breast, he throws back his head, and then bends his body to the right and to the left, uttering all the while a curious musical hiccough." Surely his lady should be flattered by such adulation.

When it comes to housekeeping, the Flicker retires to an old stub or tree trunk, but his proceedings may be watched if he is convinced of your good intentions. The sight of the large entrance hole always stirs delightful anticipations, for Monsieur 'Pique-bois-Jaune,' as he is called in Louisiana, is a character worth studying. Mr. Brewster has given us a most interesting description of a nest he watched,[1] and Mr. Manley Hardy, who has also studied the birds familiarly, tells us that he has been permitted to feed the young with strawberries while they were still in the nest! He was obliged to put the berries in their bills at first, but afterwards the nestlings would come up to the hole and look out when they heard him coming, acting, he flattered himself, 'just as if the old birds were feeding them.'

[1] *The Auk*, vol. x. pp. 231-236.

The parents feed the young by regurgitation, which is very fortunate, as bringing food by the billful to such large broods would be a good deal like feeding a giant with a teaspoon. Audubon once found a nest containing eighteen young birds and three eggs.

Though the Flicker young have the good taste to like strawberries, the family food is ants. In times of grasshopper plagues, the Woodpeckers very philanthropically turn to and help kill off the pests; but at ordinary times they work more for the housewife and florist, destroying the ants that invade the pantry and foster insect lice. Almost half of the total food of the Flicker is ants, 3,000 of which were found in each of two stomachs — stomachs whose owners apparently were not greatly in need of a tonic! This explains what the birds are doing when they are seen on the ground, and scared up from ant-hills in old pastures. The ground habit of the Flicker is so dominant that his dress conforms to the color of the earth; his tongue, too, is unusually long and has a rough surface to which his sticky saliva glues the ants which he picks up or probes out of the ant-hills.

FIG. 65.
Ant, eaten by Flicker.

FIG. 66.
Flicker, showing long tongue extended.

Like many innocent birds, the Flicker has been

accused of eating corn, but in reality only 5 out of 230 Flicker stomachs contained any, and the bird is one of the most useful we have.

FIG. 67.

Red-headed Woodpecker: *Melanerpes erythrocephalus.*

Head, neck, and breast uniform deep red; rest of under parts white; upper part of back black, wings showing white in flight. *Young*, red replaced by dark gray. *Length*, 9¾ inches.

GEOGRAPHIC DISTRIBUTION. — Eastern North America; breeds from Florida to northern New York and Manitoba; winters from Virginia and, in good beechnut years, from northern New York southward.

As we drive through the country we are sometimes surprised by the sight of a strikingly brilliant bird with a red head and patches of white on its wings flying ahead of us. It is such a dazzling beauty that, while we fear for its life if it linger along the public highway, we must wish for a closer acquaintance. Fence posts are among its favorite hunting places, and while it clings to them it is much less conspicuous than one would imagine so brilliant a creature could be; but it can sit very still on occasion, and its black back might easily pass for a fence-post shadow, while its red head seen against the green loses its color.

It is interesting to watch the Red-head hunt from a fence, for he combines the ways of the Flycatchers and more conservative tree-trunk Woodpeckers. First, perhaps, he makes short elliptical sallies into the air for insects, returning to his post with his prey; then he flies down to the ground for a grasshopper, and again shoots up straight in the air for perhaps a rod, coming down almost as straight; and finally, as if tired of such flycatcher-like antics, falls to hammering on his rail.

The Red-head is particularly fond of the injurious big white grub in its adult stage of June bug, the prionus form, and eats more grasshoppers than any other Woodpecker. It also eats wasps and weevils. To be sure, it does harm by eating some useful insects and a little grain and fruit, but the fruit does not amount to much. As it eats a large quantity of wild fruit, it could probably be diverted from the cultivated varieties by planting wild ones where they do not exist. The best of these would probably be dogwood, mulberry, elderberry, choke-cherry, and wild black cherry. In the north, the principal food of the Red-head is beechnuts, and when they are plentiful it stays north during the winter. A great many interesting observations have been made on the bird's storing habit, and though it is not so remarkable as the corresponding habit of the western Woodpecker, it is still surprising. Whole handfuls of beechnuts have been taken from a single knothole, and have been found in cracks in gate posts, behind slivers on fence posts, and in cracks at the ends of railroad ties.[1]

Fig. 68.
Prionus Beetle, eaten by Red-headed Woodpecker.

Estimating the value of the Woodpecker family, Professor Beal says they are "the only agents which can successfully cope with the insects of forest and partly of fruit trees, and for this reason if for no other they should be protected in every possible way."

[1] *The Auk*, vol. iv. p. 193; *Bulletin of the Nuttall Ornithological Club*, vol. iii. p. 124.

It is a rare pleasure to have a pair of Redheads nest on one's premises. At Rockford, Illinois, on the grounds of Rockford College, the handsome birds are so tame that the college girls can watch them without danger of worrying them; but in most places they have been so much annoyed that they are chary of their friendship, and when you go to their neighborhood hide behind a tree trunk and look out at you suspiciously from the corner of one eye, scolding with a loud rattling *krit-tar-rah* which, if you approach too near, Mr. Widmann says is indistinguishable from that of the tree-frog.

Major Bendire says that some of their nesting-holes show remarkably neat workmanship, the edges of the entrance-hole being beautifully beveled off, and finished inside as smoothly as with a fine rasp. On the treeless prairies he has found them obliged to nest in telegraph poles and similar places provided by man. Unlike the Flickers, the Major says the Red-heads do not feed their young by regurgitation, but bring them their grasshoppers '*au naturel.*'

Fig. 69.

Hairy Woodpecker: *Dryobates villosus.*

Male, upper parts black, spotted and *striped* with white; red
band on back of head; under parts white. *Female*, similar,
but without red on neck. *Young*, with crown red. *Length*,
about 9½ inches.

GEOGRAPHIC DISTRIBUTION. — Eastern United States, from
northern border south to North Carolina. Closely allied
races occur throughout the west, and from the table-lands
near the city of Mexico to northern Canada.

The Hairy is one of the two commonest black and white Woodpeckers. It is usually shy and not often seen about houses. In the nesting season the birds are noisy, the male spending his leisure time drumming on a resonant dead limb, being, as Doctor Fisher well puts it, a maker of instrumental music. When playing his piano, "the louder the noise produced, the more satisfactory it appears to be to the performer," we are assured by Major Bendire. As the best of us can speak only in the tongue we know, the Woodpeckers announce their love on the drum. If the tattoo falls softly on the ear of the lady, the happy Woodpecker pair set about looking for a home. They choose their tree with such good judgment, Major Bendire tells us, that hard knots are rarely encountered in their excavations. He says that both birds work on the nest, and it takes them about a week to prepare it. "The entrance-hole is as round as if made with an augur." Both birds incubate, and when the young appear feed them by regurgitation, the conventional method it seems with Woodpeckers when their young first hatch, though the Redheads and a few others feed by the bill as the brood grow up. The Major thinks that the Hairy Woodpeckers remain mated through life.

In regard to their food he says : " The Hairy Woodpecker, like most of its relatives, is an exceedingly beneficial and useful bird, which rids our orchards and forests of innumerable injurious larvæ, like those of the boring beetles. It never attacks a sound tree. Although commonly known as Sapsucker, this name is very inappropriate; it is not in search of sap, but of such grubs as are only found in decaying wood; nevertheless . . . many are shot under the erroneous belief that they injure the very trees they are doing their best to protect. In central New York, and undoubtedly in other sections as well, where a few decades ago one could see some of the finest apple orchards to be found anywhere, you may look in vain for them now. Nearly every tree of any size now shows abundant and unmistakable signs of decay, caused by the increase of the insects which live in them and the decrease of such birds as destroy these pests. In Oneida and Herkimer counties, New York, the top of nearly every black ash tree is dead, and the trees are slowly decaying, undoubtedly due to some species of boring beetle."

Downy Woodpecker: *Dryobates pubescens* and allies.

Adult male, upper parts black, spotted and striped with white; under parts white; a scarlet band on the nape. *Adult female*, similar, but without the scarlet patch. *Young*, with crown red. *Length*, about 6¾ inches.

GEOGRAPHIC DISTRIBUTION. — North America, from Labrador and Alaska to Florida and California; resident throughout their ranges.

The gentle little Downy Woodpecker is a bird

we may have always with us, even in the stormiest winter weather, all for the slight trouble of nailing a piece of suet or fresh pork on a tree. Though we can gain its company by feeding it, the Downy is quite capable of looking after itself in winter, living like the Chickadee on what it extracts from cocoons, together with insect eggs and larvæ which it gets from the bark. As Major Bendire says: " Unfortunately, it is also considered a Sapsucker, and many of these exceedingly useful little Woodpeckers are killed yearly through lamentable ignorance, under the supposition that they injure the fruit-trees by boring in the bark, while in fact they render the horticulturist inestimable service by ridding his orchard of innumerable injurious insects, their eggs and larvæ, and few of our native birds deserve our good will more than the little Downy Woodpecker. The most stringent protection is none too good for it."

Besides the accusation of being a Sapsucker, Downy is accused of eating fruit. The falsity of this charge is shown by the fact that, of 140 stomachs examined by the experts of the Biological Survey in the Department of Agriculture, only 3 contained fruit; apple being found in 2 and strawberries in 1. On the other hand, almost 75 per cent. of the bird's food is insects. Eleven Woodpeckers taken in Kansas in winter contained 10 per cent. of grasshopper eggs. The little

DOWNY WOODPECKER

bird also destroys May beetles, plant lice, and ants. A single wood-borer will often kill an entire tree, and one fifth of the Downy's animal food consists of caterpillars, many of which bore into wood and live on stems and leaves. Indeed, the Downy is the most beneficial of all the useful Woodpecker family. Its bill is a good excavating tool, and its barbed tongue also bears witness to its effective search for insects (Fig. 71).

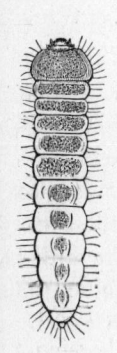

FIG. 70. Wood-boring Larva.

Downy's song is a thin rattle, his call note a sharp *peek-peek*, a most grateful sound when it breaks the winter stillness. Seeing the birds about during snowstorms, we wonder what becomes of them in the still colder nights, but the Downy takes good care of himself. Doctor Mearns says, in his interesting account of the bird's habits: "At night he is comfortably housed in a hole, which he digs expressly for that purpose. Always . . . so far as my experience goes, he places the entrance to his burrow so as to face the sunny south." One little chap whom the Doctor visited one night shortly after sunset was " snugly ensconced

FIG. 71. Tip of Tongue of Downy Woodpecker, for spearing Insects and their Larvæ.

within the cavity, with his bill warmly tucked away amongst the feathers, which were ruffed up so as to look like a black and white ball, with a red-naped head tucked in the middle. While sleeping, his whole frame heaved at every breath, so profound was his slumber."

Glancing back over the four Woodpeckers we have taken up — the four commonest of the family, the Flicker, Red-head, Downy, and Hairy (Fig. 64, p. 127; Fig. 67, p. 131; Fig. 69, p. 135), — we find it easy to discriminate between them. The Hairy and Downy are the most typical Woodpeckers, living almost exclusively on tree trunks, whose colors they match. The Red-head has more of the Flycatcher habit of hunting, and descends to fences; while the Flicker is still less of a true Woodpecker, spending most of his time on the ground looking for ants, so having the ground browns on his back in place of the conventional Woodpecker black and white. All four birds nest in tree trunks, as do the Bluebirds, Chickadees, and Nuthatches. Like those of the Swifts, the Woodpeckers' tails are stiff and pointed for bracing (see Figs. 212 and 213, p. 353), but the Flicker's is less stiff than those of the other Woodpeckers. Its bill is also modified from the Woodpecker type; and its tongue, which is one of the longest (see Fig. 66, p. 130), is provided with large salivary glands and sharp points on the surface, to which the mucilaginous saliva holds the ants for which it probes.

Waxwing; Cedar-bird: *Ampelis cedrorum.*

(Plate VIII. p. 142.)

GEOGRAPHIC DISTRIBUTION. — North America; in the east breeds from Virginia and the highlands of South Carolina north to Labrador; winters from the northern United States to Central America.

If you were to ask a dozen persons which were their favorite birds you would probably get widely varying answers, it is so largely a matter of personal associations. But there are certain birds to whom every one is attracted, and the gentle, smooth-coated, fawn-colored Waxwings stand high on the list.

In the fall, one may sometimes be fortunate enough to see one of their large bands, several hundred, the majority of which are young birds; and in winter one may have the rare pleasure of discovering a little bare tree filled with apple-like forms, which on closer view prove to be the gently lisping beauties, the sight of which always arouses pleasant memories. In the early summer, when other birds have gone to nesting, small companies, often of five, seven, nine, or eleven, will still be seen together; but by July they may be found in pairs, building in the orchards. Although it is always a pleasure to see them, they are particularly well worth watching at the nest. They are birds of remarkable affection and intelligence, and their habits are peculiarly interesting. By raising and lowering their crests they gain great variety of expression, and when about the nest often assume protective attitudes, drawing themselves up to look like long-necked bottles or sticks of wood, and sitting absolutely motionless till one would imagine longer endurance impossible. Bird literature contains many anecdotes of their affection and phenomenal conjugal devotion. Doctor Brewer tells of one which, when its mate was entrapped, became so preoccupied with anxiety it allowed itself to be taken in the hand, and when set at liberty would not leave till its companion was freed to go with it. In caring for the young, the Waxwings show great watchfulness. They feed by regurgitation.

Their food has been much discussed. In some places they are known as Cherry-birds, but cultivated cherries have been found in only 9 out of 152 stomachs examined, which, as Professor Beal says, "hardly justifies the reputation which the bird has gained as a destroyer of cherries." He ad ls that this supposed cherry habit, "to the careless and unobservant, would condemn the bird to destruction, but the closer observer looks further." Investigation shows that more than half of the whole food of the Cedar-bird consists of wild fruit which has no value, and that one eighth of its food consists of insects, among which are some of the worst pests of the country. Furthermore, since the nestlings are fed largely on insects, the greatest number of insects are eaten when fruit

PLATE VIII. — WAXWING

Crest and whole body soft fawn-color; area around bill velvety black; tail tipped with yellow band; wings often tipped with flecks of red, like sealing-wax. *Length*, about $7\frac{1}{4}$ inches.

is most abundant. The Cedar-bird eats caterpillars, spiders, and grasshoppers, but does most marked good in destroying the elm leaf-beetle that strips our village and city trees of leaves. Mrs. Mary Treat writes of one town in which the elms had been ruined for several years before the Cedar-birds came, and which were afterward comparatively free from beetles. From one calculation, it is shown that 30 Cedar-birds would destroy 9,000 worms during the month when the cutworm caterpillar is exposed.

To prevent the Cedar-bird from eating cultivated fruit, and to attract it to secure its help in destroying caterpillars, it would be well to plant the common bushes upon whose berries it feeds, such as blackberry, wild cherry, choke-cherry, sour gum, flowering dogwood, rough-leaved dogwood, chokeberry, red cedar, Juneberry, hackberry, black haw, black elder, huckleberry, frost grape, barberry, mistletoe, or pokeberry.

The Waxwings stand in a family by themselves among eastern birds, coming between the Swallows and the Shrikes. They are unique among North American birds in having wax-like appendages on the tips of their wing-feathers (Fig. 72). As we run over the groups of birds we have had, we see how the Cedar-birds differ from them in general characters. In the matter of coloration, the earth, leaf, and stubble browns of the ground birds are modified in them, for they approach more nearly the soft tints of the Doves, whose gentle ways they also share. Like the Red-headed Woodpeckers, they are erratic, wandering birds, here one year, somewhere else the next. As they travel in flocks they may be classed with the Swallows, Swifts, Blackbirds, and Bobolinks,

Fig. 72.
Wing of Waxwing, showing wax-like tips.

rather than the solitary Flycatchers, Vireos, and Woodpeckers. Ordinarily the Waxwings are put with the songless birds, and credited only with two low calls, a short whistle and the 'beady note' of Thoreau; but Mr. Nehrling says that both male and female sing. Careful notes on this point would be of value, and any study given the birds will be more than repaid, as they are unusually individual.

Goldfinch; Yellow-bird; Thistle-bird: *Spinus tristis.*

(See Frontispiece.)

Adult male, bright yellow; cap, wings, and tail black, marked with white. *Adult female*, brownish, tinged with yellow; without black cap; wings and tail blackish. *Adult male in winter*, similar to female. *Length*, about 5 inches.

GEOGRAPHIC DISTRIBUTION. — United States northward into Labrador, Manitoba, and British Columbia; breeds from Virginia, Kentucky, and California northward; winters mainly within the United States.

Like the Waxwings, the Goldfinches are late builders, and when other birds are going about silently, preoccupied with nesting cares, it is a peculiar pleasure to hear the light-hearted *per-chic-o-ree* of a band of wandering Yellow-birds as they come undulating through the sky. Few songs have the sweetness of their calls, or can awaken the same response in our hearts. For, like the Chickadee, the Goldfinch is one of the gentle, trustful birds that hold a place of their own in our affections.

When going about in wandering bands they brighten our days, and when nest-building claim still more our sympathetic attention. They are on the lookout for soft lining materials, and will frankly accept any bits of colored worsted or string that we may offer, repaying us by letting us enjoy their sweet family life. When the blue eggs are laid upon their thistle-down bed in the compact round nest in the apple-tree, the father bird watches us anxiously till he knows that he can trust us near his mate, but when once sure of our good faith, will feed her in our presence. How tenderly he calls out as he comes to her! The quality of his note has changed entirely since spring. Instead of the *per-chic-o-ree* that told only of his delight in his free life in the air, his call is now a rich, tender *dear, dear, dear-ie*, and a gentle, homelike *dear, dear, dear*. Mrs. Mabel Osgood Wright gives us a hint worth taking in the matter of attracting the Goldfinches. She says: "If you wish them to live with you and honor your trees with their nests, plant sunflowers in your garden, zinnias, and coreopsis; leave a bit of wild grass somewhere about with its mass of compositæ. Coax the wild clematis everywhere that it can gain footing; and in winter, when these joyous birds, gathered in flocks, are roving, hard-pressed for food, scatter some sweepings of bird-seed about their haunts, repaying in this their silent season their summer melody."

When nesting-time is over, the dainty birds again gather in bands, the males changing their canary-colored coats for the safer but dingy garb of their mates, and so go about through fall and winter doing public service by eating the seeds of the brown weeds that stand above the snow. In one place a flock of a thousand has been seen feeding on the seeds of ragweed, effectually limiting its spread there for another year. As every one knows, the 'thistle birds' are especially fond of thistle seeds. They also eat the seeds of the common 'beggar's tick' which is so troublesome in bottom lands, and the larvæ of the destructive wheat midge. In summer the Goldfinches feed their young mainly on insects, such as beetles, plant lice, larvæ, flies, and small grasshoppers.

Fig. 73.

Thistle, seeds eaten by Goldfinch.

But though we owe them gratitude for material benefits, in winter we think more of the good cheer they bring us. On a cold November day, when the bare trees are outlined against a gray sky, the sudden calls of a flock of these little Goldfinches will be like a burst of sunshine, bringing back all the gladness of summer. But with a *tweety-tweety-tweety* they start up and fly on, the gray clouds settle back, and the rain falls again on the black and dripping branches.

Purple Finch: *Carpodacus purpureus*.

(Plate IX.)

GEOGRAPHIC DISTRIBUTION. — Eastern North America; breeds from Minnesota and southern New York northward; winters from the northern states to the Gulf.

Purple this tuneful little Finch assuredly is not, but rather a warm old rose as if he had been dipped in pokeberry juice, as Mr. Burroughs so aptly suggests. The Finch part of the name is less deceptive and bears out the evidence of the cone-shaped bill; for the Purple Finch belongs to the Sparrow and Finch family of seed-eaters, whose partial vegetarianism enables them to winter north of the Gulf and who, like the Goldfinch, wander about in flocks looking for food. Doctor Mearns says of their flocks: " On some occasions they are quite wild, and, on being approached, all rise at once on wing with a loud, rushing noise, accompanied by certain peculiar wild notes, which produce quite a startling effect. . . . When feeding in flocks, the rustle of their wings is constant, and their united chirping produces a singular effect. . . . I have found immense flocks in March, eating the seeds of hemlock and spruce. . . . Like the Blue Jay and some other birds, they appear to be unusually lively during a rainstorm; and in winter, at the commencement of a snowstorm, they sometimes hie to the loftiest treetop, and begin to sing, as if from pleasure or excitement."

PLATE IX. — PURPLE FINCH

Adult male, dull rose-red. *Adult female*, brownish, streaked above and below. Resembles the Sparrows, but has a notched tail. *Length*, about $6\frac{1}{4}$ inches.

In summer the song of this pretty, rosy Finch is one of the common village sounds, but may easily be mistaken for that of the Warbling Vireo, until the two are heard together, when it proves to be much louder and of richer quality than that of the Vireo. The call note of the Finch is a metallic *kimp, kimp*, unlike any of the Vireo's notes.

The Purple Finch is one of the birds that should be watched closely during courtship. Its songs and dances are — apparently — of more interest to beholders than to its prospective mate!

Indigo Bunting: *Passerina cyanea.*

Adult male, whole body blue. *Adult female*, plain olive-brown above, dusky below; wings and tail black. *Young*, similar to the female but darker. *Length*, about $5\frac{1}{2}$ inches.

GEOGRAPHIC DISTRIBUTION. — Eastern United States; breeds as far north as Minnesota and Nova Scotia; winters in Central America.

In early June one of the predominating eastern songs is that of the Indigo-bird, —

Chrit-ty — chrit-ty — chrit-ty chrit, chrit, chrit, chree.
Chrit-ty — chrit-ty chrit, chrit, chrit, ta, tee.
Chrit-ty — chrit-ty — chrit, chrit, chrit, chrit, chree.

It seems commonplace enough when other birds are singing, but when the hot weather has silenced the main choir the Indigo's solo rings out with great good cheer. He often takes a solitary tree, and as if mounting a ladder flies higher and higher up its branches as he sings.

When he stops in the middle of his song to attend to domestic duties, you may be able to surprise him in his castle in some bushy fence corner, where his brown mate will meet you with an inhospitable, anxious air, crying *cheep*, and twitching her tail as nervously as if an innocent ornithologist could be a murderer. Have a care, though, if you would look at her pretty eggs, for a faint pathway through the bushes is enough to betray the poor bird's secret to her enemies, and the nest is so low and so easily upset that, as I know to my sorrow, with the best intentions one may do great harm while examining it. A sight of the eggs will repay the greatest care, however, for they are exquisitely delicate, shading from pure white to faint green or blue.

Though birds of such beautiful eggs, color, and song, as all men are mortal, the Indigos must needs attend the homely affairs of the inner man; but after descending to grasshoppers, caterpillars, and cankerworms, they again mount to the tree-tops and sing to the passing clouds their song of summer.

'Peto Bird;' **Tufted Titmouse**: *Parus bicolor.*

(See Fig. 77, p. 153.)

Crest and entire upper parts gray; under parts white; sides washed with brown. *Length*, 6 inches.

GEOGRAPHIC DISTRIBUTION. — Eastern United States; breeds from the Gulf states to southern Iowa and northern New Jersey; resident throughout its breeding range.

Like the Cardinal, the Titmouse is to be found in the National Zoölogical Park in Washington throughout the year, and the songs of the two may easily be mistaken, although the *pe-to* whistle of the Titmouse is distinctive and its *day-day-day-day-day-day-dait* proclaims it a Chickadee. Like the Cardinal, the Titmouse has a high crest, but there the resemblance ends, for the Titmouse is a small bird robed in Quaker gray, and the Cardinal a large bird decked out in cardinal plumes. Then, too, the bill of the Titmouse is small and black like the Chickadee's, while the Cardinal's is swollen and red (Fig. 28, p. 65).

In the southern part of Illinois, Mr. Ridgway says, no bird is more abundant at all seasons of the year. He says they are "roving in restless, noisy troops through the woods, scolding at every intruder and calling to one another in harsh tones." He adds that in winter "they become very familiar, approaching with confidence the immediate vicinity of dwellings — and, in company with Snowbirds, Carolina Chickadees, Nuthatches, Blue Jays, and other familiar species, glean their portion from the refuse of the table."

As the Titmice, like other Chickadees, nest in cavities in trees, they can readily be induced to live in bird-houses provided for them. They find plenty of food in winter, as they live not only on acorns, which they take under their claws and hammer open, but also find a store of food in the eggs, larvæ, and chrysalids of insects that live on bark and branches.

Key to Nuthatches and Titmice.

1. Back bluish gray; tail short. Found on tree trunks.
  2. Under parts reddish brown; crown black; side of head with black and white lines from bill to nape. Migrant . . . p. 76. RED-BREASTED NUTHATCH.

  2'. Under parts white; crown black; sides of head without lines . . p. 73. WHITE-BREASTED NUTHATCH.

1'. Back dull gray; tail long. Found on branches.
  3. Head crested; crown and throat not black. Song, *pe-to, pe-to, pe-to* . . . p. 151. TUFTED TITMOUSE.

  3'. Head not crested; crown and throat black.
  4. Wings and tail edged with white. Northern.

  p. 67. CHICKADEE.

  4'. Wings and tail not edged with white.

  p. 71. CAROLINA CHICKADEE.

NUTHATCHES AND TITMICE

Fig. 74.
Chickadee.

Fig. 75.
Red-breasted Nuthatch.

Fig. 76.
White-breasted Nuthatch.

Fig. 77.
Tufted Titmouse.

REPRESENTATIVES OF THE FAMILY OF NUTHATCHES AND TITS.

Fig. 78.

Blue Jay: *Cyanocitta cristata*.

Crest and upper parts purplish; wings and tail blue, marked with black and white; under parts gray, with black collar extending up across the back of the head. *Length*, about 11¾ inches.

GEOGRAPHIC DISTRIBUTION. — Eastern North America; breeds from Florida to Newfoundland; westward to Texas and Manitoba; generally resident throughout its range.

The Blue Jay, one of our handsomest and most vivacious birds, like the Nuthatches and Chickadees, may be attracted in winter by suet hung on the trees. Some New England farmers make beds of chaff on which they throw out corn for the Jays, and the birds come for the corn while the snow lasts, but as soon as bare ground appears they are off to find food they like better — mast, the large seeds of trees and shrubs, including acorns, chestnuts, and beechnuts.

This preference for mast, though depriving us of the Jay's society, is a good thing for the bird,

BLUE JAY

as it proves that he only takes corn when nothing better offers. Statistics bear this out. In October and November, when most corn is to be had, the Jay stomachs that have been examined show only 1 per cent. of corn against 64 per

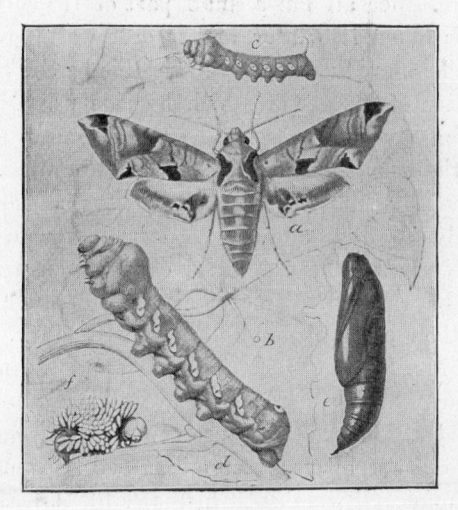

Fig. 79.

Sphynx Moth, eaten by Blue Jay.

cent. of mast, while 19 per cent. of the bird's total food is noxious insects, such as grasshoppers and caterpillars. Figures clear his name in other matters, for it has been noised abroad that he robs birds'-nests, but remains of birds' eggs were found in only 3 out of 280 stomachs, and young birds in only 2, which, to say the least, proves that he is not as black as he has been painted. Cats do much more harm than Jays in this respect; but we do not even license our cats, much less shoot our vagrants. In summing up the Jay's economic status, it is seen that he does little harm to agriculture, since all but a small part of the corn he eats is taken in winter, and is only waste grain, while he more than makes up for this by the large quantity of insects of which he rids us. He is particularly fond of the sphynx moth family, notably the member that is destructive to grapes.

Mrs. Olive Thorne Miller has always befriended the abused Jay, and in 'A Bird-Lover in the West' gives some delightful chapters on a nest that she watched. This was in the top of a pine-tree, though the birds build ordinarily lower. In Ohio Mr. H. C. Oberholser has found the nests in thorny bushes. The eggs are olive or brownish, thickly marked with brown spots.

The Jay's power as a mimic is well known, and mice may well tremble at his hawk-like cries.

The Jay belongs to the family of Crows and Jays, and has the powerful bill and feet of the family. (See Figs. 135 and 136, p. 218.) He uses his feet as the Crow does — to hold his food while he hammers it with his bill.

Like the Crows, the Jays are social birds, and live in flocks when not nesting. An extreme and most remarkable instance of their devotion to each other is given in 'The Auk' by Mr. Frithof

Kumlien. He found an old feeble Jay, with feathers faded, claws worn, bill dulled, and eyes blurred and dim, who was being protected and cared for by his companions. Some of them were always near to warn him of danger, and besides this, the faithful band would bring him food and carefully lead the old blind bird to a spring for a daily bath. ('Auk,' vol. v. p. 434.)

Fig. 80.

Belted Kingfisher: *Ceryle alcyon*.

Adult male, crest and upper parts bluish gray; under parts white; breast with bluish gray band. *Adult female*, similar, but sides and band on belly brown. *Length*, about 13 inches.

GEOGRAPHIC DISTRIBUTION. — North America, in the east breeding from Florida to Labrador, and wintering from Virginia to South America.

Not the least of the pleasures of living beside a river or lake is the chance of seeing one of these original birds on his way back and forth to his fishing grounds. Sometimes he flies so low

Fig. 81.
Belted Kingfisher.

you can see his reflection in the water; but again goes high above, cleaving the air so swiftly that, before you have had time to rejoice at his loud, stirring rattle and made up your mind to follow him, he has left you far behind.

Mr. Burroughs says that if you do "follow his rattle, . . . he will show you the source of every trout and salmon stream on the continent," adding that he always fishes alone, "true angler that he is, his fellow keeping far ahead or behind, or taking the other branch."

This is in line with Mr. Widmann's theory of

the inability of some birds to indulge the social instinct, for the Kingfisher's feeding habits may well necessitate private preserves. Whatever seabirds may do, trout-stream fishermen can ill afford to go in flocks. To be sure, though the king of fishermen, this sensible bird does not always restrict himself to a diet of fish. In the east, if opportunity offers, he eats crustaceans, grasshoppers, crickets, and beetles of the June bug family; and in Arizona, where rivers are scarce and deserts plenty, he lives mainly on beetles, grasshoppers, and lizards.

Like the Vireos, Flycatchers, and Hawks and Owls, the Kingfishers have the power of ejecting pellets of the indigestible bones and scales which they have swallowed whole. These are found around the burrows where they nest.

FIG. 82. Undeveloped foot of Kingfisher.

Like the Bank Swallows, though their feet are undeveloped (Fig. 82), they use them as trowels for excavating holes in sandbanks. Major Bendire says that while it may take a pair three weeks to excavate their nest, he has known them to make a tunnel five feet long in a little over three days. He says the male sometimes burrows a second hole over three feet deep, in which to sleep. By flashing a mirror into one of the burrows, Mr. Fuertes has seen one of the brooding birds on her nest. The young are hatched without feathers, and remain in the nest several weeks. Audubon says that when they are in the nest the mother, if disturbed, will sometimes fall on the water as if severely wounded, while her mate on a branch above shows his perturbation by jerking his tail, raising his crest, rattling, and flying anxiously back and forth.

Though shy at the nest, the Kingfisher, if treated with respect, becomes used to the genus homo. At Lake Placid, when moored in a boat alongshore, I have had one perch almost over me, and dive so near that the water spattered my paddle.

Yellow-billed Cuckoo: *Coccyzus americanus*.

(Fig. 83, p. 161.)

Upper parts *brownish gray*, with a slight greenish gloss; wings and outer tail feathers *black*, conspicuously tipped with white (thumb-marks); under parts white; under mandible yellow. *Length*, about 12¼ inches.

GEOGRAPHIC DISTRIBUTION. — North America; breeds from Florida to New Brunswick, and winters in the West Indies and Central America.

The cry of the 'Rain Crow' is a familiar country sound, but the bird who makes it is less well known. It is a bird that keeps closely hidden, flying out of one tree or bush only to cross to other cover, and moving so silently and swiftly that it might well escape detection. But it is a bird that every student and lover of the curious should hunt out and study patiently, for like the Waxwing it is an original character. As Mr. Burroughs says, "something remote seems ever weighing upon his mind." In 'Little Brothers of the Air,' Mrs. Olive Thorne Miller gives an

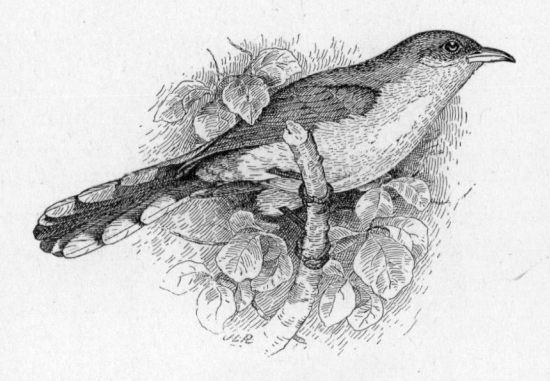

Fig. 83.

Yellow-billed Cuckoo.

account of the performances of a pair of Cuckoos which she watched nesting, and who tried by the most remarkable but characteristic posturing and ventriloqual calling to intimidate, mystify, and lure her away from the brood.

Great care must be taken in watching Cuckoo nests, as the birds are very apt to desert them when discovered. The Yellow-bill is one of the poorest nest-builders; and while the young often do fall out of the nest, the wonder is that any are ever able to stay on top of the loose mat of twigs

YELLOW-BILLED CUCKOO

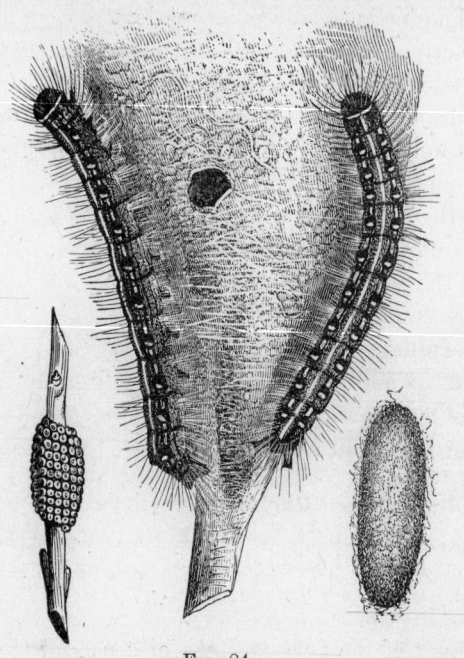

Fig. 84.
Tent-caterpillar, eaten by Cuckoo.

prepared so carelessly for them. The eggs of both Yellow and Black-billed are greenish blue.

The Cuckoos might well be called caterpillar birds, for they are so given to a diet of the hairy caterpillars that the walls of their stomachs are actually permeated with the hairs, and a section of stomach looks like the smoothly brushed top of a gentleman's beaver (Fig. 85, p. 163).

The Yellow-billed is especially fond of the destructive caterpillars that make the large web nests in our fruit-trees. Remains of 43 of these caterpillars were found in the stomach of one bird shot at six o'clock in the morning. But it was not only this early bird that got the worm, for in 21 stomachs examined there were 355 caterpillars and 23 grasshoppers, in addition to a collection of saw-flies, potato bugs, and other insects. One stomach contained 217 fall web-worms!

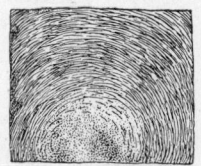

FIG. 85.
Section of Cuckoo Stomach.

Black-billed Cuckoo: *Coccyzus erythrophthalmus.*

Upper parts grayish brown, with slight green gloss; wings and tail the same, only slightly tipped with white; under parts white; bill black. *Length*, about 11¾ inches.

GEOGRAPHIC DISTRIBUTION. — North America east of the Rocky Mountains; breeds as far north as Labrador and Assiniboia, and winters in Central and South America.

The Black-billed Cuckoo is very much like the Yellow-billed, but lacks the reddish brown wings, black tail, yellow mandible, and the heavy thumb-marks on the tail of the Yellow-billed (Figs. 86, 87, p. 164). The call of the Yellow-billed is given as *tut-tut, tut-tut, cl-uck-cl-uck-cl-uck-cl-uck-cl-uck-cl-uck, cow, cow, cow, cow, cow, cow;* while the Black-billed, it is said, has the cow notes connected, and has altogether a much softer voice.

BLACK-BILLED CUCKOO

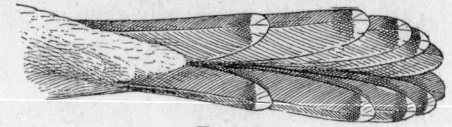

Fig. 86.

Tail of Black-billed Cuckoo.

Fig. 87.

Thumb-marks on tail of Yellow-billed Cuckoo.

The nests and eggs are similar, though the Black-billed's nest is not quite so loosely put together.

The Cuckoos are among the first birds on Mr. Forbush's list of those that eat the caterpillars of the gypsy moth, which for some years back has been ravaging New England trees. Of the Black-billed's stomachs examined by the Biological Survey, 16 contained 328 caterpillars, and in addition 15 grasshoppers and some spiders.

Fig. 88.
Gypsy Moth, eaten by Cuckoo.

The Cuckoos and Kingfishers are in the same

order, and although so unlike except in anatomy, stand apart from all other birds. By running over the orders of birds we have had, their unlikenesses will easily be seen.

Land Birds, — Order I. Grouse, Quail, etc. Order II. Pigeons and Doves. Order III. Birds of Prey. Order IV. Cuckoos and Kingfishers. Order V. Woodpeckers. Order VI. Hummingbirds, Swifts, etc. Order VII. Perching Birds: 1. Flycatchers; 2. Crows and Jays; 3. Blackbirds and Orioles; 4. Finches, Sparrows, etc.

Key to Adult Male Cuckoos and Kingfishers.

1. Crested. Back bluish. Under parts white with blue belt. Found by water.

    p. 157. BELTED KINGFISHER.

2. Not crested. Back not bluish. Upper parts brownish; under parts plain white. Found in undergrowth.

    a. Tail black, with distinct white thumb-marks on under side. Under manible yellow.

    p. 160. YELLOW-BILLED CUCKOO.

    a'. Tail brown, without distinct thumb-marks; bill black.
    p. 163. BLACK-BILLED CUCKOO.

Fig. 89.

Rose-breasted Grosbeak: *Zamelodia ludoviciana*.

Male, head, throat, and back black; under parts, rump, and marks on wings and tail white; breast and under wing coverts with patches of rose-red. *Female*, brownish, sparrowy-looking bird, with white line through crown and over eye. Saffron yellow under wings. *Length*, about 8 inches.

GEOGRAPHIC DISTRIBUTION. — Eastern North America; breeds from Eastern Kansas and the higher altitudes of Virginia and North Carolina northward to Maine and Manitoba; winters in Central and South America.

In June the New England villages ring with the songs of birds — the merry bubbling of Wrens, the monotonous short sentences of the Red-eye, the smooth-flowing roundelay of the Warbling Vireo, the *che-beck* of the Least Flycatcher, the trill of the Chipping Sparrow, the shrill twittering of passing Swifts, the pipe of the flashing Oriole, and the rich rounded pendulum song of the Rose-breasted Grosbeak. Except perhaps the Oriole's, it is the loudest and most musical of all the many songs, and may be easily traced to its source — often in the dense green of an apple-tree top. If the song stops before you have sighted your bird, he may be found by the odd thin *ick*, *eek*, or *peek* which is his characteristic call. The first glimpse of his black head and the rose-colored patch on his breast is enough to identify him; while the large, streaked brown bird who flies away with him may be recognized by her size, — she is too large for a Sparrow, — by the white line over her eye, and by her abnormally large beak, for the Grosbeak bill gives the bird its name and is an exaggeration of the Finch type.

This powerful crusher is put to most excellent use in the potato field for killing the Colorado potato beetles, of which the birds are particularly fond. The Grosbeaks have been accused of eating peas, but the stomachs of those killed while about the vines contained but few peas, and enough potato bugs and other harmful insects to pay for all the peas taken in a whole season. The garden where these Grosbeaks were found adjoined a potato patch, which was so infested with bugs that the vines were completely riddled.

The Grosbeaks visited the field every day, and when their young were old enough to travel the whole family appeared on the scene, where their proceedings were watched and chronicled by Professor Beal. The young birds stood in an ex-

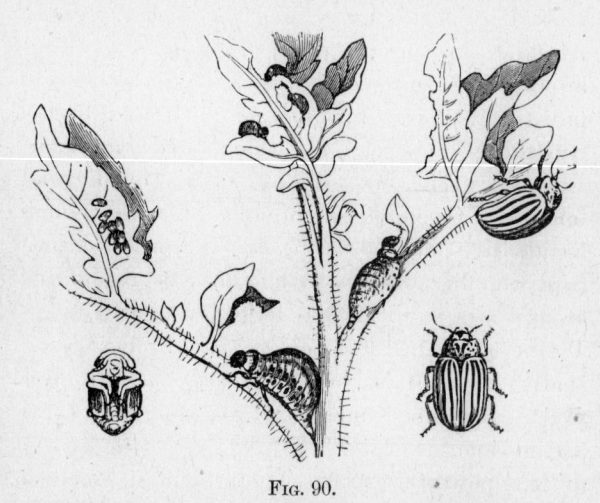

Fig. 90.

Colorado Potato Beetles, eaten by Rose-breasted Grosbeak.

pectant row on the topmost rail of the fence, and their parents flew briskly back and forth bringing them beetles. A few days later Professor Beal revisited the scene of the massacre, and " not a beetle was to be found, either old or young ; the birds had swept them from the field and saved the potatoes."

But while we appreciate his services, our affection for the Grosbeak is not based on his fondness for potato bugs. He is a striking and beautiful creature and his song is a delight; moreover, aside from his beauty and song, he is a most lovable bird. One of the pleasantest nesting episodes I have ever known was that of a Grosbeak family. The pretty, pale blue eggs with their brown markings were laid in a nest of twigs in a pear-tree, close beside a carriage drive, and the trustful birds seemed to realize that they were among friends. The father was most devoted, brooding the nest and feeding the young. All his thoughts seemed to centre about the pear-tree; the little home there was clearly the point around which everything in his world revolved. When he came to the nest, it was with a low, sweet greeting; when he left, it was with a soft farewell; if danger threatened he was on the spot, and his anxious cries filled the air; when all was quiet again and he had flown away, his cheering song came back to his mate on the nest, as if to assure her that he was near. The rich music that was always ringing about the home, the tender watchfulness and affection of the old birds, and the quiet happiness of the mother of the family on her nest under the green leaves, all seemed suited to the cheery orchard with its mellow sunshine and its ripening fruit.

Scarlet Tanager : *Piranga erythromelas*.

Adult male, whole body bright scarlet; bill, wings, and tail black; under wings white. *Adult female*, upper parts light olive; wings and tail brownish; under parts greenish yellow. *Young male and adult male in winter*, similar to female, but wings and tail black. *Length*, 7¼ inches.

GEOGRAPHIC DISTRIBUTION. — Eastern North America; breeds from southern Illinois and Virginia to Manitoba and New Brunswick; winters in Central and northern South America.

Whenever we hear a thin *eek* in a treetop, though its maker is invisible, we can say with assurance that a Grosbeak is there; and so, when we hear a call of *chip-churr* in the green leafy woods, we know that we are listening to that most brilliant of North American birds, the Scarlet Tanager. It may or may not be an easy matter to find him, for, though on the migrations he is often seen in low bushes, his choice is usually for the massive green treetops. His song is the best clue, for it is a loud, swinging-pendulum song, — like the Grosbeak's, only less smoothly rounded, — and by getting its direction, as the bird moves about, you can catch at least a passing glimpse of his glowing coat and glossy black wings and tail. And there are moments when a glimpse is enough. It is all very well if alone in a leafy vale, with nothing to do but dream under the enchanter's

FIG. 91.
Bill of Tanager.

lay, but alas for the unhappy leader of a bird class endeavoring to concentrate attention upon invisible and fleeting Warblers! At sight of the first red feather all other birds are forgotten, and one may as well bid farewell to Warblers and follow meekly where the beauty calls. Rest assured, no other bird will be worth looking at while he is by! In Washington, where both Scarlet Tanagers and Cardinals are seen, especially when the Tanagers are on their way north, the two red birds are sometimes confused, though in reality they are very unlike. The Cardinal may always be told by his high crest (see Fig. 28, p. 65), and the Tanager by his black wings and tail, while, in addition, the Cardinal is much the larger of the two, and his red coat a cardinal rather than a scarlet shade.

As the Tanager lives inside the woods and hunts mainly in dense foliage, he is much less exposed to enemies than birds which live out in open fields or even in village trees, so can well afford to wear colors that would be fatal to Sparrows and such commoners who pitch their tents on the plain. The Tanagers build low, however, and the mother bird could not be scarlet without greatly endangering the nest. Accordingly nature has provided her with a leaf-colored suit that is a perfect disguise. If danger threatens she flies into the leaves, and you may hunt a merry hour before discovering her, unless she moves in unleaf-like style.

Tanagers are as good actors as Bobolinks, and will lead you a dance if you are looking for their nest. The only one I ever found belonged to an æsthetic pair who built on the leafy arch of a slender sapling which had been bowed to earth by a falling tree. It was made of fine twigs, but we never saw the pale greenish blue eggs that should have been laid in it, for at an unlucky moment my big dog gave a sneeze that betrayed our presence, and the nest was promptly deserted.

The devotion of the old birds to their young is spoken of by Wilson, and he gives a touching instance of it. A nestling was taken and carried half a mile, where it was caged and hung out in a tree. The distressed father followed it all the way and stayed by to feed it in the cage, constantly uttering "cries of entreaty to its offspring to come out of its prison," cries so sad that the kind-hearted man who had captured the bird "took out the prisoner, and restored it to its parent, who accompanied it in its flight to the woods with notes of great exultation."

Summer Tanager: *Piranga rubra.*

Male, body and tail rose-red; wings brownish. *Adult female and young*, upper parts greenish yellow; under parts yellowish. *Length*, 7½ inches.

GEOGRAPHIC DISTRIBUTION. — Eastern United States to the Plains; breeds from Florida to southern New Jersey, wandering casually to Nova Scotia; winters from West Indies and Mexico to South America.

"In at least the southern half of Illinois the Summer Redbird is an abundant species in dry upland woods. It is moreover a very familiar species, nesting habitually in trees along the roadside and even in the midst of towns. For this reason it is much more frequently seen than the Scarlet Tanager. . . . Besides being a more abundant and familiar species, its notes are much louder. The ordinary one sounds — as Wilson expresses it, *chicky-chucky-chuck*. . . . The nest is a thin and shallow but very firm structure. . . . The eggs are usually three in number, and are similar in color and markings to those of the Scarlet Tanager, but somewhat larger." (Ridgway.)

These two birds are the only eastern members of the family in North America. They are our most brilliant birds, and, as their colors might suggest, belong to a tropical family. The two species are easily distinguished by the shade of red.

Key to Adult Spring Male Tanagers.

Common Characters. — Entire body red.

1. Bill, wings, and tail black; body bright scarlet. Found in northern woodlands. Call, *chip-churr* . . . . . p. 170. SCARLET TANAGER.
1'. Bill, wings, and tail not black; body and tail rose-red; bill and wings brownish. Found in southern woodlands. Call, *chicky-tucky-tuck* . . p. 173. SUMMER TANAGER.

White-throated Sparrow: *Zonotrichia albicollis.*

(See Fig. 92, p. 176.)

Adults, upper parts brown, streaked with black; *chin with a squarish white patch;* breast gray; belly whitish; central white crown stripe *narrower* than inclosing black stripes. *Young*, white of throat duller; black and white stripes replaced by gray and brown. *Length*, about 6¾ inches.

GEOGRAPHIC DISTRIBUTION. — Eastern North America west to the Plains; breeds from Montana, northern Michigan, and occasionally Massachusetts, northward to Labrador; winters from Massachusetts to Florida. Accidental on Pacific coast.

Associated with the crisp, fresh mornings of early spring is the sound of the clear, ringing whistle of the White-throated Sparrow. *I, I, pea-bod-y, pea-bod-y* the birds call so loudly that the dogs sometimes look up in the evergreens to see who is whistling. If they could recognize the whistler they would see an attractive sight, for the White-throat is a bird of distinction. He is as much larger than the Song Sparrow as the Song is larger than the Chipping Sparrow. (See Fig. 58, p. 117, and Fig. 55, p. 113.) Like the Chippy,

WHITE-THROATED SPARROW 175

he has a plain gray breast, but in addition to this has a handsome mark in the form of a snow-white throat patch. (See Fig. 92, p. 176.) Instead of the reddish brown cap of the Chippy, the White-throat, when arrayed in his best has a handsome black and white striped crown, but in a flock one often sees many crowns that are brown and dingy white instead of black and white.

Unlike the domestic Chippy and Song Sparrows, the White-throat nests in the north or in mountain districts, so that, while his whistle may be heard by Adirondack and White Mountain tourists during the summer, it is only a semi-annual pleasure to most of us in the United States. In this way we know the handsomely crowned birds collectively rather than individually, for on their migrations they always travel in flocks.

As they go about in fall and winter, they do a great deal of good by destroying weed seed, such as ragweed, smartweed, and pigweed. In summer they also do good by eating ants, weevils, currant worms, and leaf-eating beetles. But it is hard to think of them in purely economic connection, they are so associated with the pleasures of early spring and early autumn when the goldenrod and asters brighten the dreamy Indian Summer days.

White-crowned Sparrow: *Zonotrichia leucophrys.*

Adults, back brownish gray; breast clear gray; crown conspicuously striped black and white, three middle stripes of equal width. *Young*, similar, but crown dull gray bordered by brown. *Length*, about 6¾ inches.

GEOGRAPHIC DISTRIBUTION. — Breeding from higher mountain ranges of western United States, Sierra Nevada, Rocky Mountains, and eastward, north of the Great Lakes, to Labrador; in winter, over whole of United States, and south into Mexico. (Ridgway.)

Thousands of White-crowns may be seen in the Mississippi valley, but they are rare in the

FIG. 92.　　　　　　FIG. 93.
White-throated Sparrow.　　White-crowned Sparrow.

east. Sometimes one of the distinguished looking birds will be discovered in a flock of White-throats. You can tell him from his cousins at a glance, because he has not the white patch under the chin, being uniformly gray from his bill to his tail. His crown serves still further to distinguish him. It is as striking as a soldier's cap. Moreover, he attracts attention by his general bearing, which is unmistakably that of an aristocrat. His song has much greater variety of note than the White-throat's, though in quality the clear whistle of the White-throat can hardly be surpassed.

Mr. Burroughs is enthusiastic over the White-crown, and says: "He is the rarest and most beautiful of the Sparrow kind. He is crowned as some hero or victor in the games."

FIG. 94.

Brown Thrasher: *Harporhynchus rufus*.

Upper parts reddish brown; under parts white, heavily streaked with black. *Length*, about 11½ inches.

GEOGRAPHIC DISTRIBUTION. — North America east of the Rocky Mountains; breeds from the Gulf states to Manitoba, Maine, and Ontario; winters from Virginia southward.

The beginner often confuses the Cuckoo and Thrasher, for when seen on the wing both appear to be long, slender, brown birds with white under parts and long tails. When seen from in front, however, they may be distinguished at a glance; for the breast of the Thrasher is heavily spotted, while that of the Cuckoo is pure sheeny white. (See Fig. 83, p. 161.) The backs of the two are also dissimilar when seen close at hand; for the Thrasher's is reddish brown, while the Cuckoo's is brownish gray, with a silky greenish gloss. The tail of the Thrasher is plain brown; that of the Cuckoo marked with white spots, more or less prominent according to the species. The flight and habits of the two birds are still less alike. The Thrasher has the tilting, uneven flight of the short-winged Wrens, to whom he is allied; but the Cuckoo, when he has to cross an open space, cuts the air like a projectile from a long-distance gun. The Cuckoo goes from one cover to another, where he hunts silently for caterpillars, only occasionally giving vent to his mysterious *cuck-cuck-cuck*. The Thrasher, on the other hand, goes flaunting and flapping over the top of the bushy tangle where he lives, alights on a topmost branch, and dropping his tail and throwing up his head, shouts out at the top of his lungs. The Cuckoo is mysterious and interesting, meriting the grave attention of the psychologist and economic ornithologist; but the Thrasher is just an outspoken, jolly good fellow in whom we take a personal and affectionate interest. How can you help feeling flattered when he sits up and pours out his rollicking song to you? And such a song as it is!

Though it may be and doubtless is rank heresy to say so, I must confess that I prefer it to that of his distinguished cousin the Mockingbird; but we all need champions.

In one way the Thrasher is particularly in need of friends. Splendid bird that he is, some Jeremiahs inveigh against him with solemnly wagging heads. He is a criminal to be destroyed off the face of the earth. It is hard to believe such evil of your feathered fellows, but — he has been known to taste both grain and fruit! What considerations of song or good fellowship can weigh against such reprehensible conduct? But hold! granting that it is a sin to eat a strawberry, — if you happen to be clad in feathers, — let us look up the records and lay bare his crimes in their full enormity. Taking both grain and fruit, they amount to eleven one hundredths of his food! Moreover, we are assured that the slight loss this entails is more than compensated by the destruction of an equal bulk of May beetles, which, as pointed out, if left alive would not only have done more initial harm than the Thrashers, but would have left 'a multitudinous progeny' to attack the next year's crop. The Thrasher usually works in brushy places, but it is said that "he probably does as much good there as he would in the garden, for the swamps and groves are no doubt breeding-grounds for many insects that migrate thence to attack the farmer's crops."

The thickets where the Thrasher is usually seen are also his nesting sites. His nest is a coarse, bulky affair of twigs, rootlets, and leaves; and the eggs are bluish or grayish white, minutely and evenly dotted with brown. At the nest the bird is more interesting than elsewhere. Audubon has watched his courtship, and says that he struts before the female with his tail trailing on the ground. Mr. Torrey calls him a bird of passion, " ecstatic in song, furious in anger, irresistibly pitiful in lamentation," and exclaims, " How any man can rob a Thrasher's nest with that heart-broken whistle in his ears is more than I can imagine." Doctor Brewer gives a striking instance of the passionate nature of the bird, which is also valuable testimony on the point sometimes raised as to whether a bird has intelligence to recognize the difference between its own eggs and those of others. A set of Robin's eggs were put in a Thrasher's nest and the premises watched. Presently the female returned, looked in the nest, and flew off. In a moment she was back with her mate, and both flew at the nest in a rage. They actually took the strange eggs in their claws and dashed them on the ground, venting their anger by tossing about the broken shells.

FIG. 95.

Chewink; Towhee: *Pipilo erythrophthalmus.*

Adult male, head, breast, and back black; sides chestnut; belly and corners of tail white. *Adult female*, brown replacing the black. *Young*, in first plumage, streaked. *Length*, about 8¼ inches.

GEOGRAPHIC DISTRIBUTION. — Eastern North America; breeds from the lower Mississippi Valley and Georgia northward to Maine, Ontario, and Manitoba; winters from Virginia and southern Illinois to the Gulf.

One of the choicest delights of the book-lover is to know his authors so well that he can at any moment go to his shelves and take down the volume that corresponds to his mood, and the same thing is true in knowing birds. The true bird-lover knows his birds so thoroughly that he can choose his walks with the certainty of finding the friend who will respond to his thoughts. When moved by the gladness of spring, he will turn to the daisy fields to listen to the joyful medley of the Bobolink; when in thoughtful mood, he will retire to the green shade of the forest to be thrilled and uplifted by the hymns of the Thrushes; when tired of lawn Sparrows and hungering for the wild, free side of nature, he will clear the fences and cut across lots to the nearest old juniper pasture or brushy thicket. There he will find the prince of Bohemians, the Brown Thrasher, and if he listen quietly, may hear the scratching of the Chewink among the dead leaves, and presently its quaint, simple song, as the unsuspecting bird mounts to a low branch to sing. Though totally unlike the tempestuous torrents of the Thrasher in range and delivery, the two songs have a common quality, a certain wild flavor that goes well with the old, neglected pastures and brushy tangles, and is as grateful to the nature-lover as the spring taste of the wild sorrel or ginger-root dug from the earth. To be exact, the Chewink has two songs, one much shorter than the other, but both have a peculiar quality. The call notes are even more characteristic, a *towhee* and a more nasal *whank* or *chewink*.

Like the Thrasher, the Chewink gets his food on the ground, and while he belongs to the Finch and Sparrow family, is said to do incalculable good by unearthing wire worms, beetles, and larvæ which have gone into winter quarters. " The death of a single insect at this time, before it has had an opportunity to deposit its eggs, is equivalent to the destruction of a host later in the year," we are told. The Chewink eats some unusual insects, having a liking for both hairy caterpillars and potato bugs.

From its habits one would naturally infer that the Towhee nested on the ground, and this ground nest, with its dead-leaf walls and its white eggs dulled by their uniform brown dotting, corresponds so closely with the surroundings and the lights and shades of the woods, that one may hunt a long time for the pleasure of watching the proceedings of a family of nestlings and their anxious guardians.

Field Sparrow: *Spizella pusilla.*

Bill reddish; crown and back *reddish brown;* breast buffy, unspotted. *Length,* about 5¾ inches.

GEOGRAPHIC DISTRIBUTION. — Eastern North America; breeds from Kansas, southern Illinois, and South Carolina to Quebec and Manitoba; winters from Illinois and Virginia southward.

There is a third bird which frequents the haunts of the Thrasher and Chewink, which to me seems to surpass them both in the wild flavor of its song. Mr. Burroughs describes it as being " uttered at first high and leisurely, but running very rapidly toward the close, which is low and soft," and he gives it as *fe-o, fe-o, fe-o, few, few, few, fee, fee, fee.* Though perfectly unpretentious and simple as far as note goes, there is a certain sad, ringing quality to the song which makes it haunt the memory; and in a country where it is seldom heard, it is a song that I personally would walk miles to hear. While the *feo* song is the conventional one of the Field Sparrow, it is said to have many variations. In a field in Maryland I have heard the usual song on one side and a totally different one on the other, one curiously like a tune, with three definite sets of four notes each, or rather the same note repeated four times, the three sets given in descending scale, and the tune completed by a fourth set of varied notes thrown up higher on the scale.

Fig. 96.
Amaranth, eaten by Field Sparrow.

Living in fields, the Field Sparrow does good by destroying the seeds of amaranth, chickweed, pigweed, knotgrass, and foxtail, besides eating a large number of grasshoppers, injurious caterpillars, leaf-eating beetles, and the saw-fly that produces the currant worm. Its nest is of coarse grasses and rootlets put near the ground. The eggs are white or bluish white, sometimes marked around the larger end, at others uniformly dotted with light brown spots. The bird itself can always be distinguished by its reddish brown color and its reddish bill, for its cousin the Chippy, whom it resembles in general, has a clear gray breast and a black bill.

Whip-poor-will: *Antrostomus vociferus.*

(See Fig. 98, p. 188.)

Male, wood-brown, lighter below; patch on throat and outer tail feathers white. *Female*, similar, but throat buffy instead of white, and no white on tail. *Length*, 9¾ inches.

GEOGRAPHIC DISTRIBUTION. — Eastern North America, north to New Brunswick and Manitoba; winters from Florida and the lower Mississippi valley southward.

The evening note of the Whip-poor-will is well known, but in the daytime the bird is seldom seen. When surprised on a branch it looks like a short stick of wood, for it sits low and horizontally; and the white line of its throat absolutely destroys the head form (see Fig. 98, p. 188), so that one has to puzzle to make out that it is a head, though knowing that it is attached to the body of a bird. If one is familiar with the twilight hunting-grounds of the Whip-poor-will, many interesting things may be observed. Major Bendire gives a delightful account of what he has seen at such times. He says that, when picking up its food from the roads which it frequents for dust-baths to free itself from vermin, its movements on the ground are awkward, its feet being weak and short; but its aerial movements are most graceful. He says: "I have seen one touch the back of its wings together as it swept by me, arrest its noiseless flight instantly, drop to the ground almost perpendicularly, pick up some insect, and dash away as suddenly as it halted. At such times it occasionally utters a low, purring or grunting noise like 'däck-däck,' and another sounding like 'zue-see, zue-see,' which cannot be heard unless one is close by." When the Major was in northern New York a pair of the birds were in the habit of coming about the house where he was staying, and one evening, by watching them from inside a building, he was fortunate enough to see their curious love-making. "I saw one of the birds waddling about in a very excited manner," he tells us. "Its head appeared to be all mouth, and its notes were uttered so rapidly that, close as I was to the bird, they sounded like one long, continuous roll. A few seconds after his first effort (it was the male) he was joined by his mate, and she at once commenced to respond with a peculiar, low, buzzing or grunting note, like 'gaw-gaw-gaw,' undoubtedly a note of approval or endearment. This evidently cost her considerable effort; her head almost touched the ground while uttering it, her plumage was relaxed, and her whole body seemed to be in a violent tremble. The male in the mean time had sidled up to her and touched her bill with his, which made her move slightly to one side: . . . the female acted as timid and bashful as many young maidens would when receiving the first declarations of their would-be lovers, while the lowering of her head might easily be interpreted as being done to hide her blushes."

The Whip-poor-will lays its eggs on the ground or leaves. The mother bird shows great distress if disturbed when young are in the nest. A correspondent of Major Bendire's says that she "flies or rather flops about the intruder in a circle, often alighting to tumble about upon the ground among the leaves, spreading the tail and opening the mouth, at the same time emitting a sound something like the cry or whine of a very young puppy, and also other guttural, uncouth sounds, wholly indescribable, the young themselves, in their scanty dress of dark yellow fuzz, apparently all mouth, adding to the general effect." Besides being very interesting birds, Doctor Fisher says that they are most useful, eating ants, grasshoppers, June bugs, and potato bugs.

Nighthawk : *Chordeiles virginianus.*

Male, upper parts blackish, marked with brown ; under parts whitish, barred with black ; *throat white ; wings and tail with conspicuous white bands. Female,* no white on tail, and throat buffy. *Length,* 10 inches.

GEOGRAPHIC DISTRIBUTION. — Eastern North America ; breeds from the Gulf states to Labrador ; winters in South America.

Like the Whip-poor-will, the Nighthawk is crepuscular, flying mainly in the dusky margins of the day. The two birds look much alike, but the Nighthawk has a white throat instead of a narrow white line on a black throat, and in the sky shows white bands on its crescent-like wings.

FIG. 97.
Nighthawk.

On warm summer evenings you may often see one or more coursing over the meadows, getting their food on the wing. They live largely on flies, mosquitoes, grasshoppers, and crickets ; and one bird was found with 573 large-winged ants in its stomach, in addition to parts of 72 small-winged ants and 16 grasshoppers. A

FIG. 98.
Whip-poor-will.

flock of several thousand Nighthawks may sometimes be seen in the sky in the fall migrations, and if they all are blessed with such healthy appetites it can be imagined how effectively they

Fig. 99.
Wing of Nighthawk.

thin the ranks of the unhappy insects that lie in their path.

The aerial evolutions of the Nighthawk are remarkable. It soars and it flaps, it twists and it turns, it mounts perpendicularly into the air — all with graceful ease; and in the nesting season its performances are a seven days' wonder for all beholders. When high in air it shoots down almost to the earth, and then, turning abruptly, ascends to the same heights. In diving, the air is forced through its wings, making a booming sound. Its usual note is a sharp *eek* or *peent*, and may be heard of an evening in Washington, New York, or other of the cities, for the birds find good nesting-places on the flat roofs of city houses.

The Nighthawk and Whip-poor-will belong to the same family, and their tints suggest the

GOATSUCKERS, SWIFTS, ETC.

Grouse, wood-colors being the most effective disguise for birds that nest on the ground. As a family the Goatsuckers are perhaps more crepuscular than any birds except Owls. They are in the same order with the Swifts (see Plate II. p. 24), and like them have peculiarly small bills and wide, gaping throats, whose doors they throw wide open as, like devouring monsters, they mow their way through a cloud of insects. The Whip-poor-wills, in addition to their enormous mouths, have long, stiff bristles at the base of the bill, that may be effective aids in holding squirming June bugs and such uneasy prey.

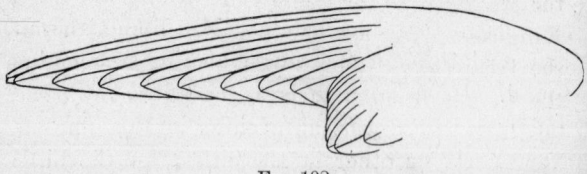

FIG. 100.
Slender wing of Hummingbird.

FIG. 101.
Short, thick wing of Sparrow.

FIG. 102.
Long, slender wing of Swallow.

The Swallows are our only birds that approach the Goatsuckers and Swifts in form of bill and

GOATSUCKERS, SWIFTS, ETC.

in feeding habits. (See Fig. 120, p. ... and 113, p. 192.)

Though the Hummingbird has branched off so far from the Swifts and Goatsuckers in form of bill (see Figs. 9 and 10, p. 26), it resembles them in its extreme development of wing (Figs. 19, p. 45, 99, p. 189, and 100, p. 190), and the undeveloped character of its feet (see Figs. 7, p. 25, and 104, p. 191), reminding us again of the dissimilarity of the whole order to the short-winged, strong-footed Grouse, Sparrows (Figs. 101, p. 190, and 103, p. 191), Wrens, and Thrashers.

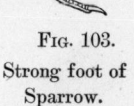

Fig. 103. Strong foot of Sparrow.

Fig. 104. Weak foot of Nighthawk.

We have now a number of new types of bill to add to those of the Hummingbird, Quail, Dove, Flycatcher, Crow, and Oriole types already noticed, for we have the sword of the Kingfisher, the fly-traps of the Goatsucker and Swallow, the seed-crackers of the Grosbeak and Sparrow, the curious nippers of the Crossbill, and the heavy drill of the Woodpecker, each in turn especially adapted to the birds' food habits.

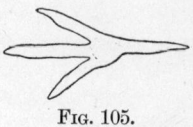

Fig. 105. Footprint of Crow.

192 GOATSUCKERS, SWIFTS, ETC.

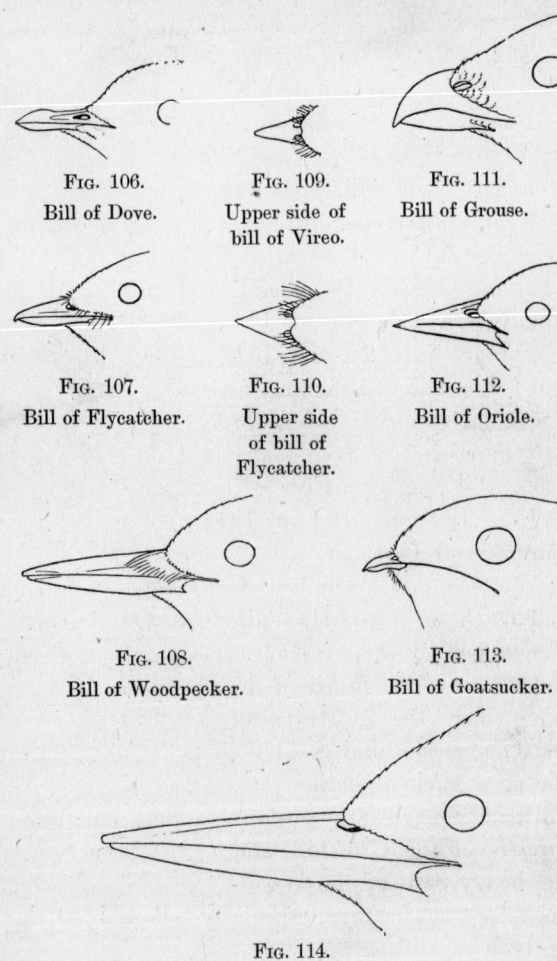

Fig. 106.
Bill of Dove.

Fig. 109.
Upper side of bill of Vireo.

Fig. 111.
Bill of Grouse.

Fig. 107.
Bill of Flycatcher.

Fig. 110.
Upper side of bill of Flycatcher.

Fig. 112.
Bill of Oriole.

Fig. 108.
Bill of Woodpecker.

Fig. 113.
Bill of Goatsucker.

Fig. 114.
Bill of Kingfisher.

KEY TO GOATSUCKERS, SWIFTS, ETC. 193

FIG. 115.
Bill of Chickadee.

FIG. 118.
Bill of Hummingbird.

FIG. 119.
Bill of Sparrow.

FIG. 116.
Bill of Crossbill.

FIG. 120.
Bill of Swallow.

FIG. 117.
Bill of Grosbeak.

FIG. 121.
Bill of Crow Blackbird.

Key to Adult Male Goatsuckers, Swifts, and Hummingbirds.

1. Bill long, with little gape. Upper parts green; throat metallic red.
p. 1.   RUBY-THROATED HUMMINGBIRD.
1'. Bill short, with wide gape.
  2. Small; needle-like spines on end of tail. Unmarked, sooty brown. Diurnal. Nests in chimneys . . . . p. 23. CHIMNEY SWIFT.
  2'. Large; no spines on end of tail. Mottled wood-brown. Crepuscular. Nests on the ground.
    3. White spot on wing; tail deeply forked, with white crescent. Seen hunting for insects high in air. Call, *peent* . . . . p. 188. NIGHTHAWK.
    3'. No white spot on wing; tail rounded; outer tail feathers mostly white. Seen hunting nearer the ground. Call, *Whip-poor-will* . . p. 185. WHIP-POOR-WILL.

Tree Swallow; White-bellied Swallow: *Tachycineta bicolor*.

Adults, upper parts steel-blue or steel-green; under parts pure white, unmarked. *Young*, upper parts brownish gray; under parts white. *Length*, about 6 inches.

GEOGRAPHIC DISTRIBUTION. — North America, north to Labrador and Alaska; breeds locally throughout its range; winters from South Carolina and the Gulf states southward.

The Tree Swallow may be known by its shining white breast. It has not yet entirely given over the habits of its ancestors, and still nests largely in hollow trees, though in some places it will accept proffers of nesting-boxes. When it does accept man's hospitality it does so without reserve, even taking up its residence in candle-boxes prepared only by having a hole made in one end, sometimes almost taking from the hand the feathers that are offered for its nest. It builds a soft nest of leaves and hay, lined with down and feathers. The eggs are pure white, unspotted.

FIG. 122.
Tree Swallow.

Unlike most Swallows, the Trees vary their insect diet with berries, being especially fond of bay-berries.

They form large roosts, and begin to gather in

the marshes near New York by the first of July. Mr. Chapman says that they sail about in circles more than other Swallows.

Rough-winged Swallow: *Stelgidopteryx serripennis.*

Sooty brown above; breast uniform light sooty. *Length,* 5¾ inches.

GEOGRAPHIC DISTRIBUTION. — North America; breeds as far north as British Columbia, Minnesota, and Connecticut; winters in the tropics.

The Rough-winged Swallow gets its name from the small, recurved hooklets set like the teeth of a saw along the edge of the outside feathers of the wing in the male. It may be mistaken for the Bank Swallow, unless it is remembered that the Bank Swallow has a dark band across the breast (Fig. 24, p. 55). The nesting habits of the two also differ.

FIG. 123.
Rough-winged Swallow.

The Rough-winged does not build in colonies like the Bank, but usually nests in isolated pairs in holes in sand-banks, stone ruins, culverts, and abutments. Near Washington, in the stone walls of the canal, it is particularly abundant. When made in sand, the entrance to the burrow is said to be round rather than elliptical, as the Bank Swallow's is, and the burrow itself is there generally a deserted Kingfisher hole or other suitable cavity. An interesting article on the Rough-winged's nesting habits, by Walter Van Fleet, is to be found in the 'Bulletin of the Nuttall Ornithological Club,' vol. i. No. i. p. 9.

Looking back over the Swallows we have spoken of, it becomes an easy matter to distinguish them. The Barn is known by its long forked tail (see Plate IV. p. 50); the Cliff or Eave by its light, buffy rump and its gourd-shaped nest (see Fig. 22, p. 52); the Purple Martin by its uniformly blue-black body; the Tree or White-bellied by its shining white breast (see Fig. 122, p. 194); the Bank by the dark band across its breast (see Fig. 24, p. 55); and the Rough-wing by its sooty back and lack of distinguishing breast-marks.

Key to Adult Male Swallows.

Common Characters. — Birds of the air, which catch their insect prey on the wing in their widely gaping bills.

1. Tail conspicuously forked. Upper parts steel-blue; under parts chocolate. Beats over meadows for insects.

p. 49.   BARN SWALLOW.

1'. Tail not conspicuously forked.
  2. Back with metallic lustre.
    3. Under parts shining blue-black.

p. 48.   PURPLE MARTIN.

3′. Under parts not shining blue-black.
   4. Under parts pure white.
p. 194. WHITE-BELLIED SWALLOW.

4′. Under parts washed with brownish, *rump light* . . . . . p. 52. EAVE SWALLOW.

2′. Back without metallic lustre.
   5. Dark band across breast . p. 54. BANK SWALLOW.

5′. No distinct band across breast.
p. 195. ROUGH-WINGED SWALLOW.

Winter Wren: *Troglodytes hiemalis*.

Upper parts reddish brown, finely barred; under parts washed with brownish. Tail very short, carried over back. *Length*, about 4 inches.

GEOGRAPHIC DISTRIBUTION. — Eastern North America; breeds from the northern states northward, and southward along the higher Alleghanies to North Carolina; winters from Massachusetts and Illinois to Florida.

During the migrations this mite of a Wren may be met almost anywhere. Sometimes it surprises you by bobbing up from a pile of boards with its bit of a tail cocked over its back; again it peers out from a goldenrod thicket, or faces you on top of a stump in the woods. It is such a friendly, jolly little bird that you are won by its confidence; but when you come to hear it sing, you are stirred by deeper emotions. The song is a marvel from such a little bird, for it is loud, rich, and melodious.

Fig. 124.
Winter Wren.

Along the banks of the Hudson, Doctor Mearns has found the Wrens running about under the ice when the water had settled away, "creeping into every nook and crevice in search of food, sometimes remaining out of sight for many minutes together," for their food is well hidden, insects and larvæ being the chief of their diet.

The Wrens nest mainly in the northern forests, so may be seen and heard by favored Adirondack tourists. Their nest is an interesting mossy one lined with feathers, those of the Ruffed Grouse among the number, Mr. Burroughs tells us. Their eggs are white, dotted with reddish brown, and the nestlings that come out of them become bewitching, bobby little scraps.

Carolina Wren: *Thryothorus ludovicianus.*

Upper parts reddish brown; under parts buffy; wings and tail barred with black; a *conspicuous white line over the eye.* Length, 5½ inches.

GEOGRAPHIC DISTRIBUTION. — Eastern United States; breeds from the Gulf states to southern Iowa, northern Illinois, and southern Connecticut; resident, except at the northern limit of its range.

On the wooded hills of the National Zoölogical Park at Washington, there are three birds whose songs perplex the brains of the beginner by their similarity — the Cardinal, Crested Titmouse, and Carolina Wren. Each of the birds, however, has one song that is distinct and easily recognized — the two-syllabled *pe-to* of the

FIG. 125.
Carolina Wren.

Titmouse; the three syllabled *tea-ket-tle* of the Wren; and the smooth, one-syllabled, long-drawn *cue* or *quoit* of the Cardinal. The Cardinal's, though one-syllabled, is often repeated rapidly as much as eleven times. The resemblance of the three songs is not fancied. The Wren is known as the Mocking Wren, and is supposed to deliberately mimic the Titmouse, and the Cardinal is also supposed to imitate its fellows; so it is well to listen carefully before naming the songsters, unless they are singing where you can *see their bills move* as the sound pours out. Indeed, this is a wise precaution to observe wherever there is any doubt, for there is sometimes more than one bird in a tree! The Cardinal and Titmouse begin to sing in February, but the Wren sings throughout the year, except when moulting, even in the stormiest and coldest weather, for he is a brave-spirited little fellow.

Though he sings so freely, the Carolina is not always easily seen. He looks over at you quite frankly from the opposite bank of a stream, but when you have crossed he has vanished.

In some places he is less shy, and builds without hesitation in nesting-boxes provided for him. Mr. Oberholser records an interesting case in which a pair built inside a barn, entering through a knothole. Though the birds were disturbed at visitors, when the nest was taken outside the barn and put on the ground they did not forsake their young, but bravely kept on feeding them as before. When left to provide for themselves, the Carolinas often build in old Woodpecker holes. The eggs are white, marked with lavender.

Bewick's Wren: *Thryothorus bewickii.*

Upper parts dark brown; under parts grayish; wings and tail barred; outer tail feathers black; white line over eye. *Length*, 5 inches.

GEOGRAPHIC DISTRIBUTION. — Eastern United States; rare and local east of Alleghanies and north of 40°; west to edge of Great Plains; winters in more southern districts (Georgia to eastern Texas).

In southern Illinois Mr. Ridgway found this the common Wren. It lived around the houses, and sang its fine, clear song from the roofs. Mr. Nehrling describes the bird's notes as "liquid, sweet, and finely modulated." He says that in Texas the Wren has become a perfect house-bird, frequenting the log-cabin of the poor settler as well as the villa of the rich merchant. When neither nesting-boxes nor natural cavities are to be found, it will build on beams in log-houses and stables, in smoke-houses and wood-sheds. Mr. Nehrling has also found nests in stove-pipes that lay on the ground, in the pocket of an overcoat that hung on the piazza, in tool-boxes and bookcases in inhabited rooms. The nest is bulky, and is sometimes arched over, with the entrance on one side. The eggs are white, speckled with brown.

Long-billed Marsh Wren: *Cistothorus palustris.*

(Plate X.)

GEOGRAPHIC DISTRIBUTION. — Eastern North America; breeds from the Gulf states to Manitoba and Massachusetts; winters from the Gulf states, and locally farther north, southward to Mexico.

When woods and fields have lost their relish, spend a day in a marsh and the world will seem young again. The expanse of the great level stretch, 'its range and its sweep' — a dark green sea interrupted only by its narrow winding river, seemingly bounded only by the horizon where treetops meet the small round clouds bordering the soft June heavens — both the expanse and solitude of the great green plain under the sky are infinitely restful.

But, aside from this, the marsh is a little world apart, offering keen, peculiar pleasures to those who know nature only in her more familiar forms. As you wade through the reeds, the long blades make pleasant music in your ears, seething as they bow before you and rise behind you. Even the unexpected plunge into deep water takes its place along with the first taste of sweet-flag and the moment when you sight the blue patch of iris down the marsh. As for birds, they pervade the margins of the plain and give it life. At one moment you are remonstrated with by Maryland Yellow-throats, small yellow birds who whip in and out of the reeds, peering up at you anxiously

L. A. Fuertes.

PLATE X. — LONG-BILLED MARSH WREN

Crown dark brown, black on the sides; line over eye white. Back black, streaked with white; wings and tail barred; under parts white; sides marked with brownish. *Length* about 5¼ inches. (By courtesy of *The Osprey*.)

to make out if you would really harm their brood; at the next you are encircled by excited Redwings, who fancy their fledglings in danger; and then, overhead, the Bobolinks, absorbed in their own happiness,

> " . . . meet and frolic in the air
> Half prattling and half singing."

But however much you are prepared for it by the other members of the choir, the first outburst of the Marsh Wrens is almost paralyzing. You feel as if you had entered a factory with machines clattering on all sides. Perching atilt of the reeds, with tails over their backs, the excited little music-boxes run on chattering and scolding almost in your very face, diving out of sight in the cat-tails only to reappear near your hand as you search for their nests.

Search for their nests? Yes, but only with gentle thoughts. The stilt-houses of these little lake-dwellers surely merit the attention of ornithological tourists. As you examine the round green balls of nests high up on the reed-stalks, what marvelous workmen the little builders seem! They bend down the tips of the long blades and weave them in together as if basket-making were an easy matter to them. Difficult work it seems to us to be done for the pure joy of doing, but nest after nest is made around the one which is actually to hold the chocolate eggs. One covets the pleasure of seeing the Wrens at work on these stilt-houses, and the added pleasure of seeing them bring out a brood of chattering brown mites upon the world of marsh. If all their nine eggs hatch, surely they will be kept busy hunting food for the hungry little folk! But they are quite equal to the task. Along the southern coasts where the rice grows, they take the opportunity to pick up the destructive weevils that feed upon it, and wherever they are they busy themselves hunting out the small worms of the earth that cumber the ground; for that is a trait of the Wren family.

This particular Wren will never be mistaken for any of his kin, for the black diamond on his back labels him as well as if he were marked with indelible ink. The rest of the family stand pretty much by their own colors, too. The Carolina and Winter Wrens are mainly birds of the woods — the Carolina of the south, the Winter of the north. The Carolina Wren has a heavy white line over the eye; the Winter Wren lacks this, but is easily distinguished by its abbreviated tail, bent at an angle over its back. The House Wren and Bewick's are more similar in habit, being familiar door-yard birds; but Bewick's, the more southern of the two, has longer wings and tail, and a diagnostic white line over the eye.

As a family (see Figs. 126–132, p. 207) the Wrens belong with the three songful cousins, the Catbird, Thrasher, and Mockingbird, and the voices of the wrenkins form no mean part of the family chorus. They seem to live to sing, and sing to live. To the passer-by it would appear the most important part of their business in life.

Most of the Wren and Thrasher family wear brown, but some wear gray. They all match well with the earth and bushes they frequent. As they have short, round wings (see Fig. 18, p. 45), they choose to migrate by night, when the two bird-catching Hawks are soundly slumbering.

Key to Thrashers, Wrens, etc.

1. Back gray.
 2. Under parts whitish; crown gray; outer tail feathers white . . . . p. 63. MOCKINGBIRD.

 2'. Under parts slate-gray; crown and tail black.
 p. 6. CATBIRD.

1'. Back brown.
 3. Large. Wings and tail not barred; upper parts reddish brown; under parts white, streaked with black. Found in thickets . . . . . p. 177. BROWN THRASHER.

 3'. Small; wings and tail barred.
  4. No white line over eye.
   5. Under parts brownish; tail very short, usually held over back. Nests in northern forests.
 p. 197. WINTER WREN.

   5'. Under parts whitish; tail of medium length, not held over back. Nests commonly about houses.
 p. 44. HOUSE WREN.

4'. White line over eye.
  6. Back with black patch. Found in marshes.
                    p. 202. Long-billed Marsh Wren.

6'. Back without black patch.
  7. Upper parts reddish brown; under parts buffy. Commonest song, a three-syllabled *tea-ket-tle, tea-ket-tle* . . . . . . p. 199. Carolina Wren.

  7'. Upper parts dark brown; under parts whitish. Found west of Alleghanies.
                    p. 201. Bewick's Wren.

WREN AND THRASHER FAMILY 207

FIG. 126.
Brown Thrasher.

FIG. 129.
Winter Wren.

FIG. 130.
House Wren.

FIG. 127.
Carolina Wren.

FIG. 131.
Marsh Wren.

FIG. 128.
Mockingbird.

FIG. 132.
Catbird.

MEMBERS OF WREN AND THRASHER FAMILY.

Yellow-bellied Woodpecker; Sapsucker:
Sphyrapicus varius.

(Plate XI.)

GEOGRAPHIC DISTRIBUTION. — Eastern North America; breeds from Massachusetts northward, and winters from Virginia to Central America.

Nuthatches and Downy Woodpeckers are often called Sapsuckers, but the Yellow-bellied Woodpecker, the one with the red crown and throat, is the only bird that deserves the name.

The Sapsucker has the habit of drilling holes in the bark of trees, and, as his name indicates, sucks the sap that exudes from the tree. But this is not all, nor does it doom him to disfavor. Now and then an individual Sapsucker may girdle and kill an ornamental birch on a lawn; but for one which does that, numbers are at work destroying the insects that gather at the sap on the hardy forest trees which the Woodpecker will not harm. An observer of his performance says: "As the sap exudes from the newly-made punctures, thousands of flies, yellow jackets, and other insects congregate about the place, till the hum of their wings suggests a swarm of bees. If now the tree be watched, the Woodpecker will soon be seen to return and alight over the part of the girdle which he has most recently punctured. Here he remains with motionless body and feeds upon the choicest species from a host of insects within easy reach."

PLATE XI. — SAPSUCKER

Adult male, crown and throat deep red, breast black; belly
yellow; back black marked with white and yellow. *Adult
female*, similar, but throat white and crown sometimes black.
Young, crown dull blackish; breast brownish; throat whitish.
Length, about 8½ inches.

Some Sapsuckers have been experimented with to find out if they could live principally on syrup, but in each instance have died from the diet. Stomach examinations bear out this testimony. The Sapsucker is largely an insect-eater. He ranks next to the Flicker as an ant-eater, 36 per cent. of his solid food consisting of ants. He also destroys wasps, beetles, bugs, flies, grasshoppers, and crickets. He eats more flies than any other Woodpecker, and Professor Beal says that he probably fully compensates for whatever harm he does by the number of insects he consumes. To keep him from ornamental trees it might be well to plant the dogwood, black alder, Virginia creeper, wild black cherry, and juniper.

In some places, Mrs. Mabel Osgood Wright tells us, the farmers cover the trunks of their orchard trees with fine wire netting, in this way getting protection without depriving themselves of the good offices of the bird.

Aside from his food the Sapsucker is one of the most interesting of Woodpecker characters, a splendid, spirited bird whose rollicking cries call our attention and whose gay humors excite our admiration.

These martial spirits lead the drum corps of the forest. In a posted woods I have known two of them to take up positions on signs forbidding shooting, and proceed to beat their tattoos as loudly as if calling attention to the inscriptions beneath them. When living near houses they are particularly given to drumming on tin, eave-troughs offering great attractions to them. Sometimes, when the male is drumming to call his mate, Mr. Brewster says a rival appears instead, and a battle ends the performance.

Mr. Brewster has also given us many interesting facts about the nesting habits of the Sapsuckers. He says both birds work on the nest, " the bird not employed usually clinging near the hole and encouraging its toiling mate by an occasional low cry. Part of the finer chips are left at the bottom of the hole for a soft bed for the eggs. The labor of incubation, like all other duties, is shared equally by the two sexes, . . . the birds relieving each other at intervals averaging about half an hour each. . . . The bird not employed . . . has also a peculiar habit of clinging to the trunk just below the hole, in a perfectly motionless and strikingly pensive attitude." [1]

Red-cockaded Woodpecker : *Dryobates borealis.*

Adult male, crown black; a scarlet spot on each side of the nape; *back barred with black;* under parts white; sides marked with black. *Adult female,* similar, but without scarlet on the head. *Length,* about 8½ inches.

GEOGRAPHIC DISTRIBUTION. — Southern United States, westward to Texas and Indian Territory, and northward to Tennessee and North Carolina.

The Red-cockaded Woodpecker is commonly

[1] *Bulletin Nuttall Ornithological Club,* vol. i. No. 3, pp. 63-70.

seen in the pine woods of Florida and other parts of the south. Audubon says that when on a high tree it looks as if entirely black. He also says that it "glides upward and sidewise along the trunks and branches on the lower as well as the upper side — moving with astonishing alertness, and at every moment emitting a short, shrill, and clear note which can be heard at a distance." Mr. Chapman compares its call note to the *yank, yank* of the Nuthatch, but says it is louder, hoarser, and not so distinctly enunciated.

The bird is said to be highly useful in destroying worms and insects under bark and in rotten wood, excavating boring beetles and larvæ.

Red-bellied Woodpecker: *Melanerpes carolinus.*

Adult male, top of head and back of neck scarlet; back black, uniformly barred with white; under parts whitish, washed with scarlet. Adult female, similar, but with the crown gray. Length, 9½ inches.

GEOGRAPHIC DISTRIBUTION. — Eastern United States, breeding from Florida to Maryland, and in the interior to Ontario and southern Dakota; occasionally strays to Massachusetts; winters from Virginia and southern Ohio southward.

Mr. Ridgway pronounces the Red-bellied one of the commonest and tamest Woodpeckers of southern Illinois. In contests with the Red-headed he has invariably seen it vanquished. Audubon gave its call as *chow-chow*, and Major Bendire calls attention to its low, mournful cooing note which resembles that of the Mourning Dove and is made in the nesting season.

In the south the bird is common and has been seen eating oranges, but as it confines itself to decayed or very ripe fruit it only harms the growers who keep their oranges for the late market; and Major Bendire says that the little harm it does is fully atoned for by the great number of larvæ and insects which it eats at the same time. He unquestioningly puts it on the list of birds that deserve protection.

In Texas it is said to nest in telegraph poles.

Pileated Woodpecker; Cock-of-the-Woods:
Ceophlœus pileatus.

Head and crest scarlet; a whitish stripe on each side of face and neck; body blackish brown. *Length,* 17 inches.

GEOGRAPHIC DISTRIBUTION. — "Formerly whole wooded region of North America south of latitude 63°; now rare or extirpated in the more thickly settled parts of the eastern states."

When a child I visited the Adirondacks with some enthusiastic young ornithologists, and I shall never forget the excitement of the moment when a loud rapping on a high tree near the lake announced the presence of this noble Cock-of-the-woods. Our boat was speedily put ashore, and the young naturalists vanished in search of the magnificent bird. Since then, when rowing on Lake Placid, I have caught a glimpse of his splendid figure on the wooded border of the lake, but the sight is becoming rarer with the settlement of the region. In the hummocks and cypress swamps of Florida, however, Mr. Chapman tells us the

Pileated is still quite common and not wild. In describing it he notes that its flight is slow and direct rather than undulating, as is that of most Woodpeckers; and says that its call note is a sonorous *cow-cow-cow*.

Mr. Manley Hardy finds the Woodpeckers in the Maine forests, where, if not disturbed, they become accustomed to man. He so won the confidence of one pair that they would let him put his hand on their tree when they were only ten feet above.

Major Bendire gives the Pileated's food as ants and different species of boring beetles and larvæ which infest timbered tracts; and, in addition, wild berries and nuts. He says the bird does far more good than harm, and only attacks decaying and fallen timber."

This is the testimony in regard to one species of Woodpecker; but Professor Beal assures us, after the examination of large numbers of stomachs, that while farmers look on the family with suspicion because they see them on the bark of fruit-trees, it is rare that any but the Sapsucker leaves an important mark on a healthy tree; but on the contrary, when a tree is infested with wood-boring larvæ the birds dislodge and devour them. Wood-boring beetles, tree-burrowing caterpillars and timber ants begin their excavations in a small spot of decay and eat in until they honeycomb the trees. They are inaccessible to other birds, but the chisel-like bills and long barbed tongues of the Woodpeckers are especially adapted to the work of extraction. So Woodpeckers naturally become the great conservers of forests. As Professor Beal says, "To them, more than to any other agency, we owe the preservation of timber from hordes of destructive insects."

The Hairy and Downy are the most beneficial of the Woodpeckers, from two thirds to three fourths of their food consisting of insects, most of which are noxious. The Flicker, as we have seen, is the great ant-eater, nearly half of his food being ants; while the Red-headed is the grasshopper-eater, and the Sapsucker feeds on both ants and grasshoppers.

The Woodpeckers are easily distinguished. The Hairy and Downy are the two black and white ones, each having a white stripe down the back, and in the case of the male a scarlet band on the nape. They usually live on tree trunks in the woods, but the Downy sometimes nests about houses. The Flicker is the ground-colored ant-eater, and the Red-head the tricolored — red, white, and black — grasshopper-hunter. The Sapsucker is the only one with red crown, red throat, and black breast, the only one to which the name Sapsucker can be rightfully applied. The Pileated lives in remote forests, is one of the giants of the family, and may be known by his scarlet head and crest and plain, blackish brown body.

The Red-bellied and Red-cockaded are southern species, distinguished by the amount and position of red on the head. In the Red-cockaded the red scarcely shows, but in the Red-bellied the whole top of the head and back of the neck are bright scarlet.

Comparing the Woodpeckers with other groups of birds we have become familiar with, their habit of living on tree trunks would separate them from all but the Nuthatch, whose grayish blue back and small size distinguish him. The habit of nesting in tree trunks is shared with Nuthatches, Chickadees, Bluebirds, Tree Swallows, and Swifts, though the Swift nests in hollow trees. As a family the Woodpeckers are black and white, very different from the brown-toned Grouse and Quail, the Doves, Wrens, Thrashers, Cuckoos, Waxwings, and Sparrows, as from the gray Flycatchers and green Vireos; and on the other hand from the brilliant Orioles and Tanagers. Their heavy, blunt bills (see Fig. 108, p. 192) are adapted to drilling and drumming — the Mexican name for them is 'Carpentaros' — their feet in most cases have two toes behind instead of one as in ordinary birds (see Figs. 202, and 204, p. 351), which seems to better support their weight in climbing and hanging on

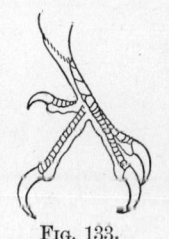

FIG. 133.

Foot of Woodpecker, two toes in front and two behind.

tree trunks, though many birds of similar habits have ordinary feet; while their tails with stiff quills and pointed feathers help them brace against tree trunks (see Fig. 212, p. 353), as do the bristly tails of the Swifts (see Fig. 213, p. 353). Though they have loud calls and are drummers, they are songless birds, and so from the standpoint of music may be classed with the Grouse, Doves, Crows, Jays, Flycatchers, Cuckoos, Kingfishers, Goatsuckers, and Waxwings, rather than with the Orioles, Finches, Sparrows, Wrens, Thrashers, Catbird, and Mockingbird.

FIG. 134.
Red-headed Woodpecker.

Key to Adult Male[1] Woodpeckers.

1. Whole head and neck bright red.
    Back black; belly white; wings and rump showing white in flight . p. 131. RED-HEADED WOODPECKER.
1'. Whole head and neck not red.
    2. Plumage mainly brownish; rump conspicuously white; breast with black crescent; under side of wings and tail yellow; white rump seen in flight. p. 127. FLICKER.

[1] The female Red-head is like the male; in all the other species the females differ from the males in having the red less extensive or absent.

2'. Plumage mainly black and white ; rump not white.
3. Under parts mainly black ; size nearly as large as Crow ; top of head red and crested ; throat and stripe on side of face and neck white ; underside of wings white and black ; rest of body black. Found in forests . . . . . p. 212. PILEATED WOODPECKER.

3'. Underparts not mainly black; size of Robin or smaller.
4. Large black patch on breast ; throat red (white in female) ; belly yellow . . . p. 208. SAPSUCKER.

4'. No black patch on breast.
5. Underparts ash-gray, washed with red ; back barred black and white ; top of head red. Common in the south . . p. 211. RED-BELLIED WOODPECKER.

5'. Under parts white, never washed or tinged with red; back mainly black.
6. Crown black ; back *barred* with white ; a small red spot on each side of back of head. Found in pine woods in south.

p. 210. RED-COCKADED WOODPECKER.

6'. Crown with a scarlet band ; back *streaked* with white.
7. Length 9 to 10 inches. Common in northern woodlands . . . . p. 135. HAIRY WOODPECKER.

7'. Length 6 to 7 inches. Familiar orchard and dooryard bird . . p. 137. DOWNY WOODPECKER.

Canada Jay; Moose Bird: *Perisoreus canadensis*.

(Plate XII. p. 218.)

GEOGRAPHIC DISTRIBUTION. — Nova Scotia, northern New England and northern New York ; west to northern Minnesota ; north in the interior to the arctic regions.

Tourists in the Adirondacks, White Mountains,

and Green Mountains may be fortunate enough to see the Canada Jays, or, as they are known from a corruption of their Indian name, Wiss-ka-chion, Whiskey Jacks; but when camping out one is most likely to see them. They are the constant attendants and companions of the lumbermen, trappers, and hunters along the Canadian border. In northern Maine Mr. Manley Hardy reports that "they will enter tents and often alight on the bow of a canoe where the paddle at every stroke comes within eighteen inches of them." They seem without fear of man, and help themselves freely to anything eatable about camp. They are remarkably

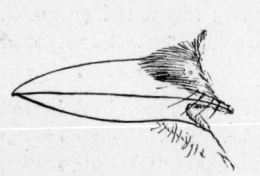

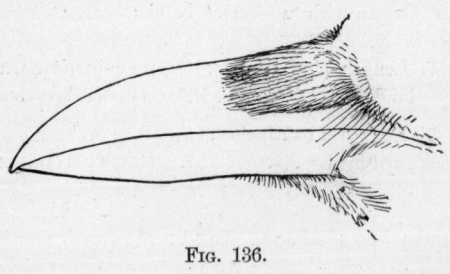

FIG. 135.
Bill of Blue Jay.

FIG. 136.
Bill of Crow.

attractive birds, and give life and interest to the dark, evergreen forests which they inhabit.

Like the ordinary Jay they are hoarders.

PLATE XII. — CANADA JAY

Forehead white; back of head and nape blackish; rest of body mainly gray. *Length*, 12 inches.

Audubon says they store away berries and nuts in hollow trees, or between the layers of bark on decaying branches, the provision secured enabling them to pass the winter in comfort and rear their young before the snow is off the ground.

With the Canada Jay we finish the family of Crows and Jays. The two Crows can be told apart by the smaller size of the Fish Crow and its harsh guttural note, while the Blue Jay will never be confused with its gray Canadian cousin. As a group they are powerful birds of marked characters and striking plumage, with heavy bills and strong feet. (See Figs. 135, 136, p. 218.) They walk rather than hop, and use their feet to hold their nuts as they drill them open.

It will be a help to run over the birds that we have already spoken of, for we have filled several gaps since the last enumeration.

Land Birds: I. Grouse and Quail. II. Pigeons and Doves. III. Birds of Prey. IV. Cuckoos and Kingfishers. V. Woodpeckers. VI. Goatsuckers, Hummingbirds, Swifts. VII. Perching Birds: 1. Flycatchers; 2. Crows and Jays; 3. Blackbirds and Orioles; 4. Finches and Sparrows; 5. Tanagers; 6. Swallows; 7. Waxwings.

FIG. 137.
Blue Jay.

Key to Crows and Jays.

1. Plumage black.
    2. Lustrous, with purple and green reflections. Voice hoarse (*car*). Found by water, or not far inland.

    p. 16. FISH CROW.

    2'. Larger, less lustrous, sometimes dingy. Voice clear (*caw*). Found everywhere.

    p. 11. AMERICAN CROW.

1'. Plumage blue or gray.
    3. Head crested; upper parts purplish; a black band around head and throat; wings and tail blue, marked with black and white . . . . p. 154. BLUE JAY.

    3'. Head not crested; upper parts gray; top of head white; nape blackish. Found in northern coniferous forests . . . . p. 217. CAÑADA JAY.

Junco; Slate-colored Snowbird: *Junco hyemalis*.

Adult male; upper parts, throat, and breast slate-gray; belly and outer tail feathers white. *Adult female,* similar, but duller gray. *Length,* about 6¼ inches.

GEOGRAPHIC DISTRIBUTION: Eastern North America; breeds from Minnesota and the mountains of New York and New England northward, and southward along the summits of the Alleghanies to Virginia; winters southward to the Gulf states.

About Thanksgiving time, in northern New York, flocks of wandering Crossbills sometimes drop in upon us, and then, too, as we are shut indoors, we think more of the companies of gray and white Snowbirds that come to our doorsteps for their share of our feast. They should receive it from generous hands, for as winter comes on they are not the least

FIG. 138.
Junco.

of the blessings for which we have to be thankful. Like the White-throated Sparrows, they are numbered with the birds whose feeding habits enable them to go in sociable flocks, for they are birds of catholic taste. In addition to their insect diet, which covers a large supply of ants, cutworms, weevils, leaf-eating beetles, and grasshoppers, they also eat the seeds of such weeds as pigweed, chickweed, knot-grass and foxtail, besides a great deal of ragweed (Fig. 139) which, while nuts to them, is a brow-knitting pest to the farmer. Mr. Nehrling after running over the Junco's catalogue, says that he is "like all our native Sparrows ... a very useful bird to the farmer and horticulturist;" and the ornithologist adds, "I cannot refrain from repeating that in treating the birds with kindness we exhibit the greatest kindness to ourselves.

Fig. 139.
Ragweed, eaten by Junco.

We can appreciate all Mr. Nehrling says of the Junco, for the little Snowbird is among our most cheery winter friends, responding to all our advances and coming to our very doorsteps for proffered food. Even their *tsip* is pleasant, and as they sit pluming themselves in the trees in the warm sunshine they often express their content in a gently warbled chorus that is most grateful to the ear.

Snowflake; Snow Bunting: *Plectrophenax nivalis.*

Mainly white; upper parts, wings, and tail marked with black; in winter washed with rusty. *Length*, about 7 inches.

GEOGRAPHIC DISTRIBUTION. — "Northern part of the northern hemisphere, breeding in the arctic regions; in North America, south in winter into the northern United States, irregularly to Georgia, southern Illinois, Kansas, and Oregon."

My only memories of these white northern visitors are connected with snowshoe walks over the fields in blinding snow-storms, when flocks of the white birds would appear and alight on the ground for a moment, then with a wild *cheep* go whirling on to disappear in the cloud of wind-blown snowflakes. One

FIG. 140.
Snowflake.

"must have been bred in the north," Mr. Chamberlain says, "to enjoy a snowstorm as the Buntings do, to find with them exhilaration in the biting air, and delight in the swish and swirl of the drifting flakes. These birds seem to be at their happiest in a storm, and whenever one comes their way they join in its whirl and scurry just for the fun of its fierce revelry, birds and flakes mingling in the same wild dance."

Dickcissel; Black-throated Bunting: *Spiza americana.*

Adult male, throat black; breast yellow, with a black central patch; back brownish, streaked. *Adult female*, duller, without black on throat or breast. *Length*, 6 inches.

GEOGRAPHIC DISTRIBUTION. — Eastern United States, mostly in the Mississippi valley; breeds from Texas to southern Minnesota and North Dakota; winters in Central and South America; breeds east of the Alleghanies now only in the south locally and rarely.

As the Snowbird's name recalls storm-blown snow-fields, so the Dickcissel's brings up pictures of the sunny level grain fields of Illinois. As he sits on a stake with the sunshine pouring down upon him, his song has all the brightness of the great open prairies he overlooks. "See, see, Dick, Dick-Cissel, Cissel" he calls from morning till night, well earning his popular name of 'Little Field Lark.'

FIG. 141.
Dickcissel.

The attractive bird is a deserving agriculturist as well as a cheering bird of song, for he makes it his business to do away with caterpillars and cankerworms, feeding his young considerately upon grasshoppers.

Savanna Sparrow: *Ammodramus sandwichensis savanna.*

Above brownish black; under parts streaked with black; pale yellow mark over or in front of eye and on bend of wing. Fall birds washed with yellowish brown. *Length,* about 5¾ inches.

GEOGRAPHIC DISTRIBUTION. — Eastern North America; breeds from Missouri and northern New Jersey north to Labrador and Hudson Bay, and winters from southern Illinois and Virginia southward to Cuba and Mexico.

Mr. Ridgway characterizes the Savanna Sparrow as "one of the inconspicuous little birds which hide in the grass or run stealthily along the fences or furrows, having nothing special in their appearance or habits to attract particular attention."

Sometimes, as you cross a meadow, one of the little brown striped creatures will start up from under your feet, and you will look down to find a nest with bluish spotted eggs in it.

Dr. Jonathan Dwight describes the Savanna's song as "insignificant — a weak, musical little trill following a grasshopper-like introduction of such small volume that it can be heard but a few rods. It usually resembles *tsĭp-tsĭp-tsĭp, sē'ē-ē-s, r-r-r.* More singing is heard toward sunset. . . . Each male seems to have a number of favorite perches, weeds or fence posts, which are visited as inclination dictates."

Speaking of the Sparrow's food, Mr. Nehrling says: "Like all our small birds these Sparrows are exceedingly beneficial, their food consisting, during the breeding time, mostly of insects, and in fall and winter they eat large quantities of the seeds of noxious weeds. Unfortunately," he goes on to say, " these and other song birds are killed by the thousand in the south by the negroes for the kitchen, and on the French market in New Orleans large masses of these birds are offered for sale during the whole winter. This shameless slaughter of our native song birds should be stopped by stringently enforced laws for their protection."

Yellow-winged Sparrow; Grasshopper Sparrow: *Ammodramus savannarum passerinus.*

Above blackish, with brown and buff streaks; crown blackish with buff line through centre; *below unstreaked*, washed with buffy. *Tail, even, pointed; bend of wing yellow.* Length, about 5¼ inches.

GEOGRAPHIC DISTRIBUTION. — Eastern North America; breeds from the Gulf states northward to Massachusetts, southern Canada, and Minnesota; winters from North Carolina to Cuba and Central America.

Mr. Ridgway says that in Illinois this little bird is known " in all cultivated portions of the State, as well as on the open prairie. To the rural population it is known as the 'Grass-bird,' 'Ground-bird,' or 'Grasshopper-bird,' the latter appellation being derived from its grasshopper-like song, which it utters from the end of a fence-stake, the top of a tall weed-stalk, or as it sits upon the summit of a haycock in the meadow. The greater portion of its time is passed in the grass, in which it runs from the intruder, unseen, like a mouse; or, if pressed too closely, rises suddenly and flies a greater or less distance in a zigzag manner." Mr. Chapman gives its song as *pit-túck, zee-e-e-e-e-e-e-e*.

In Maryland I have watched the Grasshopper while it sang undisturbed on a fence rail only a few rods away; but when it wanted to fly down to its nest it would crane its neck and jet its quaint short, pointed tail nervously.

Tree Sparrow; Winter Chippy: *Spizella monticola.*

Top of head reddish brown; *small black spot on centre of breast;* back streaked with reddish brown; breast washed with brownish; upper half of bill black, lower half yellow. *Length,* about 6¼ inches.

GEOGRAPHIC DISTRIBUTION. — Eastern North America; breeds in Labrador and the region about Hudson Bay; south in winter through eastern United States; west to the edge of the Great Plains.

There are two birds with which the Tree Sparrow might possibly be confused — the Chipping and Field Sparrows, although it is much larger than either. If one knows what to look for, however, the Field can easily be distinguished by its reddish bill, and the Chippy and Tree told apart by the indistinct black spot on the centre of the breast of the Tree. Of course none of the three can be confused with the Song Sparrow, because its breast is heavily streaked, while theirs are plain.

In the fall, when most of the other birds have left northern New York, the Tree Sparrow appears in the woodland pastures; and in Illinois it is one of the commonest and most friendly winter residents, as Mr. Ridgway says, coming "familiarly about the door-yards and gardens, gleaning from the snow in company with Snowbirds (*Junco hyemalis*) and other winter residents. During the warmer days of winter, or even if the weather be cold though clear, the rich medley of soft jingling notes uttered by a number of individuals of this species is not excelled for sweetness by any bird notes." Mr. Bicknell gives two of its call notes, the customary *chip* and "a low double note, which is uttered mainly while the birds are feeding." He says that "this simple and slightly musical sound from many birds busily feeding together produces a low conversational chirping, so pleasantly modulated as to seem an

FIG. 142.
Foxtail Grass, eaten by Tree Sparrow.

unconscious expression of contented companionship."

The Tree Sparrow is a striking illustration of the good done by seed-eating birds, for Professor Beal has calculated that in Iowa alone this little bird destroys 875 tons of noxious weed seeds every year.

Swamp Sparrow: *Melospiza georgiana.*

Crown and wings chestnut; back light brown heavily streaked with black; sides washed with brown; middle tail feathers darker on shafts. In winter, head streaked with black and brown. *Length*, about 6 inches.

GEOGRAPHIC DISTRIBUTION. — Eastern North America; breeds from northern Illinois and Pennsylvania northward to Labrador; winters from southern Illinois and Massachusetts to the Gulf.

"While wintering in the south, Swamp Sparrows frequently belie their name, and I have often found numbers of them in dry 'old fields' of broom sedge; but at the north they are more consistent, and one rarely sees them beyond the confines of a wet meadow, or, more preferably, a large grassy marsh with reed-bordered streams.

"Swamp Sparrows may be distinguished from their cousins, the Song Sparrows, by their unstreaked breasts and totally different notes. Their usual call note is a sharp *cheep*, not unlike that of the White-throated Sparrow, and quite different from the rather nasal *chimp* of the Song Sparrow. Their song is a simple, sweet, but somewhat monotonous *tweet-tweet-tweet*, repeated many times, all on one note, and sometimes running into a trill." (Chapman.)

Fox Sparrow: *Passerella iliaca*.

Head and shoulders mixed reddish brown and slate-gray; cheeks, wings, and tail warm reddish brown; breast heavily marked with rufous. *Length*, about 7¼ inches.

GEOGRAPHIC DISTRIBUTION. — Breeds from the Gulf of St. Lawrence, Magdalen Islands, and Manitoba to Alaska and the Arctic Ocean; winters from Virginia southward.

Doctor Brewer discovered Fox Sparrows on the grounds of the Capitol in Washington, in winter, and similar pleasures may be in store for many observant city dwellers. The first sight of the bird is surely a memorable experience. What with his large size, his striking fox-colored back and tail, together with the remarkable combination of slate-gray and fox on his head, he seems a new, strange creature.

FIG. 143.
Fox Sparrow.

And when he sings, one's surprise and admiration increase. His song is so loud, ringing, and liquid that it puts him at once at the head of the musical Sparrow family. "It is a revelation to hear it at sundown on some vernally softened evening of early springtime," says Mr. Bicknell; "little swarms of gnats hover in the balmy air; from the twilight meadows comes the welcome, half-doubtful piping of the first hylas — no other sound. Then perhaps from some dusky thicket a bird's song! An emotional outburst rising full-toned and clear, and passing all too quickly to a closing cadence, which seems to linger in the silent air. . . . It breaks forth as if inspired from pure joy in the awakened season, though with some vague undertone, scarcely of sadness, rather of some lower tone of joy."

Pine Grosbeak: *Pinicola enucleator.*

(See Fig. 117, p. 193.)

Adult male, slaty gray washed with dull rose-red. *Adult female*, slaty gray slightly washed with yellowish. *Young*, like the female. *Length*, about 9 inches.

GEOGRAPHIC DISTRIBUTION. — Northern portions of the northern hemisphere, breeding in North America from the mountains of New England, Colorado, and California north to the limit of trees, migrating in winter irregularly to the northern United States.

One of the rare pleasures of a winter among the snow-fields of the north is the visit of a flock of Pine Grosbeaks. The handsome, rosy-coated birds are not common visitors, and the sight of a red flock of them clustering around the cones of an evergreen is a picture to brighten many a dull day. They wander about the country in winter, and when a flock suddenly appears in a neighborhood it creates general interest and curiosity, for the birds are so large and richly colored that they are hard to overlook. Indeed, queries often appear in the country newspapers as to what the remarkable strangers may be.

Coming in this way, we naturally want to show them some hospitality, and Mrs. Mabel Osgood Wright tells us that we can please them by offering them cracked corn that has been soaked in boiling water.

They are gentle birds, whose knowledge of man is so limited that they have no fear of him, and will often let themselves be taken in the hand. One such trustful bird that came to us in northern New York was caged, but although he made a gentle pet, I can never think of him without regret for he had a wild woodland way of lifting his wings and uttering a low, plaintive, haunting call that told of his yearning for his free life of winter wandering, and his longing for a sight of the great forests and snow-fields of his northern home.

Mr. Chamberlain has had the good fortune to hear the Grosbeak's love-song near St. John in June, and describes it as "an exquisitely sweet and tender strain — sung in such soft tones it must be intended for one ear alone, for it cannot be heard a dozen yards away. The bird does not sing thus because he lacks strength of voice, for his winter song is loud and vigorous, . . . just such a breezy carol as you might expect from a stalwart fellow who loves the north wind and revels amid the snow."

Pine Finch; Pine Siskin: *Spinus pinus*.

Brownish, streaked with black above and below; *wing and tail feathers marked with yellow at base. Length,* 5 inches.

GEOGRAPHIC DISTRIBUTION. — North America generally; breeds in the British provinces, the higher mountains of the western United States, and sparingly in the northeastern states; winters as far south as the Gulf.

" Few birds are more erratic in their habits than the Siskin, or Pine Linnet. Occurring to-day, perhaps, in such numbers that one soon tires of shooting them, they are gone on the morrow, and years may elapse before one is seen again. There is, in their melancholy *che-a,* uttered at intervals as small flocks pass in

FIG. 144.
Pine Finch.

short, waving swoops far overhead, something sadly suggestive of the cold bleak winds that sweep their northern homes." (Merriam.)

Although so erratic in occurrence, when it does come, the Pine Finch is to be welcomed, not only by the bird-lover but by the agriculturist, for it is said to be fond of useless and pernicious weeds, ragweed being on its list.

American Crossbill: *Loxia curvirostra minor*.

Adult male, tips of bill crossed; body dull red. *Adult female*, dull olive-green, yellowish on rump. *Young*, similar to the female, or mixed red and green. *Length*, about 6¼ inches.

GEOGRAPHIC DISTRIBUTION. — Northern North America; resident sparingly north in the eastern United States to Virginia and the southern Alleghanies.

The Grosbeaks, Pine Finches, and Crossbills are all wandering, erratic birds, flocks of which may appear any winter's day. The Crossbills, as they fly overhead, announce themselves with a metallic *kimp, kimp, kimp*, suggestive of the note of the Purple Finch. When they settle on the ground they go to picking up food so quietly, and with such an air of being at home, that they might almost be a flock of little tame Pigeons. For like the Grosbeaks, Siskins, and other northern birds who see little of man, they are sad commentaries on the unnatural wildness of most of our birds. In looking at a flock, the first thing one notices about them is their variety of coloring; they shade from the bright reds of the adult males to the dull greenish yellows of the young and female. The second thing that attracts the eye is the curious crossed bill. It seems such a poor tool, you wonder how the birds can ever manage to pick up their food with it; but when you see them cling to a cone and extract

FIG. 145.
Bill of Crossbill.

its seeds you realize that the bill is most wonderfully adapted, from the simple Finch type, to suit their peculiar needs.

In the cold winter of 1875-76, Mr. Nehrling tells us, the parks of Chicago and the suburbs of the city swarmed with Crossbills and other northern birds. They came into his garden and to the windows of his house in Oak Park, picking up crumbs, pieces of fat and tallow, hemp, millet, canary-seed, cuttle-fish bone, and salt. Indeed, the Crossbills are particularly fond of salt, a salt pork rind furnishing them a veritable feast.

The Crossbills nest irregularly, but usually in February, when the cold of winter is most intense and the snows the deepest. As Mr. Nehrling says, one would think it impossible, not only that the eggs could be kept from freezing, but that the callow young could endure the rigors of the season.

There is a white-winged species of Crossbill that goes farther north than the American, but it is sometimes seen in flocks with the American, and the two species are similar in habits. The white-winged is said to eat cankerworms.

Redpoll Linnet: *Acanthis linaria*.

Adult male, cap bright red; rump and breast pinkish; back brownish; chin black. *Adult female*, red confined to cap. *Young*, similar to female but without red cap. *Length*, about 5¼ inches.

GEOGRAPHIC DISTRIBUTION. — Breeds in the northern part of the northern hemisphere; in winter migrates irregularly southward, in America, to Virginia, Illinois, Kansas, and Oregon.

At the time when the Crossbills visited Chicago, the Redpolls were also abundant there, and Mr. Nehrling describes them as climbing like titmice, "head downward, along the branches of shrubs and weed-stalks, always uttering a peculiar *chett* or *chett-cherrett*." He says that these "exceedingly lively and beautiful birds are especially striking objects among the snow-laden branches of firs, spruces, and pines, and imbue such a cold and dreary winter landscape with joy and happiness." But their very beauty and trustfulness prove their destruction. Together with numberless Warblers, Finches, Creepers, and Nuthatches, when they confidingly enter the villages and cities, the street boys rush out and kill them mercilessly with stones and sling-shots, with air-guns and sticks. Mr. Nehrling exclaims against this thoughtless cruelty of children, whom, he well says, should be taught to carefully preserve the beautiful in nature.

FIG. 146.
Redpoll Linnet.

The flight of the Redpolls is not very high, and they move along in undulating lines. In general habits they are said to resemble the Goldfinch. Like the other winter Finches, they live on weed seed, and Mr. Oberholser has seen flocks of several hundred feeding on a field grown up with ragweed, one of the worst of pests.

Lark Sparrow: *Chondestes grammacus.*

Stripes on crown and sides of head chestnut, striking; tail black, feathers showing white in flight; black spot on breast. *Length*, 6¼ inches.

GEOGRAPHIC DISTRIBUTION. — Interior of North America, eastward to Alabama, Ohio, and Michigan; breeds from Texas northward to Manitoba; accidental on the Atlantic coast (Massachusetts, Long Island, New Jersey, District of Columbia, Florida).

In Ohio the Lark Sparrow is found in " sparsely wooded pastures or neglected fields bordered with low trees," Doctor Wheaton tells us, and he considers its song unrivaled in the Sparrow choir. He calls attention to its habit of walking, rather than hopping as the other Sparrows do, and says that in parts of Illinois it is known as the 'Quail

FIG. 147.
Lark Sparrow.

Head,' from a superficial resemblance in color and its Quail-like habit of running after its fellows with lowered head, drooping wings, and expanded tail. In other places this Sparrow is known as the 'Road Bird,' from its habit of running along roadsides and feeding in roads.

Doctor Wheaton gives an interesting instance of a Lark Sparrow's appealing to him for help. Flying ahead of him, the bird led him to a garter snake, circling around it several times as if pointing it out. When the snake had been killed, the bird "perched upon a fence stake and filled the air with its grateful notes." But, alas, after giving thanks, the poor Sparrow discovered that unwittingly the doctor had thrown the dead snake almost on to the nest. In vain it tugged and dragged at the body till again its friend came to its assistance, when, the snake being tossed out of sight, it once more burst out into grateful song.

The nest of the Lark Sparrow is a deep, root-woven structure like those of many Ground Sparrows, often sunk in a little hollow on the ground, but sometimes placed in bushes or even trees.

The eggs are dingy white, marked, like Orioles' eggs, with irregular lines.

Sharp-tailed Sparrow: *Ammodramus caudacutus* and races.

Above, dark olivaceous; cheeks gray, inclosed by a dark brown ring; tail feathers narrow and sharply pointed; breast and sides buff, *distinctly streaked with black;* middle of throat and belly white. *Length,* about 6 inches.

GEOGRAPHIC DISTRIBUTION. — Atlantic coast north to New Brunswick; marshes of Mississippi valley north to Dakota and Manitoba.

This species is confined exclusively to the salt-water marshes of our coast, where it may be found in large numbers. It runs about among the reeds and grasses with the celerity of a mouse, and is not apt to take wing unless closely pressed. Mixed flocks of the several varieties of the Sharp-tail, together with the Seaside Sparrow, gather in the fall among the sedges, and may be observed hiding in the grass, or clinging to the tall stalks of the cat-tails. In the breeding season it is usually associated with the Seaside Sparrow on the same marsh; but it prefers the drier parts, and builds its nest in the tussocks on the bank of a ditch, or in the drift left by the tide, rather than in the grassier sites chosen by its neighbor.

FIG. 148.
Tail of Sharp-tailed Sparrow.

" From some bit of driftwood or a convenient stake its infrequent song may be heard morning and evening. It is short and gasping, and only less husky than the somewhat similar performance of the Seaside Sparrow." (Dr. Jonathan Dwight, Jr.)

The Sharp-tailed Sparrow is one of the birds whose tails must have been modified by their habits. The Swift, as we have seen, is an extreme example of the specialized tail (see Fig. 214, p. 353), and the Woodpeckers' tails are pointed for bracing. (See Fig. 213, p. 353.) But the pointed type is found in Meadowlarks, Bobolinks (see Fig. 211, p. 353), and some of the Sparrows that live among the grasses. (See Fig. 148, p. 239.) Why others, like the Vesper Sparrow, whose lives are spent in the same meadows, have the unmodified square form (see Fig. 60, p. 119) is one of the many interesting questions for field students to gather statistics on. Is the habit of steadying the body by pressing the tail against grass-stalks or reeds confined to birds with pointed tails?

Seaside Sparrow : *Ammodramus maritimus* and races.

Bill long and pointed; above, grayish olive; below, buffy streaked with gray; throat white, inclosed by gray and dusky lines; yellow line over eye and on bend of wing. *Length*, 6 inches.

GEOGRAPHIC DISTRIBUTION. — Salt marshes of Atlantic and Gulf coast; breeding as far north as Massachusetts, and wintering from Virginia southward.

" Like most marsh-loving birds, Seaside Sparrows are so consistent in their choice of a home that it would be quite useless to look for them anywhere but in a marsh, and that a salt one, generally within sound or at least sight of the sea. The baymen call them 'Meadow Chippies.' ... They pass much of their time on the ground among the reeds and grasses, but mount a stalk to sing their short, unattractive song of four or five notes. Sometimes they flutter into the air a few feet above the reeds and deliver their song while on the wing.

"The absence of distinct streaks on the breast, and lack of rufous in their olivaceous or grayish plumage, will distinguish them from the Sharp-tailed, Swamp, Savanna, or Song Sparrows, the only ones which are likely to be found in their haunts." (Chapman.)

Clay-colored Sparrow : *Spizella pallida*.

Similar to the Chipping Sparrow, but grayish rather than reddish brown on back; under parts white and buffy. *Length*, 5½ inches.

GEOGRAPHIC DISTRIBUTION. — Northern plains and prairies; breeds from northern Nebraska, central Iowa, and northern Illinois northward; winters from southern Texas southward.

This little Sparrow of the plains is said to be very much like the eastern Chipping Sparrow both in song, habits, and familiarity.

Bachman's Sparrow: *Peucœa æstivalis bachmanii*.

Upper parts rufous, buffy line over the eye; breast and sides brownish buff, unstreaked. *Length*, about 5¾ inches.

GEOGRAPHIC DISTRIBUTION. — Lower Mississippi valley north to southern Indiana and southern Illinois; west to northern Texas; east to Georgia, South and North Carolina; south in winter, in the Atlantic states, to southern Florida.

Bachman's Sparrow is a shy bird, frequenting half-cleared fields or open woods, where, when alarmed, it will dive into the nearest shelter, or skulk, wren-like, along the fences, dodging from rail to rail. In Florida, where it spends the winter, it is to be seen in the pine woods undergrown with oaks. Its near relative, the Pine Woods Sparrow, on the other hand, is found only in pine woods with an undergrowth of scrub palmetto. The songs of both birds are remarkable. Bachman's sings even during the heat of midday, but its cousin of the pine woods needs the inspiration of matins and vespers. Mr. Chapman describes the song of the Pine Woods Sparrow as being very simple, but possessing "all the exquisite tenderness and pathos of the melody of the Hermit Thrush."

Bachman's Sparrow completes the number of the Finches and Sparrows that we shall take up. The family, being the largest of our bird families, is greatly varied, but its members as a rule have the conical seed-eater bill (see Fig. 119, p. 193), and, by combining an insect and vegetable diet, are able to winter in the United States, living upon the seeds of the weeds that protrude above the snow; while exclusively insectivorous birds, such as Cuckoos, Goatsuckers, Hummingbirds, Swifts, Flycatchers, and Swallows, must go to the tropics to find their winter food.

As a family the Finches and Sparrows are musical birds, some of them such remarkable songsters that they rank with the Orioles, Wrens, Thrashers, and Mockingbird.

The Sparrows live for the most part in open fields, where their dull brown streaked coats protect them; while the Finches, largely bright-colored birds, such as the Indigo-bird and Cardinal, live in the cover of trees, where their conspicuous coats are less noticeable. As the Sparrows spend much of their time on the ground, they are birds of strong feet (see Fig. 21, p. 50) and short round wings (Fig. 149), in sharp contrast to the birds that get their food on the wing (Figs. 99, p. 189; 100 and 102, p. 190). The commonest Sparrows are easily distinguished.

FIG. 149.
Wing of Song Sparrow.

The Chipping Sparrow (see Fig. 55, p. 113), and the Clay-colored, its cousin of the plains, are the two dooryard Sparrows, as Mr. Torrey would call them, and rank with the smallest of the family. The Song Sparrow is a size larger; its breast is streaked, and has usually a black spot in the centre (Fig. 154,

p. 252). It comes next to the Chippy in friendliness. The Vesper is seen on roadside fences, and when it flies may be recognized by its white outer tail feathers. (See Fig. 60, p. 119.) Its loud, sweet song is also a striking character. The White-throated and White-crowned Sparrows stand by themselves, and the two may be known apart by the white chin patch of the Whitethroat, though both have handsome striped black and white crowns (Figs. 150 and 152, p. 252). The Tree and Field Sparrows are the less domestic cousins of the Chippy and Clay-colored. The Field may be known by its reddish bill and its plaintive song, which generally runs down the scale; while the Tree may be recognized by its larger size, the small, indistinct black spot on its breast, and the fact that it is only a winter visitor going to Labrador and the Hudson Bay country to nest. The Savanna, Grasshopper, Sharp-tailed, and Seashore Sparrows belong to the same genus, and are birds of the open meadows, or, in the case of the Sharp-tailed and Seashore, of salt marshes. Their tails are worn and pointed (see Fig. 148, p. 239), presumably because they use them to brace against the reeds and grasses, steadying themselves as they perch. A fine, insect-like song characterizes the Grasshopper Sparrow, together with the fact that its under parts are unstreaked, while those of the Savanna are heavily streaked. In the north, the Grasshopper is found in old daisy or sorrel fields. The Seaside and Sharp-tailed, while occurring together, may be told apart by the absence of distinct streaks on the under parts of the Seaside. The Lark Sparrow, the Dickcissel, and Bachman's Sparrows are birds of the interior of the United States; and the Lark is known by the heavy chestnut markings on the sides of its head (see Fig. 147, p. 237) and the white markings of its tail, while the Dickcissel, the meadow songster, may be known by its black throat and yellow breast (see Fig. 159, p. 253), which suggest similar marks in the Meadowlark (see Fig. 45, p. 106), after which it is nicknamed. Bachman's is a bird of the woods or clearings rather than the meadows, and will be recognized by its noted song. The Swamp Sparrow is in the same genus with the Song Sparrow, but may be told from it by its unstreaked breast and different song, together with the fact that in the north it is found almost exclusively in marshes or wet meadows. The Fox Sparrow is such a striking northerner that when seen on its migrations it can never be confused with any other Sparrow. (See Fig. 143, p. 230.) As its name suggests, it is fox-colored, being heavily marked with reddish brown on its breast and having reddish wings and tail. The slate-gray of its head mixed with this fox-color make an unusual combination hard to forget.

Of the rest of the family the Chewink (see Fig. 153, p. 252) has the sparrow-like habit of scratching on the ground for its food, and its russet sides match the dead leaves about it, while its black back is inconspicuous from above. The Goldfinch (Frontispiece) and Indigo Bunting carry their names in their colors, as do the Cardinal (see Fig. 155, p. 253) and the Rose-breasted Grosbeak (see Fig. 151, p. 252). The rest of the Finches we have looked at are winter visitors, including the two Snowbirds, the Slate-colored Junco and the Snowflake (see Figs. 156 and 158, p. 253), the Redpoll (Fig. 157, p. 253), Crossbill (Fig. 145, p. 234), Streaked Pine Finch (Fig. 144, p. 233) and large, rosy Pine Grosbeak (Fig. 117, p. 193).

Key to Adult Male Finches and Sparrows.

Common Characters. — Bill stout and conical.

I. STRIKINGLY–COLORED BIRDS.
- A. BLUE CONSPICUOUS IN PLUMAGE.
- B. YELLOW CONSPICUOUS IN PLUMAGE.
- C. BLACK OR SLATE–GRAY CONSPICUOUS IN PLUMAGE.
- D. RED CONSPICUOUS IN PLUMAGE.

II. DULL–COLORED STREAKED BIRDS.
- A. UNIFORMLY STREAKED ABOVE AND BELOW.
- B. NOT UNIFORMLY STREAKED ABOVE AND BELOW.

I. STRIKINGLY–COLORED BIRDS.
A. BLUE CONSPICUOUS IN PLUMAGE.

Entire body indigo blue. Call *cheep*, accompanied by twitching of tail from side to side. Female brownish.
p. 149. INDIGO BUNTING.

KEY TO FINCHES AND SPARROWS

B. YELLOW CONSPICUOUS IN PLUMAGE.
1. *Throat with black patch.*
Breast yellow; back brownish, streaked. Found in meadows in the Mississippi valley.

p. 224. DICKCISSEL.

1'. *Throat without black patch.*
Entire body canary yellow; cap, wings, and tail black.

p. 145. GOLDFINCH.

C. BLACK OR SLATE-GRAY CONSPICUOUS IN PLUMAGE.
1. *Mainly black and white, large.*
 2. Upper parts black; sides russet; belly and corners of tail white. Scratches among leaves on ground. Female brown in place of black . p. 181. CHEWINK.

 2'. Upper parts washed with brown. Seen in flocks on the snow, November to March . p. 223. SNOWFLAKE.

1'. *Not mainly black and white; small.*
Slate-gray, belly and outer tail feathers white.

p. 221. JUNCO.

D. RED CONSPICUOUS IN PLUMAGE.
1. *Bill crossed.*
Small winter visitants. Seen in flocks with greenish yellow females and young, often eating seeds of cones.
 2. Body dull red; no black or white on back or wings.

p. 234. AMERICAN CROSSBILL.

 2'. Body pink; back marked with black; wings black and white . . . p. 235. WHITE-WINGED CROSSBILL.

1'. *Bill not crossed.*
 3. Body mainly red.
  4. Body bright cardinal; head with high crest. Female largely brownish . . . . . p. 65. CARDINAL.

  4'. Body washed with dull rose-red; head without crest.
   5. Size small; resident. Female sparrowy, streaked.

p. 148. PURPLE FINCH.

5'. Size large ; winter visitors. Come in flocks with gray females and young.

   p. 231.   PINE GROSBEAK.

3'. Body not mainly red.
  6. Upper parts black (head, throat, and back black). Size large ; bright crimson patches on breast and under wings. Females sparrow-like.

   p. 166.   ROSE-BREASTED GROSBEAK.

  6'. Upper parts brown (finely streaked).
    Size small ; cap bright crimson, chin blackish ; rump and under parts dull crimson. Seen in flocks in winter . . . . p. 236.   REDPOLL.

II. DULL-COLORED STREAKED BIRDS.

A. Uniformly streaked above and below ; yellow on base of wing and tail feathers ; size small. An erratic winter visitor. Usually in flocks about evergreens.

   p. 233.   PINE FINCH.

B. Not uniformly streaked above and below ; no yellow on base of wing and tail feathers. Brownish birds. Length 5 to 10 inches . . . . SPARROWS.

Key to Sparrows.

1. *Crown conspicuously striped.*
  2. Chin with square white patch. Song a loud, clear whistle, *I, I, pea-body, pea-body.*

   p. 174.   WHITE-THROATED SPARROW.

  2'. Chin without white patch.
    Crown with conspicuous black and white stripes.

   p. 176.   WHITE-CROWNED SPARROW.

KEY TO SPARROWS

1'. *Crown not conspicuously striped.*
3. Crown mainly reddish brown or chestnut.
    4. Corners of tail conspicuously marked with white; breast unstreaked, but with small black spot in centre; cheeks chestnut. A large, handsome Sparrow of Mississippi valley region. p. 237. LARK FINCH.

4'. Corners of tail not white.
    5. A conspicuous reddish brown patch on wing. Forehead black; breast grayish, without marking; throat white . . . . p. 229. SWAMP SPARROW.

5'. No reddish brown patch on wing.
    6. Forehead black anteriorly; white wing bars *not* conspicuous; bill black. Common doorstep Sparrow . p. 113. CHIPPING SPARROW.

6'. Forehead without black; white wing bars conspicuous.
    7. Breast with indistinct black spot; upper half of bill black, lower half yellow. Common winter visitant . . . . . p. 227. TREE SPARROW.

7'. Breast without spot; entire bill reddish brown. Song, a minor whistle. p. 183. FIELD SPARROW.

3'. Crown not mainly reddish brown or chestnut.
8. Under parts not streaked.
    9. Outer tail feathers white; back and breast slate-gray; belly abruptly white. Common in flocks in winter . . . . p. 221. JUNCO.

9'. Outer tail feathers not white.
    10. Upper parts reddish brown; breast and sides brownish, unstreaked. Found in Mississippi valley and the south.
        p. 242. BACHMAN'S SPARROW.

10'. Upper parts not reddish brown; under parts whitish. Bird of the plains.

p. 241. CLAY-COLORED SPARROW.

8'. Under parts streaked.
11. Upper parts bright reddish brown; size large; breast heavily streaked. Migrant.

p. 230. FOX SPARROW.

11'. Upper parts not reddish brown; size smaller.
12. Outer tail feathers white; upper parts brownish gray, streaked; shoulders reddish brown. Seen commonly on roadside fences.

p. 119. VESPER SPARROW.

12'. Outer tail feathers not white.
13. No yellow on bend of wing; sides of throat blackish; breast and sides heavily streaked; an indistinct blotch in middle of breast. One of the commonest, most familiar Sparrows . . . p. 116. SONG SPARROW.

13'. Yellow on bend of wing.
14. Under parts white and heavily streaked; upper parts blackish brown, streaked. Bird of northern meadows.

p. 225. SAVANNA SPARROW.

14'. Underparts not white and not heavily streaked.
15. Crown blackish (a buffy line through centre); nape rufous brown; back blackish. Bird of dry fields, especially in the south.

p. 226. GRASSHOPPER SPARROW.

KEY TO SPARROWS

15'. Crown not blackish; tail pointed. Bird of salt marshes.

16. Breast and sides *distinctly* streaked; upper parts brownish olive; head marked with buffy yellow and bluish gray.

        p. 239.   SHARP-TAILED SPARROW.

16'. Breast and sides *indistinctly* streaked; upper parts grayish olive.

        p. 240.   SEASIDE SPARROW.

252 FINCH AND SPARROW FAMILY

FIG. 150.
White-throated Sparrow.

FIG. 152.
White-crowned Sparrow.

FIG. 151.
Rose-breasted Grosbeak.

FIG. 153.
Chewink.

FIG. 154.
Song Sparrow.

MEMBERS OF THE FINCH AND SPARROW FAMILY.

FINCH AND SPARROW FAMILY 253

FIG. 155.
Cardinal.

FIG. 157.
Redpoll.

FIG. 158.
Snowflake.

FIG. 156.
Junco.

FIG. 159.
Dickcissel.

MEMBERS OF THE FINCH AND SPARROW FAMILY.

Acadian Flycatcher: *Empidonax virescens*.

Upper parts *olive green;* throat white; rest of under parts white, washed with yellowish and greenish; two conspicuous yellowish white wing bars. *Length*, 5¾ inches.

GEOGRAPHIC DISTRIBUTION. — Eastern United States; breeds from Florida and Louisiana to southern Connecticut and southern Michigan; winters in West Indies and Central America.

What distinction and flavor the discovery of a new bird gives to a day in the woods, and how the event is stamped in the memory! I can recall the very hour and spot when I saw my first Acadian Flycatcher. It was in a delightful open woods with straight, high, arching trees bordering a quietly sauntering stream in the Hudson River valley. We were idly enjoying the May beauty of the woods, when suddenly there came a loud call of '*pe-ah-yuk'*,' and, before I could even imagine what it was, my companion had disappeared up stream, and when I hurried after, was absorbedly gazing at the little Acadian. The performer was perched on a low sapling over the brook, just as the books say he does, and to my great satisfaction repeated his call again and again in most orthodox Acadian fashion, with bill pointed to the sky and wings and tail shaking — all so perfectly in accord with the records one might have imagined him on the witness stand to testify to the customs of his family.

Great-crested Flycatcher: *Myiarchus crinitus*.
(Plate XIII. p. 258.)

Crest and back olive; throat and breast gray; *belly lemon yellow*, tail showing bright reddish brown in flight. *Length*, about 9 inches.

GEOGRAPHIC DISTRIBUTION. — Eastern United States and southern Canada; breeds from Florida to New Brunswick and Manitoba; winters from southern Florida to South America.

The Flycatchers are no songsters, but may be known by their calls. The Great Crest, like most birds, has moments of private meditation and soliloquy, but he usually whistles from a treetop in the woods so loudly you can hear him from the highway. '*Whuir, whuree, whit-whit,*' he calls in such a hearty, healthy tone of satisfaction that it stirs one's blood.

The force and originality of this tribal call note is not belied by the habits of the birds. Hardy and pugnacious, Colonel Goss says they fight fiercely for their mates, and have a habit of plucking the tail feathers of their rivals to disfigure them in the eyes of their lady loves! But this is not all. When the war is over, the birds build in a hole in a tree trunk, like so many Woodpeckers; and for nest lining they get the cast-off skins of snakes! Whatever may be the historic reason for this peculiar habit, the lamented Mr. Frank Bolles watched two nests in which the skin was apparently used to scare away intruders. The morning he found the first nest it had one egg and no snake-skin, but that evening he was startled to be met by the raised head of a snake (skin) in front of the nest, and on examination found that the body of the snake — six or seven inches long — was coiled around the eggs. The second year the birds built in the same place, and after each of Mr. Bolles's visits to the nest fresh pieces of skin were added. That this was done with an eye to his intentions Mr. Bolles believed from the evident disapproval of the birds, for they scolded him severely whenever he came, and as long as he remained in sight. A similar use of the skin is suggested in the instance quoted by Major Bendire, in which the skin was arranged to hang out of the hole. Mr. Burroughs throws a sidelight on the question by stating that he has found onion skin, fish scales, and even oiled paper in nests where there was no snake-skin. If originally protective, the instinct seems to have run to seed as a morbid taste for the grotesque in house-furnishing!

Though the Great Crest is a wood's bird, it often nests in orchards, and Mr. Nehrling thinks might easily be induced to build in bird-boxes. Aside from the keen interest attaching to it, it is a useful bird to have about the premises, as it eats numbers of caterpillars, grasshoppers, and harmful beetles.

Olive-sided Flycatcher: *Contopus borealis.*

Upper parts blackish brown, throat and middle of belly whitish; rest of under parts like back; lower half of bill pale; white tufts on sides of rump. *Length,* about 7½ inches.

GEOGRAPHIC DISTRIBUTION. — North America; breeds in the east from Massachusetts and Minnesota northward; winters in Central and South America.

Adirondack visitors sometimes have the good fortune to see this interesting bird. One summer when rowing on Little Otter, one of the small lakes on the edge of the Adirondacks, I heard the loud call, and traced it to the bird at the top of a dead tree overlooking the lake. There he sat in solitude, surveying the landscape, at intervals shooting out in true Flycatcher style after passing insects. His call, which Mr. Torrey hears as *que-que'-o,* has less of command than the Great Crest's; in fact it is rather plaintive, more on the cast of the Wood Pewee's; and in listening to it on Little Otter, as my floating boat displaced the water-lilies of the quiet lake, the solitary bird's cry seemed to harmonize well with the sombre depths of the silent evergreen forest.

Alder Flycatcher: *Empidonax trailii alnorum* and race.

Upper parts *olive-brown;* under parts white, washed with dusky; wing bars soiled whitish. *Length,* about 6 inches.

GEOGRAPHIC DISTRIBUTION. — North America; breeds from Arizona, Missouri, southern Illinois, northern New England, and casually Connecticut, north to New Brunswick and Alaska; winters in Central America.

This Flycatcher is a shy bird of the alders rather than a bird of the village, as is the 'Least,' its double. And instead of the call of *che-beck'*, with which the Least relieves his feelings, Traill's finds it sufficient to say *pep*. Its song is said to resemble that of the Acadian, being an '*ēē-zēē'-ē-ŭp*,' jerked out so rapidly that the performer doubles himself up, fairly vibrating with the explosive effort.

Contrasting still further the members of the Flycatcher tribe which we have looked at, we find that the Kingbird is the tormentor of Hawks and Crows, and is marked with a white band across the end of its tail. (See Plate XIII. 4.) Though the Phœbe and Wood Pewee are confusing at first, they can be discriminated by the more marked wing bars of the Wood Pewee (see Plate XIII. 2), aside from the calls and habits of the two birds, which are quite distinct; the Wood Pewee having the *pee-ah-we* call instead of *phœ-be*, and the Pewee nesting on a high branch instead of under a shed, house, bridge, or barn. The Great Crest and the Olive-sided are the two birds of the

PLATE XIII. — FLYCATCHERS

1. Great-crested Flycatcher. 2. Wood Pewee. 3. Phœbe.
4. Kingbird. 5. Least Flycatcher.

forest; the Olive the more remote of the two, for the Great Crest sometimes nests in orchards. The Pewee, too, is sometimes found in woods. The Least, the Acadian, and Traill's, or the Alder, are closely related, but their call notes and their haunts will distinguish them. Traill's is a bird of the north; the Least, of the south.

As a family, the Flycatchers contrast sharply with the Sparrows; the big heads and shoulders and the broad, flat, bristly bills of the Flycatchers (Fig. 38, p. 92, and Fig. 110, p. 192), being most unlike the small round heads and shoulders and conical bills of the Sparrows (Fig. 119, p. 193). And while the lowly Sparrows pick up seeds from the ground or low weeds, the Flycatchers mount to the high places to look for insects. On dead twigs or treetop perches they lie in wait for their prey, shoot out upon it, capture it with a snap of their hooked beaks, and instantly return to await the next hapless flies. In this habit of lying in ambuscade the Flycatchers differ from many of the other insectivorous birds, such as Swallows, Swifts, and Nighthawks, who fly through the air snapping up insects as they go. Indeed, their feeding habits more nearly resemble those of the Waxwings, the Red-headed Woodpecker, and Kingfisher, all of whom make short sallies and return to their trees. As the Flycatchers live on insects most of them make extended migrations, leaving the north early in the fall and returning late in the spring.

Fig. 160.
Phœbe.

Key to Flycatchers.

1. *Crested.*
    Throat and breast gray ; belly light yellow ; tail reddish brown. Call loud and shrill.
    p. 255. GREAT-CRESTED FLYCATCHER.
1'. *Not crested.*
  2. Back greenish.
      Throat white ; wing bars conspicuous. Southern. Call, *peet,* or *pee-a-yuk'.*
      p. 254. ACADIAN FLYCATCHER.
  2'. Back blackish or brownish.
    3. Tail with white bar across end ; crown with concealed orange patch. Chases Hawks and Crows.
        p. 83. KINGBIRD.
    3'. Tail without white bar ; crown without color patch.
      4. Without noticeable wing bars.
        5. Whole bill black ; under parts pale grayish and whitish ; no white tufts on sides of rump ; common about houses, barns, and bridges. Call, *phœ-be'* . . . . p. 87. PHŒBE.

        5'. Lower half of bill pale ; under parts nearly same color as back, with whitish line down middle of breast and belly; conspicuous white tufts on sides of rump. Breeds in northern forests. Call, *pu-pio'* . . p. 257. OLIVE-SIDED FLYCATCHER.

4'. With noticeable wing bars.
   6. Length more than 6 inches. Common. Note, *pee'-ah-wee'* . . . . p. 90. WOOD PEWEE.
   6'. Length less than 6 inches.
      7. Throat pure white. Retiring. Found in alder thickets northward.
                        p. 258. ALDER FLYCATCHER.

      7'. Throat not pure white. Familiar; found in trees about houses. Note, *che-beck'*.
                        p. 80. LEAST FLYCATCHER.

Horned Lark; Shore Lark: *Otocoris alpestris* and eastern race.

(Fig. 161, p. 262.)

Upper parts pinkish brown; tail black, outer feathers marked with white; forehead, horns, sides of throat and breast black; rest of under parts whitish. *Length*, 7¾ inches.

GEOGRAPHIC DISTRIBUTION. — Breeds in northern Europe, Greenland, Newfoundland, Labrador, and Hudson Bay region southward to upper Mississippi valley and Massachusetts; in winter, southward to about latitude 35°.

Sometimes, as you drive along the country roads, you will see perched on a fence a small chocolate-colored bird with curious black, horn-like plumes on the sides of its head; and again, in winter, you may meet a flock of the same singular little birds in the middle of a city street. I have had one of these pleasant encounters in Washington. The birds start up before you with a plaintive cry, swing round, and then surprise you by settling down again only a few yards farther away; and if you stand quietly will let you enjoy watching them.

In America the Horned Larks are alone in the family of which the famous Skylark is one of the European members; but while their song is wholly unpretentious, it is quaint and attractive, and is often given as the bird springs from the ground toward the sky, quite in the manner of the Skylark.

Fig. 161.
Horned Lark.

The characters of the Horned Larks are distinct. They are protectively colored, matching closely the soil where they are seen; and in the west, where they habitually run along the bright-colored roads, their coloration is striking. They run and walk rather than hop, and have the further habit of keeping in flocks when not nesting.

It has been complained that the Lark eats newly planted wheat and oats, but the examination of 59 stomachs shows that it does not do any appreciable damage to grain crops, and on the other hand it does great good by eating weed seed. As Professor Beal says, "Any bird which eats freely the seeds of such pests as pigweed, bitterweed, amaranth, and sorrel should be given the most perfect protection unless it is clearly shown to have bad habits which offset the benefit thus conferred."

Birds of Prey.

There is a rooted prejudice against both Hawks and Owls, although, as investigations prove, as a group they rank among the most valuable of all birds. They are persecuted unceasingly, and yet, as Doctor Fisher says, the majority of them labor day and night to destroy the enemies of the husbandman.

Turkey Vulture : *Cathartes aura.*
(Fig. 163, p. 264.)

Head and neck naked, the skin bright red; rest of body blackish; tail and wings brownish. *Length*, about 30 inches.

GEOGRAPHIC DISTRIBUTION. — Temperate North America, from New Jersey, Ohio valley, Saskatchewan region, and the State of Washington southward to Patagonia. Of more or less regular occurrence in New Jersey as far north as Princeton in the interior and Sandy Hook on the coast. Casual northward on the Atlantic coast to Maine.

The Buzzards serve man by acting as scavengers, and the occupation, in the warm countries where they occur, is no sinecure.

In New Orleans and other southern cities northern tourists see the novel sight of Buzzards sitting in rows on the fences, and in many places may observe them walking along the streets or roosting on housetops. In both west and south they are one of the commonest birds in the sky and may be recognized from below by the black body figure set in a bordering of gray wing. The wing tips are separated like the teeth of a comb. The shadows of the birds often cross your path as they circle silently around and around in the sky with heads turned down to scan the earth for carrion. On account of the character of the food of the Buzzards, their bills and feet are modified from the Hawk types. The bill is less sharply pointed and powerful; while the feet, instead of having curved talons, have an elongated middle toe well adapted to walking on the ground, or steadying the large body as the bird stands on the carrion it is devouring.

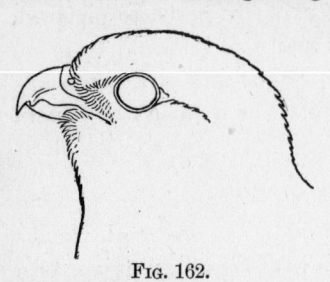

Fig. 162.
Powerful bill of Hawk.

Fig. 163.
Modified bill of Vulture.

Doctor Ralph gives a grotesque picture of the Vultures he has seen in the south "floating down

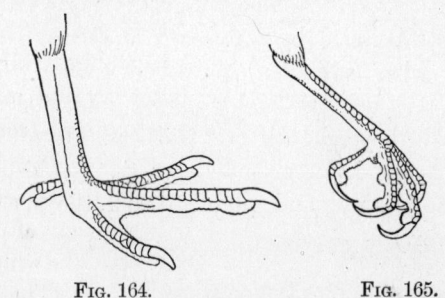

FIG. 164.
Walking Foot of Vulture.

FIG. 165.
Grasping Foot of Hawk.

a stream on a dead alligator, cow, or other large animal, crowded so closely together that they could hardly keep their balance, and followed by a number on the wing." [1]

Black Vulture: *Catharista atrata*.

Head and neck naked; the skin blackish; plumage blackish; tail rather short, and square at end. *Length*, about 24 inches.

GEOGRAPHIC DISTRIBUTION. — Breeds from North Carolina southward through Mexico to South America.

"Both in their mode of flight and in their movements upon the ground this species differs materially from the Turkey Buzzard. The latter walks steadily while on the ground, and when it mounts does so by a single upward spring. The Black Vulture is ill at ease on the ground, moves

[1] Bendire's *Life Histories of North American Birds*, p. 162.

awkwardly, and when it essays to fly upward takes several leaps in a shuffling sidelong manner before it can rise. Their flight is more labored, and is continued by flapping several times, alternated with sailing a limited distance. Their wings are held at right angles, and their feet protrude beyond their tail feathers. In all these respects the differences between the two birds are very noticeable, and plainly mark the species." (Brewer.)

Key to Vultures.

Common Characters. — Head and neck naked ; plumage glossy black.

1. Skin of head and neck bright red.

        p. 263. TURKEY VULTURE.

1'. Skin of head and neck blackish.

        p. 265. BLACK VULTURE.

Goshawk : *Accipiter atricapillus.*

(Plate XIV.)

GEOGRAPHIC DISTRIBUTION. — Breeds from the northern United States northward, and winters as far south as Virginia.

Fortunately the Goshawk is rare in the United States except in fall and winter, for it is the most

PLATE XIV. — GOSHAWK

Adults, upper parts bluish gray; under parts finely barred with wavy gray and white. *Young*, upper parts brownish, tail barred with black; under parts whitish, streaked with black. *Length*, 22 inches.

destructive of the American birds of prey; its size, strength, and daring, together with its rapid flight, making it most dangerous to game-birds and poultry. It will actually dart down at the very foot of the farmer and carry off a fowl. Major Bendire denounces it as " savage and bloodthirsty in disposition, a veritable terror to all smaller birds, and more than a match for others considerably larger than itself," and he declares that it loves to destroy life for the sake of killing.

In his 'Hawk and Owl Bulletin,' Doctor Fisher gives an interesting account of its habits. "In the fall," he says, "this Hawk is common along the smaller watercourses, where it is very destructive to wild ducks and other water-fowl, and is able to strike down a bird as large as a full-grown Mallard. If its prey is a bird of this size it rarely eats more than the flesh from the breast, leaving the rest of the carcass untouched. . . .

"Of the upland game-birds the Ptarmigan in the north and the Ruffed Grouse in the middle districts suffer severely from the attacks of this powerful Hawk. . . . In some parts of the country the Goshawk hunts the Ruffed Grouse so persistently that it is known by the name of 'Partridge Hawk,' and this bird probably has no worse enemy except man."

Sharp-shinned Hawk: *Accipiter velox*.

(Plate XV.)

GEOGRAPHIC DISTRIBUTION.— North America; breeds throughout the United States, and winters from Massachusetts to Central America.

Unlike the Goshawk, the Sharp-shinned is one of our commonest birds of prey. Fortunately it is so small that it does little harm in the poultry-yard except in carrying off very small chickens. Doctor Fisher says that its food is made up almost entirely of wild birds and young poultry; 96 per cent. of the contents of the stomachs examined consisted alone of birds. However, as the doctor says, when a pair of the Hawks find a farm where young chickens are easily obtained, they devote themselves to the family until there is no family left, or they themselves meet with a tragic death.

The one redeeming quality of the Sharp-shinned is its fondness for House Sparrows. Doctor Fisher tells us that in winter it even visits towns and cities for them, being not uncommon in Central Park and the larger parks of Washington.

Doctor Ralph finds that its numbers are not decreasing as rapidly as those of other Hawks, and attributes it to the retiring habits of the Sharp-shinned, as well as their quick movements, which make it difficult to shoot them. They do

PLATE XV. — SHARP-SHINNED HAWK

Adults, end of tail square; upper parts and tail slaty; tail banded with black; throat white, streaked with blackish; rest of under parts barred with white and reddish brown. *Young,* similar, but under parts white, streaked with brown or black. *Length,* male, $11\frac{1}{4}$ inches; female, $13\frac{1}{2}$ inches.

not, he says, circle through the air in search of food, but skulk around in thick trees and bushes, and pounce on their prey when least expected. When they seize a bird or mammal, no matter how small it may be, they always fly at once to the ground with it. When they wish to carry their prey to any distance, they do it by short flights just above the ground. They have a peculiar habit of stretching out their legs as far as they can, as soon as they seize their quarry, as if they were afraid of what they had caught."

The nests of the Sharp-shinned are very large for the size of the bird, and are in trees, from fifteen to forty feet from the ground. The eggs vary from bluish white to cream buff heavily spotted with brown.

Cooper's Hawk: *Accipiter cooperi.*

(Fig. 166, p. 270.)

End of tail decidedly rounded; crown blackish; rest of upper parts dark brown; under parts barred with reddish brown and white. *Length,* male, 15½ inches; female, 19 inches.

GEOGRAPHIC DISTRIBUTION. — Breeds from the Gulf of Mexico to Newfoundland, and winters from Massachusetts to Mexico.

Doctor Fisher has found that the food of Cooper's Hawk, like that of the little Sharp-shinned, consists almost entirely of wild birds and poultry, and as Cooper's is larger and stronger, it does much more harm in the dove-cote and hen-yard. Indeed, its devastations amount to more than all other Hawks together. It fully merits the name of Chicken Hawk, and its name should be written in black.

Colonel Goss, in his 'Birds of Kansas,' gives

Fig. 166.
Cooper's Hawk.

a hint for the identification of these Hawks, and an interesting experience of his own with them. "Their ordinary flight is a quick flapping of the wings," he says, "relieved occasionally by sailing.

Their slender build and long, rudder-like tail enables them to swiftly wind their way through the trees and to snatch a squirrel or a lizard from the branches with as much apparent ease as they swoop down upon their prey in the open lands. Rabbits, mice, small birds, Bob-whites, and Ducks help to make up their bill of fare. They often boldly enter the door-yard, where I saw one of the birds strike a hen, while in defense of her brood, with a force that killed her, and then grasp in its claws a half-grown chicken and triumphantly carry it away."

This is the last of the three brigands of the family, and after following their gory records it is pleasant to turn to the citizens of better repute.

Red-tailed Hawk: *Buteo borealis*.

(Plate XVI. p. 272.)

GEOGRAPHIC DISTRIBUTION. — Eastern North America, breeding throughout most of its range.

It is important to discriminate between the slender, long-tailed, darting Accipiters — the three black sheep of the Hawk family, the Goshawk, Sharp-shinned, and Cooper's Hawks — and the large, heavily-built, shorter-tailed, and slow-flying Buzzard Hawks or Buteos, which number among them the Red-tailed and Red-shouldered Hawks; for the larger and most useful Hawks have been confused with the small, injurious ones, and the name Hen Hawk and Chicken Hawk applied ignorantly to the members of the beneficial genus. Doctor Fisher says that the name Hen Hawk is responsible for much of the false opinion regarding the Red-tail, and states that, "while fully 66 per cent. of the Red-tail's food consists of injurious mammals, not more than 7 per cent. consists of poultry, and it is probable that a large proportion of the poultry and game captured by it and the other Buzzard Hawks is made up of old, diseased, or otherwise disabled fowls, so preventing their interbreeding with the sound stock and hindering the spread of fatal epidemics." Among other things, the Red-tail eats ground-squirrels, rabbits, mice, and rats.

This splendid bird is one of our commonest Hawks, and, when circling in the sky, can often be recognized by its fan-shaped reddish tail.

Though these Hawks are known less familiarly than the small birds, there is always something virile and interesting about them, and it is a never-failing interest to watch them soar, and to speculate over the unsolved problem as to how they do it. Nuttall notes that they sometimes amuse themselves by ascending to a vast elevation like the aspiring Eagle, and says that this predilection for the cooler regions of the atmosphere is shared by most rapacious birds, apart from any survey for prey. In his delightful way, the old ornithologist describes one such flight. "On a fine evening, about the middle of January, in South

PLATE XVI. — RED-TAILED HAWK

Adults, upper parts dark brown; under parts white, streaked with brown; *tail reddish brown*. *Young*, similar, but tail brown and banded with black. *Length*, male, 20 inches; female, 23 inches.

Carolina," he says, "I observed one of these birds leave its withered perch, and soaring aloft over the wild landscape, in a mood of contemplation, begin to ascend towards the thin skirting of elevated clouds above him. At length he passed this sublime boundary, and was now perceived and soon followed by his ambitious mate, and in a little time, by circular ascending gyrations, they both disappeared in the clear azure of the heavens; and though I waited for their reappearance half an hour, they still continued to be wholly invisible."

Red-shouldered Hawk: *Buteo lineatus*.

Adults, upper parts dark brown; *shoulders reddish brown;* tail black, with four to five white cross-bars; under parts barred with reddish brown and white. *Young*, tail without distinct cross-bars; under parts whitish, streaked with dark brown. *Length*, male, about 18¼ inches; female, about 20¼ inches.

GEOGRAPHIC DISTRIBUTION. — Eastern North America, west to the Plains, north to Nova Scotia and Manitoba.

This valuable bird has also been damned by the name of Hen Hawk and Chicken Hawk, though not a single fowl has been found in the many stomachs examined by Doctor Fisher. The doctor's testimony is enforced by the record of a case in which a pair of the Red-shoulders reared their young for two years in a small, swampy piece of woods about fifty rods from a poultry farm containing 800 young chickens and 400 ducks, and in all the two years were never seen attempting to catch one of the fowls. (See 'Hawk and Owl Bulletin,' p. 63.)

As for birds, Doctor Fisher says that this Hawk flies too slowly to be able to catch them. Instead, it eats, among other things, mice, snakes, grasshoppers, earthworms, snails, spiders, and centipedes. Indeed, 90 per cent. of its food is composed of injurious mammals and insects.

In view of these facts, it seems strange that the bird's good work should be interfered with, but, as Mr. Chapman explains, "The farmer sees a Hawk sailing in wide circles above him, uttering its fierce, screaming cry. . . . While he is watching it a sly, low-flying Accipiter slips by him and makes a sudden dash into the poultry-yard. The farmer does not discriminate; a Hawk is a Hawk, and, shaking his fist at the bird in the air, he vows vengeance at the first opportunity."

Aside from the economic interest attaching to the Red-shoulders, their domestic relations are worth study. Nuttall, who saw pairs of the birds in the south in winter, tells us that they call affectionately for each other, and that the male, when discovering his mate, caresses her much in the manner of the Dove.

Broad-winged Hawk: *Buteo latissimus*.

Adults, upper parts dark brown; tail with two light bars; under parts *heavily* barred with reddish brown. *Young*, tail with three to five indistinct bars; under parts white, streaked with brown. *Length*, male, about 16 inches; female, about 16¾ inches.

GEOGRAPHIC DISTRIBUTION. — Eastern North America, south to northern South America; breeds throughout eastern North America from New Brunswick and Saskatchewan southward to Florida and Texas.

This is another of the beneficial Buteo family, and its food consists principally of insects, small mammals, reptiles, batrachians, and occasionally a young or disabled bird.

It is a quiet bird, and during the early summer, Doctor Fisher notes, it "often may be seen sitting for hours on the dead top of some high tree. At other times it is found on the smaller trees in the deep woods, along streams, or on the ground, where its food is more often procured. Although sluggish and unusually heavy in its flight, it is capable of rapid motion, and sometimes soars high in the air."

The Broad-wing is the common Hawk of the Adirondacks, and nests about small lakes, where it can find the mice, shrews, and squirrels upon which it lives. Its call note is said to resemble that of the Kildeer Plover.

Sparrow Hawk: *Falco sparverius*.
(Fig. 167, p. 277.)

Adult male, upper parts reddish brown and bluish, barred with black; tail reddish brown, with a broad black band near end; *black stripes on sides of head;* under parts reddish brown, somewhat spotted with black. *Female,* back, wings, and tail barred with black; under parts streaked with brown. *Length,* 10 inches.

GEOGRAPHIC DISTRIBUTION. — Breeds from Florida to Hudson Bay, and winters from New Jersey southward to northern South America.

This little striped-faced Hawk is often found perched on a dead limb of a tree, or seen, like the Kingbird, hovering in mid air over a field, holding itself up with rapidly beating wings and tail. In both cases it is probably watching for its dinner, waiting to pounce on some unsuspecting grasshopper or cricket, for they supply its table in summer. In winter it may sometimes be seen on poles about haystacks, lying in wait for a more substantial meal of mice.

In some sections the Sparrow Hawk is known as the 'Killy Hawk,' from its cry of *killy-killy-killy-killy.*

Curiously enough, while the other Hawks build large twig nests high in trees, the Sparrow Hawk hides its brood inside a hollow branch, or even in a Woodpecker's deserted nest, sometimes putting up with a hole too small for it, one which it has much ado to get in and out of.

In watching the aerial performances of the

Sparrow Hawk, one understands how the flight of birds is modified by their feeding habits. The Ruffed Grouse *walks* to pastures new, and, as it springs from under your feet and goes whirring

FIG. 167.
Sparrow Hawk.

away, is merely seeking new cover, which it easily reaches after a short flight by descending in a curve to the earth. The Kingfisher wings his way with the level, rapid flight of one who has many miles to travel for his meal — whose mind is fixed on a distant goal. Flycatchers, Waxwings, and Red-headed Woodpeckers, on the other hand, make short parabolas, leaving their perches only to seize the insects that happen by. The Sparrows and Wrens make short, labored flights from one clump of weeds or bushes to another, using their wings merely to transport them to neighboring feeding-grounds, never loitering in the air. But the Swift, the Swallow, and the Nighthawk have business in the air, and their flight is a series of curves, zigzags, or other evolutions, as they hunt back and forth, snapping up the insects that are in the skies. The Kingbird and Sparrow Hawk also have business in the air, but they use it, not as a dining-table, but as a perch, hovering on wing while they scrutinize the ground beneath for their food.

Marsh Hawk: *Circus hudsonius.*

(Plate XVII.)

GEOGRAPHIC DISTRIBUTION. — North America in general, south to Panama.

The female and young Marsh Hawks can always be known as large, dark birds with white at the base of the tail, for the round white spot can be seen rods away as the Hawk slowly beats over the face of the meadow in its search for mice. The adult male is still more strikingly

PLATE XVII. — MARSH HAWK

Adult male, upper parts gray; under parts pearl gray or white; *base of tail white.* *Adult female,* upper parts dark brown; under parts reddish brown, streaked; *base of tail white.* *Young,* similar to female. *Length,* male, 19 inches; female, 22 inches.

marked, and unless you have been warned, you will find it hard to believe him a Hawk, for he is a most distinguished-looking beauty, as pearly gray as a Sea Gull.

In his 'Hawk and Owl Bulletin,' Doctor Fisher deplores the fact that for its occasional poultry dinner the Marsh Hawk is shot, as he says, at sight, quite "regardless or ignorant of the fact that it preserves an immense quantity of grain, thousands of fruit-trees, and innumerable nests of game birds by destroying the vermin which eat the grain, girdle the trees, and devour the eggs and young of the birds."

It is "unquestionably one of the most beneficial, as it is one of our most abundant Hawks," the doctor states, "and its presence and increase should be encouraged in every way possible, not only by protecting it by law, but by disseminating a knowledge of the benefits it confers. It is probably the most active and determined foe of meadow mice and ground squirrels, destroying greater numbers of these pests than any other species, and this fact alone should entitle it to protection, even if it destroyed no other injurious animals."

Although the Marsh Hawk is usually seen flying low over the ground, in the spring he imitates the Nighthawk, doing his wooing in the sky with many most remarkable flourishes, presumably adapted to the taste of the ladies of the marshes.

Sometimes he mounts aloft for the express purpose of dropping to the earth in a series of somersaults; at others, as Mr. Thompson describes it, "he flies across the marsh in a course which would outline a gigantic saw, each of the descending parts being done in a somersault and accompanied by the screeching notes which form the only love-song within the range of his limited vocal powers."

He is not only an ardent wooer but a devoted mate, carrying food to the brooding bird, who flies out to meet him and dexterously seizes the morsel which he drops in her talons.

Osprey; Fish Hawk : *Pandion haliaëtus carolinensis.*

(Plate XVIII.)

GEOGRAPHIC DISTRIBUTION. — North America; breeds from Florida to Hudson Bay and Alaska; winters from South Carolina to northern South America.

"This species lives in colonies, and also in pairs, along our coasts, returning year after year to the same nesting ground. Its food consists solely of fish, which as a rule it captures alive. Winging its way slowly over the water, it keeps a keen watch for fish which may appear near the surface. When one is observed it pauses, hovers a moment, and then closing its wings, descends with a speed and directness of aim that generally insure success. It strikes the water with great force, making a loud *splash*, and frequently dis-

PLATE XVIII. — FISH HAWK

Upper parts brown; head, nape, and under parts white. *Length*, about 23 inches.

appears for a moment before rising with its prey grasped in its powerful talons. As a rule, it carries its food to some favorite perch, there to devour it. It is said that Fish Hawks have been known to strike fish so large that, unable to release their hold, they were drawn under water and drowned.

"When protected, Fish Hawks, like many other birds, to a large degree lose their fear of man. In the 'Auk,' for October, 1892, will be found a valuable article by Dr. C. S. Allen, on the habits of this species, as observed by him on Plum Island, N. Y., where for forty years the birds had been protected by the owner of the island." (Chapman.)

In the Adirondacks, on an inlet between two of the lakes of the 'Fulton Chain,' a pair of Fish Hawks had a nest for many years, and though sportsmen's boats passed under their very tree on the way up the lakes, the birds, protected by the chivalry of the guides, were so tame they would perch beside the nest unmoved while the gunners looked up at them.

It is said that the Fish

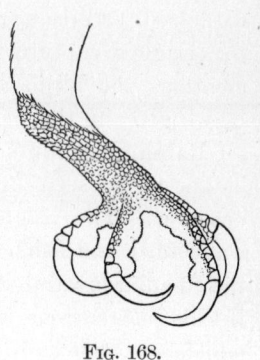

FIG. 168.

Grasping foot of Fish Hawk.

Hawks sometimes combine to drive away the Bald Eagles, but never attack them singly.

The foot of the Fish Hawk is remarkably adapted to holding its slippery prey, the toes having pads with horny spikes in addition to sharp curved nails (Fig. 168, p. 281).

Bald Eagle: *Haliæetus leucocephalus*.

(Plate XIX.)

GEOGRAPHIC DISTRIBUTION.—North America, breeding throughout its range.

The Bald Eagle, being our national emblem, is familiar to all good Americans, but in the north the sight of the splendid bird itself is a rare and exciting one. In Florida the tourist is more often privileged to see it, and if the privilege is not abused, many interesting performances may be witnessed. Wilson gives a spirited account of the Eagle's capture of a wild Swan, and also mentions the bird's habit of making the Fish Hawk give up the fish it has caught, while Doctor Ralph gives hints of most interesting nesting habits to be seen by the close and unobtrusive observer. The Eagle lives largely on wounded water-fowl and fish. In the west and southwest the Spaniards value it for the number of squirrels it kills. A curious case is recorded of an Eagle which was shot and found to have on its neck a locket in the form of the bleached skull of a weasel, hanging by its firmly set teeth. In the

PLATE XIX. — BALD EAGLE

Head, neck, and tail white; rest of plumage dark brown.
Length, male, about $32\frac{3}{4}$ inches; female, $35\frac{1}{2}$ inches.

greater part of the country the Eagle is harmless and should be protected; but in places where it cannot get its natural food, and so carries off sheep and other domestic animals, it should not be allowed to become too abundant.

Swallow-tailed Kite: *Elanoides forficatus.*

(Plate XX. p. 284.)

GEOGRAPHIC DISTRIBUTION. — United States, north to North Carolina and Minnesota, and casually to Massachusetts, Manitoba, and Assiniboia, southward throughout Central and South America, breeding locally throughout its range.

As its name suggests, the Swallow-tailed Kite has a forked tail like that of the Barn Swallow. The Barn Swallow, the Nighthawk, and the Long-tailed Pigeons rank with it in contrast to the Short-tailed Sparrows, Wrens, and Swifts; and as the Kite has long, slender wings, it is enabled to live almost exclusively in air. Just what part the tail plays in the flight of birds is a most interesting question. Though many of its peculiar developments seem to be of purely æsthetic value, merely sexual characters, other tails appear to have weight in the more ordinary affairs of life — such as steering for a fly. Careful observations will do much to clear up all such problems, it is to be hoped, within the next few years of extended field-work.

The Kite, in any case, is a true aeronaut. As it flies it will actually reach down and eat the snake that it holds in its talons; and it has also been seen by Doctor Merriam to dart down and pick a wasp's nest from the underside of a leaf, flying off eating the contents as it went.

In cotton fields the Kites turn their acrobatic skill to good purpose, descending to feed on the cotton worms. They also eat a great many grasshoppers, but their favorite foods are snakes, lizards, frogs, and insects. In Florida, where snakes can readily be dispensed with, the Kites eat so many they are known as 'Snake Birds.'

This is surely a good record, and puts the Kites on the 'white list' of Hawks. Indeed, the more we study the beneficial Hawks the more we are impressed with the contrast between them and the three black sheep on the black list. It is indeed fortunate that the blue Goshawk is with us only in fall and winter, and that the Sharpshinned is so small it can manage quarry little larger than small birds; for that narrows down the evil done by the black-listers to the depredations of Cooper's Hawk (see Fig. 166, p. 270), the true Chicken or Hen Hawk, who destroys both poultry and Doves, and whose sins are so many that they are borne by a large number of those who are innocent of game dinners. That we make no mistakes in identification in future, and lay the blame only where it belongs, let us look carefully over the white-list birds once more. While the injurious Hawks are slender, long-

PLATE XX. — SWALLOW-TAILED KITE

Head and under parts white; upper parts and long, forked tail black, with metallic reflections. *Length*, 24 inches.

tailed, and swift-flying (see Plate XIV. p. 266, Plate XV. p. 268, and Fig. 166, p. 270), the beneficial Buteos are large, shorter-tailed, and slow-flying (see Plate XVI. p. 272), and are often seen soaring high in the sky. Of their number the Red-tailed hunts in open ground, the Red-shouldered and Broad-winged mainly in woodland. The Broad-wing may be further discriminated by its smaller size. The Sparrow Hawk is the small Hawk with dark face-stripes seen hovering over the meadows (see Fig. 167, p. 277), while the Marsh Hawk is the large, white-rumped mouser seen beating low over the field. (See Plate XVII. p. 278.) The Turkey and Black Vultures are the two scavengers; both are primarily southern birds, and the Black Vulture is rarely seen north of the Carolinas. The Kite is the Hawk Swallow (see Plate XX. p. 284); and the Fish Hawk (see Plate XVIII. p. 280) hunts over rivers, lakes, and along seashores, and is sometimes forced to give up its prey to the Bald Eagle. (See Plate XIX. p. 282.)

Key to Falcons, Hawks, and Eagles.

1. Head and neck mainly white.
    2. Tail as well as head white; under parts dark brown or blackish . . . . p. 282. BALD EAGLE.
    2'. Tail not white; under parts white.
        3. Tail forked; head wholly white; back glossy bluish black. Southern.
            p. 283. SWALLOW-TAILED KITE.

3'. Tail not forked; sides and back of head marked with blackish; back brown. Found near water.

p. 280. FISH HAWK.

1'. Head and neck not mainly white.
4. Small (length 10 to 13 inches).
   5. Black stripes on sides of head; under parts sparsely spotted; back and tail mainly reddish brown. Common. Hovers over meadows for grasshoppers and mice . . . . . p. 276. SPARROW HAWK.

   5'. No black stripes on back of head; under parts everywhere barred with reddish brown and white; upper parts slaty gray. Darts after small birds.

   p. 268. SHARP-SHINNED HAWK.

4'. Larger (length 15 to 25 inches).
   6. Base of tail conspicuously white.
      Upper parts dark brown; under parts brownish. Female and young . . p. 278. MARSH HAWK.

   6'. Base of tail not conspicuously white.
      7. Tail strikingly reddish; upper parts dark brown; under parts white, streaked with brown. Common, mousing over meadows.

      p. 271. RED-TAILED HAWK.

      7'. Tail not reddish.
         8. Upper parts ashy gray or bluish gray.
            9. Upper parts bluish gray; under parts finely barred with gray and white. Winter visitant.

            p. 266. GOSHAWK.

            9'. Upper parts ashy gray; under parts whitish. Adult male . . . . p. 278. MARSH HAWK.

         8'. Upper parts dark brown; under parts barred with reddish brown and white.
            10. Shoulders reddish brown. Common in woods.

            p. 273. RED-SHOULDERED HAWK.

PLATE XXI. — SCREECH OWL

Adults, small, with ear-tufts conspicuous. Reddish-brown phase:
Upper parts warm, reddish brown; under parts white, washed
with reddish brown and streaked with black. *Gray phase:*
Upper parts grayish, streaked with gray and black. *Young,*
entire plumage regularly barred with grayish or reddish brown
and white. *Length,* about 9½ inches.

10'. Shoulders not reddish brown.
11. Tail long, with three light bands; under parts lightly and uniformly barred. Destroys poultry . . . p. 269. COOPER'S HAWK.

11'. Tail short, with two light bands; breast heavily barred with brown; under parts lightly barred. Found in woods.
p. 275. BROAD-WINGED HAWK.

Screech Owl: *Megascops asio.*

(Plate XXI.)

GEOGRAPHIC DISTRIBUTION. — Eastern North America, northward to New Brunswick and Minnesota; generally resident throughout its range. Various forms are found throughout the wooded portions of the United States and Mexico.

Of the small Owls, the Screech Owl is the only one with large ear-tufts, and so may be easily known, although its color varies, being sometimes reddish brown and sometimes gray. We are fortunate enough to have this little Owl as a familiar neighbor in our orchards and about our farmhouses, where it comes out at night and inspects corn-cribs and grain-stacks for mice, devouring in its time many thousands of the little pests. Doctor Fisher speaks of the pretty footprints of mice which mark the snow after a winter's night, and says that when a track stops abruptly, if the faint impression of a pair of wing-tips is visible beside it, one can guess what has happened. Besides ridding us of mice, the Screech Owl also does good by destroying House Sparrows.

Major Bendire believes that these Owls remain mated through life, and quotes an interesting account of their courtship from Mr. Lynds Jones. "The female was perched in a dark leafy tree," his informant writes, "apparently oblivious of the presence of her mate, who made frantic efforts through a series of bowings, wing-raisings, and snappings to attract her attention. These antics were continued for some time, varied by hops from branch to branch near her, accompanied by that forlorn, almost despairing wink peculiar to this bird. Once or twice I thought I detected sounds of inward groanings, as he, beside himself with his unsuccessful approaches, sat in utter dejection."

The Screech Owl's nesting site is almost always a hollow in a tree, often a Woodpecker's hole, and it has been known to accept a bird-box for its home. It is interesting to hear that both little parent Owls sometimes sit on the eggs at the same time. The eggs, like those of all Owls, are white.

Long-eared Owl: *Asio wilsonianus.*

(Plate XXII.)

GEOGRAPHIC DISTRIBUTION. — North America; breeds from Nova Scotia and Manitoba southward to the Gulf states and table-lands of Mexico.

In the Long-eared Owl we have one of the interesting cases where unconscious protective

PLATE XXII. — LONG-EARED OWL

Ear-tufts an inch or more long; upper parts dark brown, marked with yellowish; under parts white, longitudinally streaked with brown; facial disk yellowish. *Length*, about 15 inches.

coloration is combined with conscious protective attitudes. When the Owl is frightened, it rises up, "draws the feathers close to the body, and erects the ear-tufts, resembling in appearance a piece of weather-beaten bark more than a bird."[1] When not able to employ this device effectively, the Owl resorts to another. Major Bendire surprised one while she was killing a ground squirrel, and was startled by the sudden transformation that took place in her. "All at once she seemed to expand to several times her normal size," he says, "every feather raised and standing at a right angle from the body; the wings were fully spread, thrown up and obliquely backward, their outer edges touching each other over and behind the head, which likewise looked abnormally large." This was accompanied by a hissing noise. But in spite of this bravado, the bird found herself afraid to stand her ground, and, " collapsing to her normal size, flew off, leaving her quarry behind."

Doctor Fisher proclaims the Long-eared Owl one of our most beneficial species, for it destroys vast numbers of injurious rodents and seldom touches insectivorous birds. It is preëminently a mouser.

[1] *Hawk and Owl Bulletin*, p. 143, U. S. Department of Agriculture.

Short-eared Owl: *Asio accipitrinus*.

(Plate XXIII.)

GEOGRAPHIC DISTRIBUTION. — Nearly cosmopolitan, breeding in the United States locally from Virginia and Illinois northward.

This Owl differs widely from its relatives. It is much less nocturnal, and rarely even alights on a tree. It is a bird of the marshes and flies near the ground, like the Marsh Hawk. It lives mainly on meadow mice, gophers, grasshoppers, crickets, and other insects, and deserves the fullest protection.

A strong piece of evidence in its favor is found in Yarrell's 'British Birds.' "Undoubtedly field mice, and especially those of the short-tailed group or voles, are their chief objects of prey, and when these animals increase in an extraordinary and unaccountable way, as they sometimes do, so as to become extremely mischievous, Owls, particularly of this species, flock to devour them. Thus there are records of a 'sore plague of strange mice' in Kent and Essex in the year 1580 or 1581, and again in the county last mentioned in 1648. In 1754 the same thing is said to have occurred at Hilgay, near Downham Market, in Norfolk; while within the present century the Forest of Dean, in Gloucestershire, and some parts of Scotland have been similarly infested. In all these cases, Owls are mentioned as thronging to the spot, and ren-

PLATE XXIII. — SHORT-EARED OWL

Ear-tufts short; upper parts brown, marked with buffy; under parts streaked with dark brown. *Length*, 15½ inches.

PLATE XXIV. — BARRED OWL

Upper parts grayish brown, marked with white; breast *barred*, and belly and sides *streaked* with brown and white; bill yellow. *Length*, 20 inches.

dering the greatest service in extirpating the pests. The like has also been observed in Scandinavia during the wonderful irruptions of lemmings and other small rodents to which some districts are liable, and it would appear that the Short-eared Owl is the species which plays a principal part in getting rid of the destructive horde."

Barred Owl; Hoot Owl: *Syrnium nebulosum.*
(Plate XXIV.)

GEOGRAPHIC DISTRIBUTION. — Eastern North America, west to the Plains; northward to Nova Scotia and Manitoba; resident except at the northern limit of its range.

The larger part of the food of the Barred Owl consists of mammals, including among them the most destructive rodents with which the farmer has to contend. Heavily wooded swamps and hemlock forests are the favorite haunts of this retiring Owl. It is one of the noisiest of its family, and probably oftener heard than any other. Adirondack campers are often startled by its cry at night, although, as Major Bendire remarks, "a rapidly passing shadow distinctly cast on the snow-covered ground is often the sole cause of its presence being betrayed as it glides silently by the hunter's camp-fire in the still hours of a moonlight night." Its hoot is given as *whoo-whoo-whoo, who-whoo-to-whoo-ah*, uttered in an interrogatory tone.

Doctor Fisher tells us that "it is the commonest species of rapacious bird throughout the extensive swamps covered by cypress and other growths which abound in the coast region of the south, where as many as fifteen or twenty may be seen in a day's tramp. Although not usually seen near habitations, it sometimes wanders into large towns, either in search of food or the shelter afforded by some attractive clump of evergreens."

Great Horned Owl: *Bubo virginianus*.

(Plate XXV.)

GEOGRAPHIC DISTRIBUTION. — Eastern North America, northward to Labrador and southward to Costa Rica; resident throughout its range.

Where wild game is scarce and poultry plenty, the Great Horned Owl ranks with the three brigand Hawks, and should be studied closely, that its sins may not be laid at the door of the deserving members of the family. But where wild game is plenty the Owl's record is better, for it turns its attention to rabbits and other 'small dere' that make sad havoc with the crops.

So each case should be judged on its own merits. As Doctor Fisher says, . . , " a bird so powerful and voracious may at times be a source of great benefit, while at other times it may be the cause of great damage. Now, the serious inroads it makes on the tenants of the poultry-yard, as well as the destruction of many game and song birds, would seem to call for the total suppression of

PLATE XXV. — GREAT HORNED OWL

Ear-tufts nearly two inches long; upper parts mottled with yellowish brown and black; facial disk yellowish brown; white patch on throat; rest of under parts buffy, barred with black. *Length*, 22 inches.

the species. Again, when engaged chiefly in the capture of injurious rodents which threaten the very existence of the crops, it is the farmer's most valuable ally, and consequently should be most carefully protected."

The Great Horned Owl lives mainly in heavy forests. I have often heard it in the night at Lake Placid in the Adirondacks, and its loud, deep-toned *whoo-hoo-hoo-hoo*, *whoo*, *whooo* was a pleasant reminder of the unspoiled depths of the forest.

Barn Owl; Monkey-faced Owl: *Strix pratincola*.

(Plate XXVI. p. 294.)

GEOGRAPHIC DISTRIBUTION. — Southern and western United States; occasionally found as far north as Massachusetts; breeds from Long Island southward to Mexico.

The Barn Owl is one of the most beneficial of rapacious birds, its food consisting of rodents that are a curse to the country they inhabit — the gopher and ground squirrel in the west, the cotton rat in the south, and various species of rats and mice in the north.

An interesting account of a family of Barn Owls is given in the 'Cincinnati Journal of Natural History,' by Charles Dury. They lived in the tower of the Town Hall in Glendale. Two naturalists climbed the tower and raising the trapdoor at the top, saw a curious sight. The floor and ledges were covered with the cast-up pellets of the birds, made up of the hair and bones of the smaller rodents, mainly mice. "There must have been the débris of several thousand mice and rats," Mr. Dury assures us. "But the strangest part of the curious habitation was the flock of domestic Pigeons that were living seemingly on intimate terms with the Owls, and, judging from the old Pigeons' nests, I presume the Pigeons had actually nested and reared young there. This seems to show the food of this Owl to be almost exclusively mice and rats, and proves it to be a species of the greatest economic value."

It is interesting to know that a pair of these birds have for years nested at intervals in one or other of the towers of the Smithsonian Institution at Washington.

Snowy Owl: *Nyctea nyctea*.
(Plate XXVII.)

GEOGRAPHIC DISTRIBUTION. — Northern part of northern hemisphere; breeds from Labrador northward, in North America to Arctic Ocean, and wanders southward in winter regularly to the northern United States, and occasionally to Texas and California.

A great deal of interest is excited by the appearance of a Snowy Owl in the neighborhood in winter, for it is a large bird, dressed in the white feathers that enable it to come unawares upon its prey in its arctic home. Audubon gives a most interesting account of the way he saw these

PLATE XXVI. — BARN OWL

Upper parts yellowish brown, washed with gray; under parts white, washed with buffy and finely spotted with black; brownish ring around facial disk. *Length*, 18 inches.

PLATE XXVII.—SNOWY OWL

White, more or less barred with brown. *Length*, 25 inches.
(By courtesy of *The Osprey*.)

Owls catch fish. They would lie down flat on the rocks beside a pot-hole, as if asleep, but the moment a fish rose to the surface, would thrust out the foot next the water, and with the quickness of lightning seize the fish and draw it out.

Unlike most of the Owls, the Snowy is diurnal in habit, but it is most active in early morning and toward evening.

Looking back over this interesting group of birds, we see how easily they may be discriminated. Those with ears are the Screech Owl, the Long-eared, the Short-eared, and Great Horned (Plate XXI. p. 287, Plate XXII. p. 288, Plate XXIII. p. 290, Plate XXV. p. 292). Of these the Screech Owl is the smallest, the Great Horned the largest. The Great Horned has broad ears wide apart, while the Long-eared and Short-eared have narrow ears set close together, but the length of the ear is enough to distinguish them. The Barred Owl, the Barn, and the Snowy have round heads without ear-tufts and cannot be confused (Plate XXIV. p. 290, Plate XXVI. p. 294, Plate XXVII. p. 294).

As a group the Owls supplement the good work of the Hawks; for while the Hawks kill diurnal mammals, the Owls kill nocturnal ones. Moreover, as the Owls usually remain on their nesting grounds during the winter, they continue their good work after the Hawks have gone south.

Key to Owls.

1. Small.

    Ear-tufts conspicuous; upper parts reddish brown or grayish; under parts whitish, streaked with black and washed with reddish brown or grayish. Nests near houses. Tremulous wailing whistle.

    p. 287. SCREECH OWL.

1'. Large.
  2. Without ear-tufts.
    3. Plumage mainly white.

        Lightly barred with brownish. Winter visitant.

        p 294. SNOWY OWL.

    3'. Plumage not mainly white.
      4. Face and under parts white or buffy, with or without small black spots; upper parts yellowish brown. Southern . . . . . . p. 293. BARN OWL.

      4'. Face and under parts dull grayish brown; barred across the breast and streaked lengthwise of the belly; upper parts grayish brown.

          p. 291. BARRED OWL.

  2'. With ear-tufts.
    5. Size very large (length about 2 feet); breast with cross-bars. Found in deep forests.

        p. 292. GREAT HORNED OWL.

    5'. Size medium (length about 15 inches). Breast without cross-bars.
      6. Under parts buffy, streaked with brown. Ear-tufts inconspicuous. Frequents grassy marshes.

          p. 290. SHORT-EARED OWL.

6'. Under parts whitish, streaked with brown. Ear-tufts conspicuous. Wholly nocturnal.

p. 288. LONG-EARED OWL.

As an Order the birds of prey are peculiarly well adapted to their work of keeping down the harmful insects and mammals. Their talons are sharp and curved, for seizing and holding their prey (see Fig. 207, p. 351); their bills sharp and hooked, to tear it apart (Figs. 199, 200, p. 350); their eyesight is extraordinarily acute, their wings strong and enduring, and their digestion so rapid that they can eat great quantities of food. They save time by swallowing their food bones and all, having, like the Vireos, Flycatchers, Crows, and Kingfisher, power to regurgitate such indigestible parts as bones, feathers, fur, and hair, their stomachs — after the absorption of the softer parts of their food — working the hard parts up into round balls or 'pellets,' in which the sharp materials that might injure the mucous membrane are coated with soft fur or hair.

With all these special adaptations, the birds of prey do more good than almost any other birds, and facts regarding their food habits should be noised abroad, as they are most unjustly persecuted by those who should be their best friends.

The characters of the birds of prey are so distinct that every one must know them. With them we fill the last gap in the Orders we have examined, up to that of the Perching Birds, and it will be well to glance over the list once more before leaving them.

Order I. Grouse, Quail, Pheasants. Order II. Pigeons and Doves. Order III. Birds of Prey. Order IV. Cuckoos and Kingfishers. Order V. Woodpeckers, etc. Order VI. Goatsuckers, Hummingbirds, Swifts. Order VII. Perching Birds.

Fig. 169.

Loggerhead Shrike: *Lanius ludovicianus* and race.

Upper parts gray; wings and tail and line from bill to ear black; wings and tail showing white in flight; under parts white. *Length,* 9 inches.

GEOGRAPHIC DISTRIBUTION. — Eastern North America west to the edge of the Plains; breeds east of the Alleghanies as far north as Virginia; west of the Alleghanies breeds northward to the Great Lakes, and eastward through central New York to Vermont and Maine.

The Butcherbird is often started from a roadside tree in driving along the country, and in places where the Mockingbird also occurs, the two may be confused, although they are really quite distinct. The Shrike is a lighter, clearer gray, and has black instead of brownish wings and tail marked like those of the Mocker, with white. The Shrike has also a distinctive flight. It moves along evenly, flapping its short wings and holding its head up. When perching on a telegraph wire, as it often does, its large head and quiet, preoccupied manner are also totally different from the round head and restless ways of the talkative Mocker.

Where the honey locust or the spiny thorn trees grow the Shrike is found; for it not only hides its nest in thorn bushes, but uses the thorns for impaling its prey. What the reason for this custom may be is not certain, but it is probably a phase of the storing instinct seen in Jays and Woodpeckers. The birds take what the gods provide at the moment, and put it away against a possible time of need. Bachman says he has seen the Loggerhead occupy itself for hours hanging up small fish the fishermen had thrown on shore. But though the bird did not return for them, that proves nothing, for at the moment there was probably plenty of fresh food to be had.

In cruelty and pride of disposition the Shrikes resemble the Hawks, as they do in their way of lying in wait to pounce on their victims and tear them to pieces with their strong hooked beaks.

The Loggerhead in summer lives almost exclusively on insects, mainly grasshoppers; but in winter, when these are scarce, it becomes carnivorous, taking to a diet of mice.

Butcherbird: *Lanius borealis*.

Upper parts gray, wings and tail and line back of eye black; wings and tail showing white in flight; under parts white, finely barred with black; *forehead whitish*, without black line. *Length*, about $10\frac{1}{4}$ inches.

GEOGRAPHIC DISTRIBUTION. — Breeds in the far north (Fort Anderson, MacFarlane), and migrates southward in winter as far as California, Kansas, and Virginia.

The northern Shrike comes into the United States only in winter, and then may be known by its larger size, lack of black on the forehead, and gray rather than black in front of the eye.

This is the true Butcherbird, and on its winter visits it does good service in making way with mice and House Sparrows.

Key to Shrikes.

Common characters. — Upper parts light gray; wings, tail, and face marked with black and white.

1. Under parts white, finely barred with black; forehead whitish. Winter visitant.

    p. 300. NORTHERN SHRIKE; BUTCHERBIRD.

1'. Under parts white, not barred with black; black line on forehead. Summer resident.

    p. 298. LOGGERHEAD SHRIKE.

Yellow-throated Vireo: *Vireo flavifrons.*
(See Fig. 170, p. 305.)

Adults, upper parts *bright* olive-green; throat and breast *bright* yellow; two white wing bars. *Length,* about 6 inches.

GEOGRAPHIC DISTRIBUTION. — Eastern North America; breeds from Florida to Newfoundland and Manitoba; winters in the tropics.

We have spoken of the Red-eyed and Warbling Vireos, the commonest Greenlets of village and woodland; but often, when listening to the song of the Red-eye on the village streets, or more frequently in the woods, you will hear the rich contralto warble of the Yellow-throat. It is as much richer as the colors of the bird are deeper than those of the Red-eye. In addition to the conventional Vireo triplet, the Yellow-throat has a guttural fragment of one note repeated four times, followed by a short, rapid run down the scale. To distinguish it from both the Warbling and Red-eye, you have but to remember the yellow on its breast and its two strongly marked wing bars.

Mr. Chapman gives its song as "See me; I'm here; where are you?" but adds that the little bird "sometimes astonishes us by an intricate liquid trill which suggests the wonderful song of the Ruby Kinglet, but which unfortunately is sometimes marred by the scolding notes that precede or follow it."

The nest of this Vireo is particularly pretty, being decorated not only with spider-webs but with bits of lichen also.

White-eyed Vireo; Whip-Tom-Kelly: *Vireo noveboracensis.*

(See Fig. 171, p. 305.)

Upper parts bright olive green; under parts white; breast and sides washed with yellow; two yellowish wing bars. *Length*, about $5\frac{1}{4}$ inches.

GEOGRAPHIC DISTRIBUTION. — Eastern United States; breeds from Florida to Connecticut and Minnesota; winters from Florida southward.

In Bermuda this bird abounds and is called the 'Chick of the Village,' the people interpreting its song as "*Chick-a-dee-chick'-de-villet.*" While this is a fair rendering, the song has an interrogatory inflection given better by the phrasing, "*Now, who are you', eh?*" This suits the manner of the bird, too, for it hunts calmly through its bush till it faces you, and then accosts you quite with the air of one who has a prior right on the premises. It is a piquant, independent, original character; one which stimulates the interest, and makes us desire a better acquaintance.

Like all the Vireos, the White-eye is very tame. Doctor Mearns says he has actually taken a sitting bird from the nest before she would leave it, and that then, instead of flying off, she would return and scold most vigorously, in a tone resembling that of an irate Catbird. The nest is like the pendent basket of the Red-eye, and the eggs are white, speckled with black at the larger end.

While the Vireos have adopted a Quaker-like

costume, little individual touches in their attire help to distinguish them. The Red-eye wears a gray cap with black and white border; the Warbling keeps strictly to its plain olive gown, having no cap or trimmings of any sort; and its characteristic flowing warble comes to us from the elm-tops. Both the White-eye and Yellow-throat wear white wing bars and brighten their costume with yellow, but in the case of the little White-eye it is only a touch, while in the Yellow-throat it is a clear yellow vest.

As the Grouse, Sparrows, and Wrens wear ground-colors, and the Flycatchers the grays of the dead trees and bare twigs, so the Vireos carry the colors of their environment and are clothed in green to match the foliage in which they live. They are not green all over, however, but in compliance with the law of the gradation of tints, expounded by Mr. Abbott Thayer, are white, or white grading to yellow underneath where the least light reaches, and green above where the strong light falls.

In disposition the Greenlets are as gentle and friendly as the Shrikes and Hawks are fierce. Although they are not equally gifted, and do not rank with the greatest musicians, they stand with the singing birds as compared with the Grouse, Doves, Hawks, Woodpeckers, Flycatchers, and Waxwings, for they make up in perseverance what they lack in quality.

Besides being pleasing birds from their ready response to our friendliness, the Vireos are of great value to our trees. They may be found from morning till night searching among the leafy treetops for insects both in our forests and in our villages and towns. They probably rank next to the Cuckoo in the destruction of caterpillars, and are also of great value from their fondness for bugs and weevils, May beetles, inch-worms, and leaf-eating beetles.

With the Vireos we finish the tenth family of Perching Birds.

I. Flycatchers.   II. Larks.   III. Crows and Jays.   IV. Blackbirds and Orioles.   V. Finches and Sparrows.   VI. Tanagers.   VII. Swallows. VIII. Waxwings.   IX. Shrikes.   X. Vireos.

Key to Vireos.

1. With wing bars ; upper parts bright olive-green.
   2. Throat bright yellow.
      p. 301.   YELLOW-THROATED VIREO.

   2'. Throat white or whitish.   Song, "*Now, who are you', eh?*" . . . . . . p. 302.   WHITE-EYED VIREO.

1'. Without wing bars ; upper parts dull olive-green.
   3. Head with gray cap, bordered by black and white lines. Song, broken triplets . . p. 120.   RED-EYED VIREO.

   3'. Head without gray cap.   Song, a continuous flowing warble, heard from elm-tops.
      p. 126.   WARBLING VIREO.

Fig. 170.
Yellow-throated Vireo.
Fig. 171.
White-eyed Vireo.

Fig. 172.
Warbling Vireo.

Fig. 173.
Red-eyed Vireo.

MEMBERS OF THE VIREO FAMILY.

Warblers.

Warblers are at once the most fascinating and the most exasperating of birds. They come with a rush in the spring, but though the woods are full of them, nothing but a faint lisp from the pine-tops suggests their presence, and if, intent on other songs with which the air is ringing, you ignore this, your opportunity is lost. But if you close your ears with determination to all else, resolutely concluding to devote yourself to Warblers, the sight of a diminutive figure disappearing in a high treetop will often be your only reward.

But this is generalization — one of the most dangerous kinds of all subtle forms of false witness. Some of the Warblers, it is true, lisp faintly from the treetops, but others lift up loud-ringing voices from the ground at your feet. Indeed, they are a family of contradictions.

With most, 'motley is surely the only wear,' for their coats are patched with many colors; but some among them are as Quakerish as Vireos, with never a spot on rectrix or primary to hint of their station in life. Some of them dash about among the leaves as if life depended on one particular passing gnat; others hunt soberly over the branches, like Vireos. Though most of them hop gayly on the few occasions when they descend to earth, some staid members of the family walk sedately over the ground, bobbing their heads or tilting their tails like veritable 'tip-ups.' Part of the tribe, after thoroughly confusing our brains, fly north to nest in coniferous forests; but a few settle down and build in our parks, gardens, and shrubbery, where we can study them at our leisure throughout the summer.

In the matter of food they are more consistent, for they are all insect-eaters; destroying ants, flies, caterpillars, larvæ, plant-lice, cankerworms, and May-flies.

Yellow Warbler: *Dendroica œstiva*.

(See Fig. 191, p. 347.)

Male, upper parts greenish yellow; under parts yellow, streaked with reddish brown. *Female and young*, duller, and usually unstreaked. *Length*, about 5 inches.

GEOGRAPHIC DISTRIBUTION. — North America, except southwestern states, where a closely allied race occurs; breeds northward to the arctic regions; winters as far south as northern South America.

This little bird is closely associated in my mind with the first spring days in Central Park when the trees are veiled in varied shades of tender green, richly clustered lavender wistaria drapes the walls and arbors, and the great pleasure ground is pervaded with spring happiness. Then, as you rest on the benches, enjoying the soft air, fragrant with the breath of freshly mown grass, idly watching the happy children bravely riding the donkeys up and down the paths, or resting your eyes on the bench where the workman is taking his noonday meal with his wife and child beside him — suddenly from out the blooming shrubbery close by there rings out the loud, cheery *wee-chee, chee-chee, cher-wee* of the friendly little yellow bird. What a bright, sunny song it is! How summery it sounds! The little Warbler sings as he works, and his song seems the natural outpouring of happiness akin to the opening of leaves and flowers until you pass on and his mate starts from her nest in a bush, when you realize that the ecstatic quality of his lay is due to something more than the unfolding of the season. And as you stop to examine the beautiful little home the pretty pair have worked together to prepare for their brood, the songster becomes transformed into a home-maker whose anxieties and happiness seem almost human.

And the poor little yellow birds have more than their share of anxieties, for they of all birds are chosen for the impositions of the Cowbird. They probably suffer more than many birds under it, too, for instead of accepting their fate calmly, they build a new nest over the old, or rather a second story over the eggs of the intruder. Sometimes the shameless Cowbird lays eggs in this second nest, when the undaunted Warblers actually build a third story and start again.

Redstart : *Setophaga ruticilla.*

(See Fig. 195, p. 348.)

Adult male, black, with salmon on breast, wings, and tail; belly whitish. *Adult female and young*, brownish gray instead of black, yellow instead of salmon. The male is three years in attaining full plumage. *Length*, about 5½ inches.

GEOGRAPHIC DISTRIBUTION. — North America; breeds from Kansas and North Carolina north to Labrador and Fort Simpson; winters in the tropics.

The Redstart is the Warbler you are perhaps most likely to see on a walk in the woods. It can never be mistaken for any of its family, which is a great and shining virtue to be possessed by a Warbler! The jet-black upper parts and the salmon patches on the breast and tail of the male, and also the soft yellow that replaces them in the female, show clearly as the birds flit about the branches, or suddenly drop down through the air in pursuit of some hapless insect. Another good field character is the long tail of the restless little bird, for it is constantly opened and shut, like a gaudy fan.

The Redstart has two songs, one that hurries to its accented close, and a simpler one that suggests the *see-see-see-see* of the Black and White Creeper.

It is interesting to hear that in Cuba, where the Warblers are called 'mariposas,' — butterflies, — this one, from its brilliant colors, is called by the pretty name of 'Candelita,' meaning the little

Yellow-rumped Warbler; Myrtle Warbler:
Dendroica coronata.
(See Fig. 194, p. 348.)

Adult male, yellow on crown, rump, and breast; under parts with patches of black and white. *Adult female*, similar, but with black streaks instead of patches on under parts. Old and young, in fall and winter, dull; *upper parts streaked with black;* rump bright yellow. *Length*, about 5½ inches.

GEOGRAPHIC DISTRIBUTION. — Eastern North America; breeds from northern Minnesota and northern New England northward; winters from the middle states southward.

On the spring migration the Yellow-rump unfurls his colors and stands proclaimed, but in fall, when flocks of old and young appear together, the colors of the old birds are so much duller that it is hard to know them until you remember the combination of black back-streakings and yellow rump as belonging to the little friends who formerly faced you with a shield of black and gold.

The call note of the Myrtle is rather distinct, being a loud and unmusical *tchip*, uttered with emphasis as the birds chase about the trees, but their song is a nondescript warble that might be attributed to a dozen of their kindred.

In southern Illinois, Mr. Ridgway tells us, the Yellow-rump is often seen in midwinter in the door-yards, together with Juncos and Tree Sparrows, picking up bread-crumbs from the doorstep or hunting for spiders in odd nooks and crevices.

Black-throated Green Warbler: *Dendroica virens*.

(See Fig. 192, p. 347.)

Adult male, throat and sides black, forming an inverted V of black; *cheeks* bright *yellow; tail* strikingly marked with *white. Female and young,* similar, but with black obscured. *Length,* about 5 inches.

GEOGRAPHIC DISTRIBUTION. — Eastern North America; breeds from northern Illinois and Connecticut northward to Hudson Bay and southward along the Alleghanies to South Carolina; winters in the tropics.

In migration this is one of the most welcome birds to the would-be ornithologist, because it is so easily recognized. The black inverted V of its under parts (Λ), the yellow cheeks and large areas of white on the tail, are unmistakable.

But in the nesting-season we are glad to meet it for other reasons. At sound of its leisurely, woodsy —— ——√——, *zee-ee-ee, zee-ah-ee,* in which Mr. Torrey hears *trees, trees, murmuring trees,* the forest grows more silent, the solitude becomes more protected, and the world with its hurry and care fades away far behind the 'aisles of the forest dim;' for with such small, woodland voices Mother Nature soothes her tired children to rest.

Black-throated Blue Warbler: *Dendroica cærulescens*
and race.

(See Fig. 188, p. 347.)

Adult male, throat and band along sides black; rest of under parts pure white; upper parts bluish gray; *white spot on wing in both sexes*. *Adult female*, upper parts olive-green; under parts soiled buffy; *young male*, like adult male; *young female*, like adult female. *Length*, about 5¼ inches.

GEOGRAPHIC DISTRIBUTION. — Eastern North America; breeds from northern Minnesota and Connecticut (rarely) northward to Labrador, and south along the crest of the Alleghanies to Georgia; winters in the tropics.

Be on your guard. When you first see the female Blue you will be tempted to jump to a conclusion. But don't say that she is a female Redstart until you have looked closely at her wing, and then — you won't say it at all. The small white spot is her mark, and by its presence you may surely know her. Her mate has it, too, but with him it seems redundant, for he wears a blue coat, his head and throat are jet-black, and his under parts pure snowy white. Then, too, when he is on a branch with his side turned toward you so that his other points are not so plainly to be seen, you can tell him by the black line that runs along his side under his wing, like the tug on a horse in harness.

Like the Black-throated Green, this is one of the loveliest of all the Warblers of the woodlands. Its song has the same *z-y* leisurely quality as the

Green's, but differs from it in note, being made up of three phrases in descending scale.

Hour after hour I have followed this lovely bird through the cool beech-woods, as it hunted quietly up a woods road and back again, singing as it went. Its ways impress one as unusually deliberate for a Warbler. It treats a tree as a staircase, hopping up a branch at a time, often stopping on the landings to follow the limbs out to their tips, and then, instead of vaulting into the air or dropping off in somersaults as do many of its acrobatic relatives, stops still, turns its head over and looks up before going on up the next stair.

The mother Blue is no less interesting than the songster, and makes an exquisite little nest in a bush near the ground. The eggs are grayish white, marked with brown, chiefly about the larger end. One whom I watched at her building enjoyed her work so much she could not bear to leave her nest among the fresh sunlit green leaves, but hopped out on the edge of the bowl only to turn around and jump in again; ran up one of the supporting twigs only to turn around and run down again; and, after actually starting away, flew back for a last look at the pretty home she was preparing for her brood. Perhaps she was just trying to decide some point in architecture, but it certainly looked very much as if she were lingering lovingly about her nest.

Black and White Creeping Warbler: *Mniotilta varia*.

(See Fig. 190, p. 347.)

Black and white streaked above and below. *Length*, about 5¼ inches.

GEOGRAPHIC DISTRIBUTION. — Eastern North America; breeds from the southern states north to Fort Simpson and Nova Scotia; winters from Florida southward.

This little Warbler is so uniformly striped with black and white that beginners often dub him ' the little zebra bird,' taking great satisfaction in his unique characters. His habits are as foreign to Warbler circles as his dress, for he spends his time clambering about tree trunks and branches like a Nuthatch. There is a difference even here, however; for while a Nuthatch creeps up a tree with at least some show of regularity, the Black and White, showing his Warbler blood, zigzags back and forth and hops about, turning to peck at every bit of loose bark, promising crotch, or dead tip of a broken branch.

His song, too, is a family matter; just a simple little Warbler *see-see-see-see*, repeated a varying number of times. Sometimes it is given loudly, — as the buzz of some flies is loud, — but at others, as when he sits in a sunny crotch and plumes himself, he cons over the four little syllables in a low, soft voice, as if talking to himself about pleasant matters.

Maryland Yellow-throat: *Geothlypis trichas.*
(See Fig. 193, p. 347.)

Adult male, forehead and cheeks black, bordered by ashy gray; bright yellow below; brownish green above. *Adult female*, duller above, pale buffy below; no black mask. *Length*, about 5¼ inches.

GEOGRAPHIC DISTRIBUTION. — Eastern North America, west to the Plains; breeds from the Gulf states to Manitoba and Labrador; winters from the Gulf states southward.

There are Warblers and Warblers, and the Yellow-throat is one of them! What pleasant memories his name calls up! — visions of bushy thickets, rich swamps, or winding river banks, with an inquisitive little black-masked bird-face peering up at you out of the cover, while its mate, a dull little nondescript bird, whisks back out of sight just as you have made a mental note of her, for you would never have known her had she not taken her stand on the bush beside her lord.

But it is not only pleasant sights that are associated with the Maryland; for at his name his song again rings in your ears, always new and interesting — *witchery, witchery, witchery; wreechetty, wreechetty, wreechetty;* or *chee-wee-oh, chee-wee-oh.* Which is it? Few bird-folks say always the same thing in the same way, and the Maryland in Washington judged by the Maryland in New York may well show a southern accent.

The bird is so identified with his three syllabled *wit-che-ry* that it is a surprise when he suddenly vaults into mid air with an ecstatic love-song. It breaks away from his stereotyped notes so completely that it comes as an outpouring of long-pent-up feeling, and raises him from the rank of a prosaic hunter after worms to that of an impassioned musician and lover. In domestic relations, few birds are more affectionate than the Yellow-throat, Mr. Chamberlain tells us. The male carries food most assiduously to his mate at the nest, caressing her, singing for her diversion, and guarding her from disturbance. If the nest is approached, he " alternately scolds and pleads with marked emphasis of displeasure and anxiety." The nest is a bulky but comfortable abode made of loosely woven strips of bark, grasses, and dead leaves, sometimes roofing the top; and the eggs are white, speckled thinly at the larger end.

Red-poll Warbler: *Dendroica palmarum hypochrysea*.

Crown chestnut; back brownish green; under parts *entirely* bright yellow. *Young and adult*, in winter, cap concealed or wanting. *Length*, about 5½ inches.

GEOGRAPHIC DISTRIBUTION. — Eastern North America east of the mountains; breeds from Maine northward east of Hudson Bay; migrates southward through the Atlantic states, and winters in the Gulf states.

In the spring migration the Red-poll is often seen on the ground or on fences or bushes in company with Yellow-rumps, Pine Warblers, and Chipping Sparrows. It is common in Central

Park at that time, as it is on the City Green in the heart of New Haven; and it may be known by its chestnut crown, fine chip, and habit of wagging its tail as it works. This tilting motion is so marked that it has earned it the name of 'Wagtail Warbler.'

In Illinois Mr. W. E. Henderson has seen flocks of several hundreds feeding in a field grown up with ragweed.

Parula Warbler: *Compsothlypis americana.*

(See Fig. 189, p. 347.)

Adult male, copper-colored or blackish band on chest; back bluish gray, with a *yellow patch between shoulders.* Female and young, similar, but the chest patch duller or wanting. *Length,* about 4¾ inches.

GEOGRAPHIC DISTRIBUTION. — Eastern North America; breeds locally from the Gulf states northward to Anticosti; winters from Florida southward.

It is always a pleasure to discover this exquisite little Warbler on the migrations. Other members of the family are more gorgeous, but it is a peculiarly dainty little bird, and its manner of hunting is quiet and attractive. Sometimes it will hang head down from a hemlock bough as easily as a Chickadee. Mr. Bicknell accords it two songs; "in one the notes coalesce into a fine insect-like trill; in the other four similar notes are followed by four others."

The nest of the Parula is unique, being made habitually in the gray hanging moss. One nest in the collection of Major Bendire is a round gray ball midway in a streamer of Florida moss probably ten feet long. No better case of protective nesting could be found. In Illinois the Parula nests in swampy forests.

Chestnut-sided Warbler: *Dendroica pensylvanica.*

(See Fig. 183, p. 346.)

Adult male, crown yellow and *sides chestnut. Adult female,* similar, but duller. *Young,* upper parts bright yellowish green; under parts pure white, with sometimes a little chestnut on sides. *Length,* about 5 inches.

GEOGRAPHIC DISTRIBUTION. — Eastern North America; breeds from central Illinois and northern New Jersey north to Manitoba and Newfoundland, and southward along the Alleghanies to South Carolina; winters in the tropics.

The friendly Chestnut-sided Warbler nests with us, and is easily known by its combination of yellow crown and dark brown sides. It lives low in the bushes, and hunts with wings hanging and tail up. Its nest is not far from the ground, and is a delicate structure, often made with birch bark, like a Vireo's. The eggs are white, with a wreath of brown about the larger end.

The Chestnut has two songs, both of which resemble that of the Yellow Warbler.

In watching this Warbler I have had many delightful surprises; but the most interesting of all was the day when Mrs. Olive Thorne Miller and I happened on a Redstart's nest, the young of which were being fed by the mother Redstart and a Chestnut visitor. We watched them with keen interest for several hours. The father Redstart did not appear, and was doubtless dead.

The young were fed at dangerously short intervals; we feared they would leave the nest dyspeptics for life; and they would have been crammed still more if it had not been for the time it took the Redstart to drive off the Chestnut, and the delay her attacks caused him; for she had no wish for his kind offices, and, as Mrs. Miller remarked, like some other philanthropists that made no difference to him! When she saw him coming with food, before he was anywhere near the tree, she dashed at him with spread tail and resentment in every feather. His long-suffering meekness was philosophical. He flew before her, waited till she had spent her anger and gone off or down in the bushes for an insect, when he slipped up to the nest and fed his charges. It seemed as if she could not bear the sight of him. Again and again she drove him out of the tree. Sometimes she almost tumbled her youngsters out of the nest, flouncing at him over their heads when he was in the act of feeding them. Once or twice he came to a twig behind the nest, leaned over, and stretched the food across to the birds, as if to make sure of getting off before she caught him. But he was no coward, and took a good claw-to-claw tumble with her when she had snapped her bill at him once too often. Except for this, he seemed calm and self-possessed through all her persecution, hopping from twig to twig, running along the branches, clambering up the stalks of the bushes, and occasionally giving a thin low call; while she flashed around madly, under leaves and over branches, flying up against one tree trunk only to dart off to another. At first she made no noise, except when she snapped her bill; but later on she sang a few notes now and then while at her work.

The next day the young flew; but though the Chestnut watched where the Redstart went and tried to follow her, after he had been driven back a number of times he apparently gave up; at all events he disappeared.

Whether he finally succeeded in following the family, or went away discouraged in well-doing, we did not determine. We saw the Redstart hunting about in the vicinity of the dead treetop where she took her young, the day after they left the nest, but saw no more of the Chestnut with her.

Black-poll Warbler: *Dendroica striata*.

(See Fig. 187, p. 346.)

Adult male, crown black, rest of body largely streaked with black and white. *Adult female*, upper parts olive-green, distinctly streaked with black; under parts tinged with yellow. *Young*, brighter and less streaked. *Length*, about 5¼ inches.

GEOGRAPHIC DISTRIBUTION. — Eastern North America to the Rocky Mountains, north to Greenland, the Barren Grounds, and Alaska, breeding from the Catskills and northern New England northward; south in winter to northern South America.

The Black-poll at first glance suggests the Black and White Creeper (Fig. 190, p. 347); but instead of a striped head, has a black cap. It hunts in both bushes and treetops, and Wilson says it is partial to woods in the neighborhood of creeks, swamps, and morasses. In Ohio Mr. Oberholser finds it the commonest of the transient town Warblers, where it goes about in companies of six or seven. Mr. Torrey has found it on Mount Washington, and in the White Mountains generally. In Washington it is common during the spring migration, the little pine groves sometimes being filled with its faint notes. The song is very similar to that of the Black and White Creeper, but by careful listening you can see what Mr. Torrey means by saying that it has a crescendo and decrescendo. Sometimes the decrescendo consists of only one or two notes dropped down the scale, but again the two parts of the song are more nearly balanced. The performance varies greatly toward the end.

The Black-poll is said to be one of the most beneficial of Warblers, fairly gorging itself on cankerworms.

Canadian Warbler: *Wilsonia canadensis.*

(See Fig. 184, p. 346.)

Upper parts gray; a *necklace of black spots* on yellow of throat.
GEOGRAPHIC DISTRIBUTION. — Eastern North America; breeds from Michigan and the hills of southern New York and southern New England to Manitoba and Labrador, and winters in Central and South America. *Length*, about 5½ inches.

The Canadian is one of the most satisfactory of Warblers, for it may be recognized at sight by its necklace. In the migrations it is found low in bushes, and for a home chooses low wet woods.

Its spirited song is given by Mr. Ernest Thompson as "*rup-it-che, rup-it-che, rup-it-chitt-it lit.*"

Nashville Warbler: *Helminthophila rubricapilla.*

Adults, head gray, with *chestnut patch in crown;* back olive-green; under parts bright yellow. *Young*, duller. *Length*, about 4¾ inches.
GEOGRAPHIC DISTRIBUTION. — Eastern North America; breeds from northern Illinois and Connecticut northward to Labrador and the fur countries; winters in the tropics.

One gets so accustomed to looking for a multitude of marks on the Warblers, sure that any least dot overlooked will prove the one on which identification hangs, that when one comes upon a member of the family with no marks on wings or tail and a general uniformity of coloring, it seems as if there were nothing to identify him by, and a mental state of helpless perplexity results. But many matters in life are best treated by elimination, and the plain Warblers are not so confusing when one realizes that they are a handful to be studied apart, and free from the mass of their confusingly marked, streaked, and spotted brethren. Those we can be rid of, which is certainly something to be thankful for. Looked at by himself, the Nashville is not so bad. To begin with, his head is bluish gray, which is a mercy, for that is unusual in combination with the olive and yellow of his body. Then he has a concealed chestnut patch in this gray crown, if we can but see it. Furthermore, he hunts close to the ground, which at once distinguishes him from the little wretches which hunt so high in the treetops it is impossible to say what they wear on head or heels. It is also something to know that his ground is usually in " open woodland, young second growth, or tree-bordered fields," and that his song, " *wee-see-wee-see, wit-a-wit-a-wit,*" suggests in its first half the song of the Black and White Creeper, and in the last half that of the Chipping Sparrow. When narrowed down in this way, he ought to be easily identified, and though he has no marks it is, after all, a satisfaction to know that some Warblers are *plain!*

Black and Yellow Warbler; Magnolia Warbler:
Dendroica maculosa.

Under parts yellow, with a necklace and long pendants of black. Head bluish gray; large white patch on wings; ends of tail feathers black; middle, white. *Length*, about 5 inches.

GEOGRAPHIC DISTRIBUTION. — Eastern North America; breeds from northern Michigan and northern New England to Hudson Bay, and southward along the crests of the Alleghanies to Pennsylvania; winters in Central America and West Indies.

The Magnolia does not suffer from dearth of markings. Identifying him is like taking count of each stone in a mosaic passed rapidly before your bewildered eyes. But he usually alights in a low bush, — the gods be praised! — and two impressions will generally remain after even a hurried glimpse — large white wing patches and heavy black breast blotches. The one point to note, though, if we could but know it beforehand, is the white on the middle of the tail feathers, as most Warblers wear their polka dots at the tips of the feathers.

FIG. 174.
Black and Yellow Warbler.

In any case the Black and Yellow is a most striking and handsome bird, and one feels greatly elated over discovering him.

His song is given as a rapidly uttered and falling *chee-to, chee-to, chee-tee-ee*.

Prairie Warbler : *Dendroica discolor.*

(See Fig. 181, p. 346.)

Under parts yellow, sides streaked with black; *cheeks marked with black; chestnut patch between shoulders.* Length, 4¾ inches.
GEOGRAPHIC DISTRIBUTION. — Eastern United States; breeds from Florida to Michigan and Massachusetts; winters in southern Florida and West Indies.

Hillside pastures and old, overgrown juniper fields, whose little evergreens give character to the landscape and afford cover quite to the mind of Chewinks and Field Sparrows, prove also the best places to look for the attractive little Prairie Warbler. It may be known by the dark marks on the side of its head and the reddish patch on its back — points which can be seen when the bird is perched on a low branch.

The song of the Prairie is one of the most restful of bird songs. It is only a simple ascending scale, as far as note goes; but when listened to on a quiet juniper hillside, its delicious *z-y* quality, and the reposeful, leisurely way in which each note of the upward scale falls on the ear, make it, to me, one of the choicest of all songs. No hint of the work-a-day hurry and toil is to be found here; for a moment you step aside from the careworn world procession and stop to listen to the quieting voice of Nature, to whom hurry and striving are unknown.

The quality of the Prairie's song suggests that of the Black-Throated Green and the Black-Throated Blue, but each is distinct. The Prairie's is a slow, regular, ascending scale ⟋ ; the Green's, as given by Mr. Burroughs, is —— ——✓—— ; while the Blue's is composed of three phrases, each in descending scale, ⟍ ⟍ ⟍ .

Blackburnian Warbler: *Dendroica blackburniæ.*

(See Fig. 185, p. 346.)

Adult male, throat and breast, patch in crown and on cheeks, *bright orange;* back black; wings and *tail largely marked with white. Female and young*, similar, but duller. *Length*, 5¼ inches.

GEOGRAPHIC DISTRIBUTION. — Eastern North America; breeds from northern Minnesota, northern New York, and southern Maine northward to Labrador, and southward along the Alleghanies to South Carolina; winters in the tropics.

The Redstart's name of 'Candelita' might well be applied to the Blackburnian, for it is not only one of the most beautiful of the little Warbler butterflies, but its flaming orange-red throat might easily suggest a torch in the forest.

The song of the Blackburnian has several forms. Mr. Torrey says that one ends with *zip, zip,* another begins with *zillup, zillup,* and a third "runs up the scale to high Z."

Hooded Warbler : *Wilsonia mitrata*.

(See Fig. 180, p. 346.)

Back of head and throat black; under parts, forehead, and cheeks bright yellow; back olive-green. *Length*, about 5¾ inches.

GEOGRAPHIC DISTRIBUTION. — Eastern United States; breeds as far north as southern Michigan, western New York, and southern Connecticut, and winters in Central America.

One spring, when watching migrating Warblers in Central Park, my attention was attracted by the unusual sight of a boy peering into the bushes with opera-glasses. When he discovered me similarly engaged, he came hurrying over, asking eagerly if I had seen the Hooded Warbler he was watching. A Hooded Warbler! I had *never* seen one. What good fortune! I followed my little guide, meditating gratefully upon the enthusiasm which makes all naturalists akin, and when we reached the bush, found that the striking bird surpassed anything I had imagined. How quaint and curious he is, with his "bright yellow face peering out from its black sun-bonnet"! What distinction he gives to the inns at which he stops on his northward journey! That little bush where he hunted seemed indeed a royal bush, prouder than any in the Park. Perhaps he will visit it again; it would do no harm to look sharp as you pass that way, for where a bird stops one year he is very likely to stop the next. It was in the Ramble, one of the best of the many good places for Warblers, on a slope above one of the little ponds.

Since that first glimpse of the handsome bird I have had the delight of seeing him on his nesting grounds. What a choice place it was, too, just suited to the distinguished beauty! High-arching, vine-draped woods they were, carpeted with dense vegetable undergrowth, and made beautiful by clear brooks winding in and out through the greenery. His loud song rang out continuously, giving us the pleasant assurance of his presence, though he hunted so low in the thicket we had only rare glimpses of his pretty face.

The song is rather a hard one to describe. Mr. Nehrling gives it as *we-che-e-o*, but this is sometimes prefaced by a number of short notes.

The nest of the Hooded, as one would naturally imagine, is hung low in the crotch of a bush or sapling, and it is made of leaves, strips of bark, and rootlets. The eggs are white, thinly spotted with brown, generally in a wreath around the larger end.

Kentucky Warbler: *Geothlypis formosa*.

(See Fig. 186, p. 346.)

Upper parts olive; crown, cheeks, and broad line bordering throat black; under parts bright yellow. *Length*, about 5½ inches.

GEOGRAPHIC DISTRIBUTION. — Eastern United States; breeds from the Gulf states to Iowa and Connecticut; winters in Central America.

In the neighborhood of Washington, one of the best places for birds on the spring migration is along the eastern wooded bank of the Potomac. There, above High Island, opposite the 'amphitheatre' one day early in May we heard a song so like the famous Carolina Wren's that we hurried off in its direction. Crossing on a fallen tree that bridged the narrow arm of the Potomac, we were on the little island where the bird was singing. The song receded as we advanced, and we forced our way through the dense tangle of undergrowth to follow it till we came suddenly upon a forest garden, a great blue rug spread on the floor of the woodland and lit up by the sun coming through the skylights of the freshly leafing trees. The delicacy of the light blue phlox and its vine-like tracery of meadow rue made an exquisite spring picture. There was such a luxuriant growth of the phlox that negroes were picking it for the market. As we stood absorbed on the edge of the garden, suddenly, right before us, rang out the wren-like song we had been following, and on a low bush, with head thrown back, the bird was singing. But — the *brown* Wren was a brilliant yellow, with black, velvety bands bordering his throat! A Kentucky Warbler, we exclaimed in excited whispers, and then stood silent, afraid of startling the bird that, quite unmindful of us, now hopped down to the ground, and now mounted a bush to sing. '*Klur-wee, klur-wee, klur-wee,*' we repeated after him, to test for ourselves Mr. Torrey's phrasing of it, and indeed, at times the bird pronounced the syllables as distinctly as a person. And with what richness of tone! Surely it is a song that goes well with the songster. Mr. Torrey, referring to his notebook, copies the exclamation made in the field, "It *is* a beauty!" and no one seeing the bird for the first time in such a setting as we saw him can fail to share his enthusiasm.

But how about the Carolina Wren? We did not say much about that on the spot, but when we got home and consulted the books our self-respect was restored, for they say that the Kentucky's song resembles that of both Wren and Cardinal, the two birds whose notes are so puzzlingly similar.

Yellow-breasted Chat: *Icteria virens*.

Upper parts olive-green; under parts bright yellow; line on side of throat, and from eye to bill, white. Largest of the Warblers. *Length*, about 7½ inches.

GEOGRAPHIC DISTRIBUTION. — Eastern United States; breeds as far north as southern Minnesota and Massachusetts, and winters in Central America.

The Chat is such a secretive roysterer one rarely *sees* but the *sound* of him, but one day when I had been calling the attention of my bird class to the song of the invisible beauty, and telling them that they would probably never see him — in verification he flew up on a telegraph wire and sang before the whole row as if giving the class notes in his own proper person, unwilling to have any uncertain records on such an important matter! When the questions of yellow breast, white eye-ring and throat line were thus settled he fell back into the bush and gave the class notes they are likely to remember on his manner of life. It was not his fault if they did not tear their hair as well as rend their garments as he led them through the thicket; for he skulked ahead, singing in the back of a bush when they

FIG. 175.
Yellow-breasted Chat.

were in front, and whistling in loud, aggravating tones from the recesses of the next bush when they had forced a way through the briars for a sight of him in the first. To the excited imaginations of his followers his two loud whistles and the *tut-tut-tut-tut-tut-tut-tut* that followed were as taunting as if he were consciously poking fun at his would-be observers.

Washington, where this occurred, is blessed with an abundance of the jovial musicians, and the Zoölogical Park is as good a place to hear them as the banks of the Potomac. When not whistling, chuckling, or otherwise performing, the Chat barks like a dog. It is only fair, however, to say that in sober moments he has notes of rare richness and liquidity. Indeed, his repertoire is so varied that he is well called the 'Yellow Mockingbird.' He sings at night; serenades? Perhaps. One of his daylight amusements has been described by Mr. Torrey. "I caught the fellow," he says, "in the midst of a brilliant display of his clownish tricks, ridiculous, indescribable. At a little distance, it is hard to believe that it can be a bird, that dancing, shapeless thing, balancing itself in the air with dangling legs, and prancing, swaying motions. Well, that is the Chat's way. What more need be said? Every creature must express himself, and birds, no less than other poets, are entitled to an occasional 'fine frenzy.'"

The birds, it can well be imagined, are shy at

the nest. No ordinary mortals must be let into the personal concerns of the family. If one care to listen to a soloist at a respectful distance, that is one matter, but! If one cannot watch the birds at the nest, it is some satisfaction to examine it when they are away, for it is low to the ground, and a bulky affair of leaves, grass, and bark, and the eggs are large, white, and evenly spotted with brown. When attending to serious matters, the Chat is said to eat tent-caterpillars.

Oven-bird: *Seiurus aurocapillus*.

Crown golden brown, inclosed by two dark lines; rest of upper parts olive-green; under parts white, streaked with black. *Length*, about 6¼ inches.

GEOGRAPHIC DISTRIBUTION. — Eastern North America; breeds from Kansas and Virginia northward to Manitoba and Labrador, southward along the Alleghanies to South Carolina; winters from Florida southward.

In Washington, New England, and New York, one of the commonest and most pervading woodland songs is that of the Oven-bird. It is a repetition of the word *teach-er*, or *teach*, rising from an ordinary tone to a very loud one, so marked that the bird has been aptly called the 'Crescendo Chicken.' The chicken part of the name

FIG. 176.
Oven-bird.

comes from the fact that, instead of hopping, the

bird walks on the ground, quite in the manner of a chicken. Mr. Burroughs dubs it 'by far the prettiest pedestrian in the woods.' As it walks, the Oven-bird bobs its head much like a Dove. Although the word 'teacher' is a very good representation of one of the commonest forms of its song, there is often only one syllable instead of two — 'teach' instead of 'teach-er.' The song seems to come from under your very feet, but you may watch for a long time without getting sight of the singer. When you do he will probably be on a branch, down which he walks primly. On stopping, he throws up his head and sings. Look well at his crown as he throws it back, for if the light is right you can get a glint of the golden V set in between two dark bands, the decoration which gives him the name of Golden-crowned Thrush.

When he flies to the ground, you will very likely lose sight of him again and have a good opportunity to meditate upon the perfection of his protective coloration and gradation of tint. The thin smack which is his call note seems quite out of character, but once heard will be easily recognized. Though you think you know the Golden-crown, you have not realized what manner of bird he is until you have heard his famous love-song. It is as if a musician who had been playing scales had suddenly changed to an impassioned rhapsody. His ecstacy carries him off his feet and he flies higher and higher into the air, pouring out his rapturous love-song. I have often heard fragments of this song in the stillness of the night, when it is peculiarly poetic, as if the bird's joyous dreams had aroused him.

The nest of the Oven-bird is placed on the ground, and, though made only of dead leaves, might be a structure of stone, so skillfully are the leaves placed to make its domed roof and the side entrance, which suggest the open oven. It is a rare pleasure to see the birds at work upon it, and a coveted one to watch them through its history. The eggs are thickly spotted with brown, and the nestlings feathered with warm brown. In feeding the young, the Oven-bird can choose from its own diet of earthworms, crickets, flies, and larvæ.

Northern Water-Thrush : *Seiurus noveboracensis.*

(Fig. 177, p. 336.)

Upper parts dull grayish olive; *buffy* line over eye; under parts *yellowish;* entire under parts streaked with black, *including throat.* Length, about 6 inches.

GEOGRAPHIC DISTRIBUTION. — Eastern North America; breeds from northern Illinois and northern New England northward; winters from the Gulf states to northern South America.

This Northern Water-Thrush is seen in migrations, when it is largely silent. It is seen skulking along the muddy banks of rivers, brooks, and ponds, and usually under cover; while its larger relative, the Large-billed or Louisiana Water-Thrush does not care for cover, and prefers clear mountain streams with pebbly bottoms. The call note is a sharp, metallic *cheep*, similar to the call note of the Maryland Yellow-throat, though it is louder and more piercing.

The Water-Thrushes have the characteristic motions of the Wagtails, which are suggested by their relative the Oven-bird, with his tilting tail and bobbing head. As one watches them tilt up and down, it seems as if it must be exceedingly uncomfortable to be attached to such spring boards.

Louisiana Water-Thrush ; Large-billed Water-Thrush : *Seiurus motacilla.*

Upper parts dull grayish olive; conspicuous *white* line over the eye; under parts streaked *except on the throat.* Length, about 6¼ inches.

GEOGRAPHIC DISTRIBUTION. — Eastern United States; breeds as far north as Minnesota and Connecticut.

The Louisiana or Large-billed Water-Thrush is

FIG. 177.
Northern Water-Thrush.

FIG. 178.
Louisiana Water-Thrush.

to be told by the lack of streaks on its throat. As its name suggests, it is the more southern of the two, and so the common one in the southern United States.

Doctor Mearns gives a very sympathetic description of this interesting bird in his notes on the Hudson Highlands. "Even a casual allusion to this little bird," he says, "recalls, to the mind of the collector, a bright picture of clear mountain streams, with their falls and eddies, their dams of rocks and fallen tree trunks, their level stretches flowing over bright, pebbly bottoms, with mossy banks and rocky ferneries, and their darting minnows and dace; for only in such wild localities is the Water Wagtail at home. There you will see it sitting upon the stones, close beside the foaming water, expressing its pleasure at its surroundings by constantly repeating its single *chick*. It *runs* about (never hopping) over the stones and moss, gleaning along the sandy margin of the stream."

The song of the Water-Thrush is famous for the wild quality of its ringing notes.

Worm-eating Warbler : *Helmitherus vermivorous*.

Four black stripes on head; upper parts olive; under parts buffy. *Length*, about 5¼ inches.

GEOGRAPHIC DISTRIBUTION. — Eastern United States; breeds from the Gulf states north to southern Illinois and southern Connecticut; winters in the tropics.

In a dry, open woods near Portland, Connecticut, the Worm-eating Warbler is almost sure to nest. When going to see the bird there with Mr.

John H. Sage, we heard its song some rods away. At first it sounded like an insect; then, on nearer approach, it had the metallic quality of a rattlesnake's rattle; and when within sight of the bird its song assumed the ring of the Pine-creeping Warbler and the Chipping Sparrow, though distinctly different from both.

FIG. 179.
Worm-eating Warbler.

My first impression of the bird was that he was brown, then that he was very plump, and finally, as he turned over his head to look for a worm, that his black-striped crown was strikingly handsome — all of which points were a surprise after the pictures in the books.

He sang with his head thrown back and his bill wide open, his drooping tail shaking with the energy of the performance. For some time he sang regularly every ten seconds. He had a definite beat, singing up and down the length of a shallow ravine. As he sang he hunted quietly, hopping down the branches of a tree in ladder fashion, dropping from the tree to the ground; flying up to another tree, and again down to the ground. But though we followed him closely, and thought we examined every one of the spots he visited on the ground, we were unable to discover the rare bird's nest and spotted eggs, and had to leave with

Wilson's Warbler: *Wilsonia pusilla*.

(See Fig. 182, p. 346.)

Adult male, cap black, upper parts bright olive-green; under parts bright yellow; *no marks on wings or tail. Female and young,* similar, but generally without cap. *Length,* 5 inches.

GEOGRAPHIC DISTRIBUTION. — North America; breeds from the Sierra Nevada, Minnesota, and Nova Scotia northward; winters in Mexico and Central America.

Piquant and jaunty, this little black-capped yellow Warbler hunts low in the bushes, and comes out to peer at you, twitching its tail from side to side in pretty, half shy, half trustful and interested fashion.

For a song, it has a surprisingly harsh chatter, and its call is rather a nasal note.

As this is the last of the Warblers we will examine, it will be well to glance back over the family, to make sure of their distinguishing characters.

The Yellow Warbler may be known by its almost uniformly yellow plumage, and the reddish brown streaks on its yellow breast (Fig. 191 [1]); the Redstart by its salmon and black, and its long fan-shaped tail (Fig. 195); the Black-throated Green by an inverted V of black underneath yellow cheeks, with white in its tail (Fig. 192); the Black-throated Blue by the colors that

[1] For Figs. 180–195 see pp. 346–348.

give it its name, and the white spot on its wing (Fig. 188); the Black and White by its zebra-like stripes (Fig. 190); the Maryland by its half mask (Fig. 193); the Red-poll by its red cap and wagging tail; the Parula, or Blue Yellow-backed, by its small size, yellow patch on the back, and dark band across the throat (Fig. 189); the Chestnut-sided by its yellow cap and brown sides (Fig. 183); the Black-poll by its black cap and black and white stripes (Fig. 187); the Canadian by its gray back, yellow under parts, and *black necklace* without pendants (Fig. 184); the Prairie by its general yellow color and black cheek marks in connection with the reddish patch between its shoulders (Fig. 181); the Blackburnian by its gorgeous orange throat (Fig. 185); the Hooded by its black hood (Fig. 180); the Chat by its large size, Mockingbird-like song and brilliant yellow breast (Fig. 175, p. 331); the brown Worm-eating by its four black head stripes (Fig. 179, p. 338); the Kentucky by the black lines bordering its yellow throat (Fig. 186); and the Nashville by its gray head, yellow under parts, and reddish crown patch. The Yellow-rump and Magnolia may be distinguished by the large white patch on the wings of the Magnolia, added to the white patches on the *middle* of its tail feathers (Figs. 194, and 174, p. 324). The Oven-bird and Water-Thrushes may be told apart by their haunts, and by the stripes inclosing the orange crown of the Oven-bird (Figs. 176, p. 333; 177, and 178, p. 336); while the Large-billed Water-Thrush may be known from the Northern Small-billed by the fact that the Large-billed or Louisiana has a plain throat, and the Small-billed has the throat striped all the way up to the bill; also by the fact that the northern bird is comparatively tame and unsuspicious, while the Louisiana is a wild, shy bird.

The Warblers may be classified roughly by their levels, although, as birds have wings, it is not safe to say that they will never use them except by the yard-stick; and many birds that nest on the ground frequent treetops when migrating. The Oven-bird and Water-Thrushes live largely on the ground; and near their level, in low bushes, are generally found the Kentucky, Maryland Yellow-throat, and Red-poll; while between these and the highest treetop Warblers come the Canadian, Hooded, Chat, Prairie, Redstart, Chestnut, Wilson's, Yellow Warbler, Yellow-rumped, Black-throated Blue, the Parula, and Magnolia. The treetop Warblers we have not taken up very much, as they are rare and difficult to identify; but the Blackburnian and Black-throated Green often come under that head.

The characteristic Warbler song is an indistinct trill of little character, but a number of the songs stand out remarkably. Three songs have a marked z-y quality — those of Black-throated

Green, Blue, and Prairie. The Maryland says *witch-i-ty, witch-it-ty, witch-it-ty;* the Kentucky, *klur-wee, klur-wee, klur-wee,* or *tur-dle dee, tur-dle dee;* the Oven-bird calls *teach-er* or *teach;* and the Water-Thrushes and Chat have famous songs.

As the Warblers live exclusively on insects, they go far south in winter — many of them to South America — so that, small as they are, they perform remarkably long journeys, many nesting far to the north and wintering in the tropics. When seen on their migrations they are hurrying through, and present a very different appearance from the quiet Sparrows who have weed seeds enough to depend on if they are overtaken by a cold wave.

Field Key to Adult Male Warblers in Spring Plumage.

I. BRIGHT YELLOW, ORANGE, OR SALMON IN PLUMAGE.
II. NO BRIGHT YELLOW, ORANGE, OR SALMON IN PLUMAGE.

I. BRIGHT YELLOW, ORANGE, OR SALMON IN PLUMAGE.
1. Under parts chiefly yellow.
 2. Under parts without markings.
   Upper parts olive-green; wings and tail unmarked. Seen near the ground.
 3. Top of head black.
   4. A broad black stripe on each side of face and neck; black cap reaching bill. Song, a loud, clear whistle, *klur-wee, klur-wee, klur-wee.*
     p. 329. KENTUCKY WARBLER.

KEY TO WARBLERS

4'. No black stripe on side of face or neck; black cap separated from bill by yellow space. Female generally without black cap.

p. 339. WILSON'S WARBLER.

3'. Top of head not black.
  5. Head and neck gray, strongly contrasted with color of back; cap reddish brown.

p. 322. NASHVILLE WARBLER.

  5'. Head and neck not gray, same color as back.
    6. Broad black mask over bill and on cheeks. Song a loud ringing *wree'-chet-ty, wree'-chet-ty, wree'-chet-ty*. Female duller and without mask.

p. 315. MARYLAND YELLOW-THROAT.

  6'. No black on face or cheeks. Largest of the Warblers (length about 7½ inches). Song mixed with whistles, chucks, and calls.

p. 331. YELLOW-BREASTED CHAT.

2'. Under parts with markings.
  7. Throat black.
    Face yellow, hooded in black. Found in damp woods.

p. 327. HOODED WARBLER.

  7'. Throat not black.
    8. A ring of black, or black spots on throat or breast.
      9. Heavy white patches on wings and *middle* of tail feathers.

p. 324. BLACK AND YELLOW WARBLER.

      9'. No white patches on wings or tail

p. 322. CANADIAN WARBLER.

    8'. No ring of black or black spots on throat or breast.
      10. Under parts streaked with black, chiefly on sides; middle of back chestnut. Found in old fields and juniper pastures. Female sometimes without chestnut patch . . . p. 325. PRAIRIE WARBLER.

KEY TO WARBLERS

10′. Under parts streaked with reddish brown.
11. Streaking inconspicuous; top of head yellow or orange; back olive-yellow. Found in shrubbery in parks and gardens.

p. 307. YELLOW WARBLER.

11′. Streaking conspicuous; top of head chestnut, back brown. Twitches tail.

p. 316. RED-POLL WARBLER.

1′. Under parts not chiefly yellow.
12. Throat black.
13. Upper parts black; orange patches on breast, wings, and tail. Common in northern woodland. Female without black, and orange replaced by dull yellow.

p. 309. REDSTART.

13′. Upper parts olive-green; cheeks yellow; white patches on tail.

p. 311. BLACK-THROATED GREEN WARBLER.

12′. Throat not black.
14. Throat and breast yellow or orange.
15. Throat and breast yellow, interrupted by dark band across breast; upper parts bluish gray; yellow patch between shoulders. Female sometimes without dark band on throat.

p. 317. PARULA WARBLER.

15′. Throat and breast orange, not interrupted by band; crown patch orange; back black; wings and tail with large white blotches.

p. 326. BLACKBURNIAN WARBLER.

14′. Throat and breast not yellow or orange.
16. Under parts white, with chestnut on sides; crown yellow . . p. 318. CHESTNUT-SIDED WARBLER.

16′. Under parts white, black, and yellow; crown and rump yellow. One of the first Warblers to come north in spring, and last to go south in fall.

p. 310. YELLOW-RUMPED WARBLER.

KEY TO WARBLERS

II. No Bright Yellow, Orange, or Salmon in Plumage.

1. Top of head and whole of back uniform dark slate-blue. Throat and sides of breast black; rest of under parts white; conspicuous white spot on wing. Female olive above, dull yellowish below.

    p. 312. BLACK-THROATED BLUE WARBLER.

1'. Top of head and back not blue.
  2. Plumage mainly black and white.
    3. Cap black, rest of body streaked black and white.

    p. 321. BLACK-POLL WARBLER.

  3'. Cap not black; whole body streaked black and white. Seen on tree trunks.

    p. 314. BLACK AND WHITE CREEPING WARBLER.

  2'. Plumage mainly brownish.
    4. Under parts not streaked.
    Head with four black stripes; back olive-green. Found in dense woodland. Song suggests Chipping Sparrow.

    p. 337. WORM-EATING WARBLER.

  4'. Under parts streaked.
    5. Crown dull orange, inclosed by two black lines. Found *walking* in dry woodland. Song, a loud crescendo, *teacher, teacher, teacher,* or *teach, teach, teach*.

    p. 333. OVEN-BIRD.

  5'. Crown olive-brown, like back. Found by water.
    6. *Throat* as well as breast streaked. A northern bird.

    p. 335. WATER-THRUSH.

  6'. *Throat not streaked.* A southern bird, coming north to southern New England.

    p. 336. LOUISIANA WATER-THRUSH.

346   *WARBLERS*

Fig. 180.
Hooded Warbler.

Fig. 184.
Canadian Warbler.

Fig. 181.
Prairie Warbler.

Fig. 185.
Blackburnian Warbler.

Fig. 182.
Wilson's Warbler.

Fig. 186.
Kentucky Warbler.

Fig. 183.
Chestnut-sided Warbler.

Fig. 187.
Black-poll Warbler.

WARBLERS.

WARBLERS 347

Fig. 188.
Black-throated Blue
Warbler.

Fig. 191.
Yellow Warbler.

Fig. 189.
Parula Warbler.

Fig. 192.
Black-throated Green
Warbler.

Fig. 190.
Black and White Creeper.

Fig. 193.
Maryland Yellow-throat.

WARBLERS.

Fig. 194.
Yellow-rumped Warbler.

Fig. 195.
Redstart.

WARBLERS.

American Pipit; Titlark: *Anthus pensilvanicus*.

Upper parts brownish gray; a whitish line over the eye; under parts buffy, streaked with black; outer tail feathers white; *hind toe-nail elongated*. Length, about $6\frac{1}{4}$ inches.

GEOGRAPHIC DISTRIBUTION. — North America at large, breeding in the higher parts of the Rocky Mountains and from the Gulf of St. Lawrence northward, and wintering in the Gulf states, Mexico, and Central America.

In passing plowed fields in October, be on the lookout for a flock of these curious birds. They are invisible until you startle them, when a few rise at a time, showing white tail feathers as they go. When the whole flock is in air, if you keep quiet they may light again after circling around with their wild *cheep, cheep*, and then, although you see where they stop, it will be necessary to *bear on hard* with your eyes to distinguish them from the brown earth. When found they will surprise you by their peculiar walk, for they bob their heads as the Doves do, and wag their tails somewhat like Water-Thrushes.

Their business on the plowed ground is to pick up insects and larvæ, but they are often ruthlessly shot for sport or gun practice. I saw a wretched case of this sort one day when driving in the country. The report of a gun was followed by smoke rising over a plowed field, and then a flock of the poor little creatures rose crying into the air. The gunner came up, gazing vacantly over the field, and a farmer who was plowing there held up his horses out of idle curiosity to see what luck the sportsman had had, and would doubtless have been amazed if told that the birds shot were doing anything that affected his interests.

Brown Creeper: *Certhia familiaris americana.*

Bill curved; upper parts brownish, streaked with white; rump pale reddish brown; one light wing bar; under parts white; *tail feathers stiff and sharply pointed. Length*, about 5½ inches.

GEOGRAPHIC DISTRIBUTION. — Eastern North America; breeds from Minnesota, New York, and Maine northward; winters from northern United States south as far as the Gulf states.

This is one of the unique little birds whose ways are all his own. To be sure, the Nuthatches and Black and White Creeper affect tree trunks, but not so exclusively that their dress and tools declare their trade. The Brown Creeper is bark color to begin with, and then his bill is curved to better reach the insects and eggs under the bark of tree trunks (compare Figs. 196–200, p. 350); his hind toe-nail is elongated, to better bear his

Fig. 196.
Curved bill of Brown Creeper.

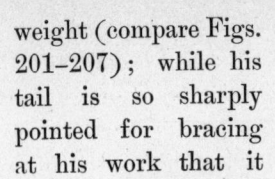

Fig. 197.
Straight bill of Wren.

Fig. 198.
Hooked bill of Shrike.

Fig. 199.
Hooked bill of Owl.

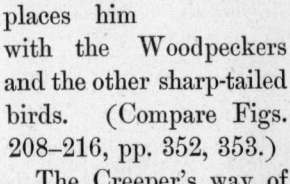

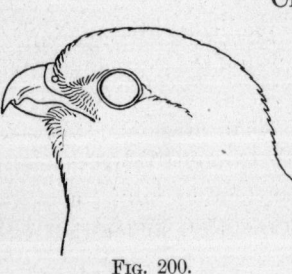

Fig. 200.
Hooked bill of Hawk.

weight (compare Figs. 201–207); while his tail is so sharply pointed for bracing at his work that it places him with the Woodpeckers and the other sharp-tailed birds. (Compare Figs. 208–216, pp. 352, 353.)

The Creeper's way of hunting differs essentially from that of the other tree trunk birds. The Woodpeckers hop up a trunk and may back down if they wish to retrace their steps; the Nuthatch goes head down; the Black and White Creeper zigzags up a trunk, hopping gayly along, branching off as his fancy dictates; but the Brown Creeper rocks sedately up the bole, getting its insect and larvæ dinner in formal fashion as it

FIG. 201.
Climbing foot of Creeper (hind toe-nail elongated).

FIG. 202.
Climbing foot of Woodpecker (two toes behind for supporting body).

FIG. 203.
Weak foot of Nighthawk.

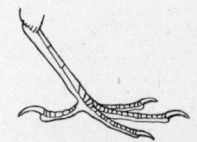

FIG. 204.
Strong foot of Sparrow.

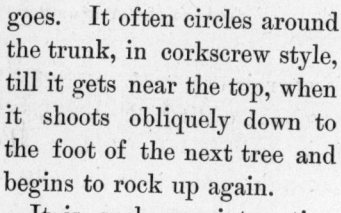

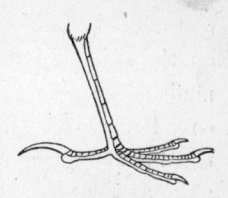

FIG. 205.
Walking foot of Pipit (hind toe-nail elongated).

FIG. 206.
Walking foot of Vulture.

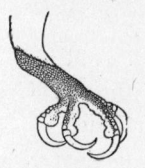

FIG. 207.
Grasping talons of Hawk.

goes. It often circles around the trunk, in corkscrew style, till it gets near the top, when it shoots obliquely down to the foot of the next tree and begins to rock up again.

It is such an interesting bird that we would be glad to have more than a mere passing woodland acquaintance with it, and Doctor Mearns assures us that by hanging a bit of pork from the balcony we can attract it to our houses.

Fig. 208.
Square tail of Vireo.

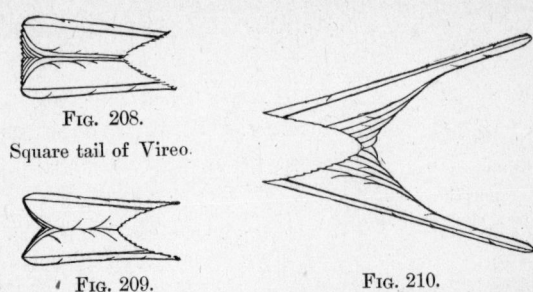

Fig. 209.
Notched tail of Pine Finch.

Fig. 210.
Forked tail of Barn Swallow.

The nest of the Creeper is one to be searched diligently, it is such an oddity in bird architecture. It is tucked in under a bit of loose bark on the side of a tree trunk, where it has a ready-made Mansard roof to keep off the rain, and a cosy home of it in all respects. Good notes on the history of one of these nests would be valuable, as the bird has been studied comparatively little.

The song of the Creeper is described by Mr. Brewster as exquisitely pure and tender, alternately rising and falling, and "dying away in an indescribably plaintive cadence, like the soft sigh of the wind among the pine boughs."

With the Creepers we complete thirteen of the families of Perching birds, and will do well to glance over the bills and feet added to our list. (See pp. 350, 351. Compare Figs. 106–121, pp. 192, 193.) We can also compare the types of

TYPES OF TAILS 353

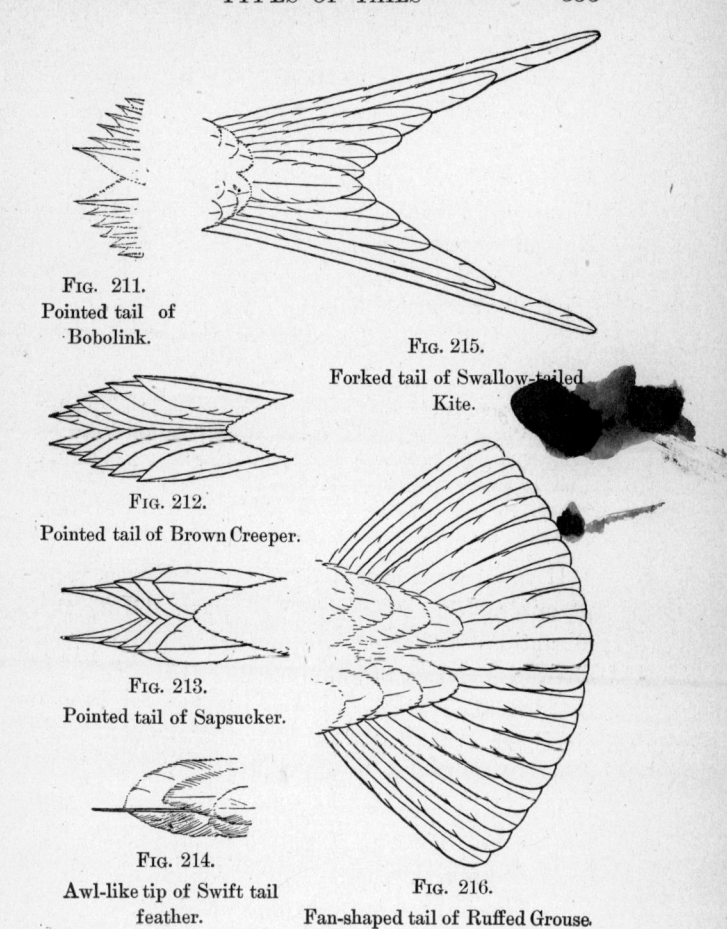

Fig. 211.
Pointed tail of Bobolink.

Fig. 215.
Forked tail of Swallow-tailed Kite.

Fig. 212.
Pointed tail of Brown Creeper.

Fig. 213.
Pointed tail of Sapsucker.

Fig. 214.
Awl-like tip of Swift tail feather.

Fig. 216.
Fan-shaped tail of Ruffed Grouse.

tails. The list stands now: 1. Flycatchers. 2. Larks. 3. Crows and Jays. 4. Blackbirds and Orioles. 5. Finches and Sparrows. 6. Tanagers. 7. Swallows. 8. Waxwings. 9. Shrikes. 10. Vireos. 11. Wood Warblers. 12. Pipits. 13. Thrashers, Wrens, Catbirds. 14. Creepers. 15. Nuthatches and Titmice.

Ruby-crowned Kinglet: *Regulus calendula.*

(See Fig. 218, p. 356.)

Adult male, crown with concealed scarlet patch; upper parts olive-green; under parts whitish. *Female and young*, similar but without scarlet patch. *Length*, about 4½ inches.

GEOGRAPHIC DISTRIBUTION. — North America, south to Guatemala; breeds from the Sierra Nevada, Rocky Mountains, and the high mountains of Arizona and eastern United States north to the arctic.

If you have thorn-apple or fruit trees on your premises, keep close watch of them during the migrations, and some morning you will find a tree alive with a flock of plump little olive-green birds that lift their wings like the Bluebird and Pine Grosbeak. They are too short and plump to be either Warblers or Vireos, and when one of them is moved by love or war, he will lift the green feathers of his cap and disclose his mark — a concealed scarlet patch — by which all men may know him to be a Ruby-crowned Kinglet.

If you come too near, he may favor you with a little chattering scold, but will pay little more attention to you, as Kinglets have small fear of

man, and are too busy about their own affairs to
be curious about their neighbors.

The song of the Ruby is one of the most remarkable of bird songs, being comparable with that of the Winter Wren. My first experience with it was when Mr. Burroughs took out a party of girls at Smith College, and pointed out the diminutive songster in the pines. Several years later, when the Ruby was in Central Park on its way north, Mrs. Olive Thorne Miller came over from Brooklyn expressly to hear it, and we spent a morning in the Ramble listening to it, marveling at the volume and the ringing quality of the notes. The following October I heard the Kinglet again, but this time the song was a low, sweet, liquid warble, smooth and rounded, but without the force or ecstacy of spring. It seemed a fitting Indian Summer meditation, though without the languor of the season, being full of the freshness of the breeze that tempers the heat of the autumn sun.

Golden-crowned Kinglet: *Regulus satrapa*.

Male, centre of crown orange, bordered by black and yellow lines; rest of upper parts olive-green; under parts whitish. *Female*, similar, but centre of crown yellow. *Length*, about 4 inches.

GEOGRAPHIC DISTRIBUTION. — North America; breeds from the northern United States northward, and southward along the Rockies into Mexico, and in the Alleghanies to North Carolina; winters from the southern limit of its breeding range to the Gulf states.

The Ruby-crowned Kinglets are the first on the ground in the fall, but some morning you will discover some beautiful Golden-crowns with the Rubies.

The song of the Golden is a high, thin *ti-ti*, very different from the chatter of the Ruby. Its song is described by Mr. Brewster in 'The Auk' as beginning with shrill, high-pitched, faltering notes, and ending with a short, rapid, and rather explosive warble.

FIG. 217. Golden-crowned Kinglet.

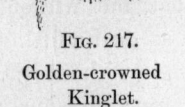

FIG. 218. Ruby-crowned Kinglet.

In winter the Kinglets may be seen in the Washington Zoo, and other places in the south, in company with Carolina Chickadees, Nuthatches, and Tufted Titmice.

Blue-gray Gnatcatcher: *Polioptila cærulea*.

Adult male, upper parts bluish gray; under parts whitish; forehead and line over bill black; outer tail feathers white; middle ones black. *Adult female,* similar, but without the black on the head. *Length,* 4½ inches.

GEOGRAPHIC DISTRIBUTION. — Eastern United States; breeds from the Gulf states to northern Illinois, southern Ontario, and New Jersey, and wanders rarely to Minnesota and Maine; winters from Florida southward.

This is one of the most piquant and original of birds and will well repay close study. He goes about with wings hanging, whipping his tail as he flirts from branch to branch, and flips out into the air after the small winged insects, reminding one of a Redstart. His call note is as distinctive as everything else about him — a nasal *tsang*. He warbles an inconsequent little song as he works.

FIG. 219. Blue-gray Gnatcatcher.

Key to Adult Male Kinglets and Gnatcatchers.

1. Upper parts bluish gray; summer residents.
    Black line on forehead; tail black, outer feathers white.
          p. 357. BLUE-GRAY GNATCATCHER.

1'. Upper parts olive-green; winter visitors.
  2. Crown reddish orange bordered by black and yellow.
          p. 356. GOLDEN-CROWNED KINGLET.

  2'. Crown with concealed scarlet patch.
          p. 354. RUBY-CROWNED KINGLET.

Thrushes.

The Thrushes are the quiet, brown, woodland choristers, the most famous of American songsters. They are named with the Skylark and Nightingale, but it is said their songs have more richness and spirituality than either of the far-famed Europeans.

Thrushes are easily recognized, for, barring the Robin, they all have plain, brown backs and white, spotted breasts.

Like the Robin they are often seen on the ground, where they feed on grubs, worms, and beetles found by turning up the leaves; but in fall they are found on the elder bushes, and it is well to take the hint and plant the berries for them.

Veery Thrush; Tawny Thrush; Wilson's Thrush: *Turdus fuscescens.*

(See Fig. 220, 2, p. 361.)

Upper parts *uniformly* warm brown; breast tawny, slightly marked with small dark spots. *Length,* about 7½ inches.

GEOGRAPHIC DISTRIBUTION. — Eastern North America; breeds from northern Illinois and Pennsylvania to Manitoba and Newfoundland, and southward along the Alleghanies to North Carolina; winters in Central America.

The Veery is a peculiarly companionable bird to those who live near its haunts. It will become so tame as to nest close to a house if not disturbed, and when sought in its natural woodland home will meet your friendly advances with confidence, answering your whistle with its own sweet wavering *whee-u*, till you feel that the woods hold gentle friends to whom you will gladly return. Hold a stiff beech-leaf at right angles to your lips, and whistle softly a series of descending *whee-u*, *whee-u*, *whee-whee-u's*, and you will get a little of the reed-like quality and phrasing of the Veery's song. To me it has all the restfulness of the sunny beech woods in summer, for it is one of my best-loved home-birds.

Olive-backed Thrush: *Turdus ustulatus swainsonii.*

(See Fig. 220, 4, p. 361.)

Upper parts uniformly *olive;* throat buffy; breast lightly spotted. *Length*, about 7¼ inches.

GEOGRAPHIC DISTRIBUTION. — Breeds from Manitoba, northern New England, and New Brunswick to Alaska and Labrador, and southward along the Alleghanies to Pennsylvania; winters in the tropics.

This northern Thrush may be heard singing on its spring migration, and its song is said to be forcibly delivered and ringing. The call note is *puk*.

Hermit Thrush: *Turdus aonalaschkæ pallasii.*

(Plate XXVIII.)

GEOGRAPHIC DISTRIBUTION. — Eastern North America, breeding from the northern Alleghanies, the mountainous parts of southern New England, southern New York, and northern Michigan, etc., northward, and wintering from the northern states southward.

The Hermit has a distinguishing reddish tail, which it raises and lowers as it gives its characteristic call of *chuck*.

The song of the Hermit has the leisurely quality which that of the Olive-backed lacks, and it fades away while the Olive's 'bubbles on' to the end.

The songs of the Wood Thrush and Hermit resemble each other in their spiritual quality; but the Hermit has a more chant-like utterance, and its first high strain arouses emotions which its regularly falling cadences carry to a perfect close. The song is one for which many of nature's devotees make long pilgrimages; and to my mind it excels that of any bird I have ever heard, being, above all others, serene and uplifting.

Key to Thrushes and Bluebirds.

1. Back blue.
   Breast reddish brown . . . . . p. 41. BLUEBIRD.
1'. Back brown or brownish.
   2. Under parts bright reddish brown . p. 17. ROBIN.
   2'. Under parts white, more or less spotted.
      3. Tail reddish brown.
         Breast thickly spotted. Found in deep woods. Call, *chuck* . . . . p. 360. HERMIT THRUSH.

KEY TO THRUSHES AND BLUEBIRDS 361

3'. Tail not reddish brown.
  4. Under parts heavily spotted; breast *white*; upper parts golden brown, brightest on head. Call, *pit-a-pit*. Most familiar of Thrushes.
     p. 22. WOOD THRUSH.
4'. Under parts not heavily spotted; breast *tawny*.
  5. Back uniformly cinnamon brown; breast spots very small and brown; sides whitish. Call *whee-u*.
     p. 358. WILSON'S THRUSH.
  5'. Back uniformly *olive*; breast spots larger and black; sides brownish gray. Migrant.
     p. 359. OLIVE-BACKED THRUSH.

FIG. 220. THRUSHES.
1. Hermit Thrush. 2. Wilson's Thrush. 3. Wood Thrush. 4. Olive-backed Thrush.

With the Thrushes we finish the list of Perching Birds, and will do well to take a final review of all the birds we have spoken of in the order in which they belong. The hen-like Grouse and Quail, the Pigeons and Doves, and the mice-destroying Hawks and Owls, carry their pictures with their names. The caterpillar-eating, long brown Cuckoos and the water-haunting blue Kingfishers are followed by the forest-preservers, the black and white tree-trunk-loving Woodpeckers. The slender-billed Hummingbird and the gaping-mouthed Swifts and Goatsuckers — Nighthawks and Whip-poor-wills — make the last order before that of the Perching Birds. Of these the Gray Flycatchers match the bare twigs on which they lie in wait for their prey; the Horned Larks have curious black horns; the Crows and Jays are powerful birds of strong bills and feet; the Blackbirds and Orioles, strikingly-colored birds, most of which spend their days devouring insects; and the Finches and Sparrows, a family which does equal public service by making way with vast amounts of weed seed. The Tanagers are our most brilliantly plumaged birds, our truly tropical visitors; the Swallows, the birds of the air; the Waxwings, the fawn-colored, crested, silent, cankerworm-eaters; the Shrikes, the impalers of grasshoppers, birds, and mice; the Vireos, the green caterpillar-birds; the Warblers, speaking broadly, the parti-colored butterflies; the Pipits, the ground-colored wagtails; the Thrashers and Wrens, the brilliant musicians;

the Creepers, the demure, systematic, tree trunk birds; the Nuthatches and Titmice, the cheery winter friends; the Kinglets and Gnatcatchers, the restless little birds that are good opposites of the quiet, dignified Thrushes and Bluebirds, who stand in the place of the most highly developed of birds.

LAND BIRDS.[1]

Order I. Grouse and Quail, p. 40.
" II. Pigeons and Doves, p. 80.
" III. Birds of Prey, pp. 285–287; 296, 297.
" IV. Cuckoos and Kingfishers, p. 165.
" V. Woodpeckers, pp. 216, 217.
" VI. Goatsuckers, Hummingbirds, Swifts, p. 193.
" VII. Perching Birds.
    1. Flycatchers, pp. 260, 261.
    2. Larks, p. 261.
    3. Crows and Jays, p. 220.
    4. Blackbirds and Orioles, pp. 111, 112.
    5. Finches and Sparrows, pp. 246–251.
    6. Tanagers, p. 174.
    7. Swallows, pp. 196, 197.
    8. Waxwings, p. 141.
    9. Shrikes, p. 300.
    10. Vireos, p. 304.
    11. Wood Warblers, pp. 342–345.
    12. Pipits, p. 348.
    13. Wrens and Thrashers, 205, 206.
    14. Creepers, p. 349.
    15. Nuthatches and Titmice, p. 152.
    16. Kinglets and Gnatcatchers, p. 357.
    17. Thrushes and Bluebirds, pp. 360, 361.

[1] The Order of Parrots, Macaws, and Paroquets and the Family of Starlings are not taken up in this book, and so are omitted from the list of Land Birds.

APPENDIX

MIGRATION

MIGRATION BLANKS. — Convenient migration blanks are issued by the Biological Survey, and may be had on application to the Biological Survey, Department of Agriculture, Washington, D. C.

The form of the blanks will be helpful for individual notebook records.

INSTRUCTIONS FOR USE OF BLANK (p. 368).

In the *first* column should be stated the exact date when each kind of bird was first seen. This entry should be made on the day the bird arrives — not from memory afterwards (general statements such as 'late in March,' 'early in April,' etc., are of no value).

In the *second* column should be stated, with as much exactness as possible, the number of each kind of bird observed during the day it was first seen.

In the *third* column should be stated the date when the same kind of bird was next seen — whether this happens on the very next day, the next week, or not till a month later.

In the *fourth* column should be stated the date when the bird becomes common. Some birds come in a body and are common from the day of their first arrival, while others straggle along and are not common for a month or more; and others still are never common.

In the *fifth* column should be stated the last date when the bird was observed. In the SPRING MIGRATION this column will remain vacant in those species which breed in the neighborhood, as it can be filled only when *all* the individuals go north. In the FALL MIGRATION it should be filled in those species which pass farther south, but must remain vacant in those which spend the winter in the vicinity of the station.

In the *sixth* column should be stated whether the species is abundant, common, tolerably common, or rare.

MIGRATION BLANK

DIVISION OF BIOLOGICAL SURVEY,
SCHEDULE NO. 3.

INLAND DIVISION.

1897.

U. S. DEPARTMENT OF AGRICULTURE.

DIVISION OF BIOLOGICAL SURVEY.

BIRDS OBSERVED AT STATION.

Name of place where observations are made, ...

Name and P. O. Address of Observer, ...

NAME OF BIRD.	When was it first seen?	About how many were seen?	When was it next seen?	When did it become common?	When was it last seen?	Is it common or rare?	Does it breed near your station?	REMARKS.

Schedules filled during the spring migration should be returned in June; those filled during the fall migration should be returned in November. Additional schedules can always be had on application.

Date of mailing this schedule, ...

MIGRATION LISTS. — When beginning to keep migration records, it will be a help to consult a local list of the same general region. For this purpose three are given here, one of the latitude of Washington, D. C., made by Mr. William Palmer; one for the latitude of Portland, Connecticut, by Mr. John H. Sage; and one for St. Louis, compiled from migration lists of Mr. Otto Widmann, in the files of the Biological Survey.[1]

SPRING MIGRATION AT ST. LOUIS, MO.

Feb. 15–March 10.[2]

Turkey Buzzard.
Flicker.
Cowbird.
Red-winged Blackbird.
Meadowlark.
Crow Blackbird.
Field Sparrow.
Chewink.

March 10–20.

Red-shouldered Hawk.
Sparrow Hawk.
Kingfisher.
Sapsucker.
Phœbe.
Rusty Grackle.
Purple Finch.
Goldfinch.
Swamp Sparrow.
Purple Martin.
Tree Swallow.
Loggerhead Shrike.
Yellow-rumped Warbler.
Bewick's Wren.

Brown Creeper.
Golden-crowned Kinglet.

March 20–31.

Marsh Hawk.
Chipping Sparrow.
Waxwing.
Ruby-crowned Kinglet.

April 1–10.

Mourning Dove.
Swift.
Barn Swallow.
Rough-winged Swallow.
Mockingbird.
Brown Thrasher.
Winter Wren.
Gnatcatcher.
Hermit Thrush.

April 10–20.

Red-headed Woodpecker.
Kingbird.
Vesper Sparrow.
Savanna Sparrow.
Lark Sparrow.

---

[1] These lists include only land birds.
[2] Dates of arrival.

White-crowned Sparrow.
White-throated Sparrow.
Lincoln's Sparrow.
Cliff Swallow.
Barn Swallow.
Yellow-throated Vireo.
White-eyed Vireo.
Parula Warbler.
Sycamore Warbler.
Oven-bird.
Louisiana Water-Thrush.
Maryland Yellow-throat.
House Wren.

Black-poll Warbler.
Yellow Redpoll.
Grinnell's Water-Thrush.
Kentucky Warbler.
Yellow-breasted Chat.
Hooded Warbler.
Canadian Warbler.
Redstart.
Catbird.
Red-breasted Nuthatch.
Wood Thrush.
Gray-cheeked Thrush.
Swainson's Thrush.

April 20–30.

Nighthawk.
Great-crested Flycatcher.
Wood Pewee.
Acadian Flycatcher.
Least Flycatcher.
Orchard Oriole.
Baltimore Oriole.
Rose-breasted Grosbeak.
Indigo Bunting.
Dickcissel.
Scarlet Tanager.
Summer Tanager.
Bank Swallow.
Red-eyed Vireo.
Warbling Vireo.
Black and White Warbler.
Worm-eating Warbler.
Blue-winged Warbler.
Nashville Warbler.
Tennessee Warbler.
Yellow Warbler.
Cerulean Warbler.

May 1–10.

Black-billed Cuckoo.
Yellow-billed Cuckoo.
Hummingbird.
Alder Flycatcher.
Bobolink.
Bell's Vireo.
Black-throated Blue Warbler.
Magnolia Warbler.
Chestnut-sided Warbler.
Black-throated Green Warbler.
Wilson's Warbler.
Wilson's Thrush.

May 10–20.

Olive-sided Flycatcher.
Yellow-bellied Flycatcher.
Blackburnian Warbler.
Connecticut Warbler.
Mourning Warbler.

THE SPRING MIGRATION

SPRING MIGRATION AT WASHINGTON, D. C.

March 1–15.[1]
Cowbird.
Red-winged Blackbird.
Rusty Blackbird.
Crow Blackbird.

March 15–21.
Song Sparrow.
Swamp Sparrow.

April 1–7.
Phœbe.
Vesper Sparrow.
Savanna Sparrow.
Grasshopper Sparrow.
Rough-winged Swallow.
Passenger Pigeon.[2]

April 7–14.
Mourning Dove.
Sapsucker.
Chipping Sparrow.
Field Sparrow.
Tree Swallow.
Yellow-rumped Warbler.
Yellow Palm Warbler.
Brown Thrasher.
Ruby Kinglet.
Blue-gray Gnatcatcher.

April 14–21.
Whip-poor-will.
Nighthawk.
Swift.
Kingbird.
Bachman's Sparrow.[3]
Chewink.
Purple Martin.
Barn Swallow.
Yellow-throated Vireo.
Blue-headed Vireo.
Black and White Creeper.
Parula Warbler.
Yellow Warbler.
Prairie Warbler.
Oven-bird.
Louisiana Water-Thrush.
Maryland Yellow-throat.
Bewick's Wren.[3]
House Wren.
Long-billed Marsh Wren.
Wood Thrush.

April 21–28.
Hummingbird.
Great-crested Flycatcher.
Olive-sided Flycatcher.[3]
Least Flycatcher.
Orchard Oriole.
Purple Finch.
Scarlet Tanager.
Summer Tanager.
Red-eyed Vireo.
Warbling Vireo.
White-eyed Vireo.
Nashville Warbler.

[1] Dates of arrival in numbers.
[2] Nearly extinct.
[3] Very rare.

Black-throated Blue Warbler.
Black and Yellow Warbler.
Chestnut-sided Warbler.
Black-throated Green Warbler.
Water-Thrush.
Wilson's Warbler.
Redstart.
Catbird.

Bank Swallow.
Worm-eating Warbler.
Blue-winged Warbler.
Golden-winged Warbler.
Blackburnian Warbler.
Kentucky Warbler.
Yellow-breasted Chat.
Hooded Warbler.[1]

May 1–7.

Yellow-billed Cuckoo.
Black-billed Cuckoo.
Bobolink.
Baltimore Oriole.
White-crowned Sparrow.
Rose-breasted Grosbeak.
Cliff Swallow.

May 7–14.

Wood Pewee.
Yellow-bellied Flycatcher.
Acadian Flycatcher.
Alder Flycatcher.
Black-poll Warbler.
Wilson's Warbler.
Canadian Warbler.
Olive-backed Thrush.

SPRING MIGRATION AT PORTLAND, CONN.

Date of arrival.		Date of departure.
Feb. 15–	Phœbe.	Oct. 6–14.
Mar. 10.	Red-winged Blackbird.	Oct. 22–Nov. 1.
	Purple Grackle.	Oct. 25–Nov. 8.
	Purple Finch.	Oct. 21–Dec. 16.
	Song Sparrow	Oct. 21–Nov. 2.
	Fox Sparrow.	Apr. 3–26.
	Robin.	Nov. 3–Dec. 9.
	Bluebird.	Oct. 26–Dec. 30.
Mar. 10–20.	Mourning Dove.	Nov. 13–30.
	Cooper's Hawk.	Oct. 6–15.
	Meadowlark.	Oct. 26–Dec. 7.
Mar. 20–31.	Sharp-shinned Hawk.	Oct. 10–29.
	Red-headed Woodpecker.	Sept. 14–Oct. 14.
	Horned Lark.	Mar. 25.

[1] Very rare.

THE SPRING MIGRATION

	Cowbird.	Nov. 6–Dec. 13.
	Rusty Blackbird.	Apr. 16.
Apr. 1–10.	Marsh Hawk.	Oct. 21–Nov. 2.
	Fish Hawk.	May 1–20.
	Yellow-bellied Woodpecker.	Apr. 20–May 10.
	Kingfisher.	Oct. 24–Nov. 22.
	Vesper Sparrow.	Oct. 15–21.
	Savanna Sparrow.	Oct. 21–26.
	Chipping Sparrow.	Sept. 28–Oct. 23.
	Field Sparrow.	Oct. 9–26.
	Tree Swallow.	Oct. 13–26.
	Pine Warbler.	Apr. 16–25.
	Ruby-crowned Kinglet.	Apr. 25–May 6.
	Hermit Thrush.	Apr. 25–May 3.
Apr. 10–20.	Broad-winged Hawk.	Sept. 17–Oct. 21.
	Swamp Sparrow.	Oct. 21–Nov. 2.
	Purple Martin.	Sept. 12.
	Barn Swallow.	Sept. 27–Oct. 19.
	Bank Swallow.	Sept. 25.
	Yellow Palm Warbler.	Apr. 23–May 17.
	Louisiana Water-Thrush.	August.
Apr. 20–30.	Short-eared Owl.	April.
	Whip-poor-will.	Sept. 21–25.
	Nighthawk.	Sept. 29–Oct. 3.
	Chimney Swift.	Sept. 23–30.
	Kingbird.	Sept. 4–10.
	Least Flycatcher.	Sept. 4.
	White-throated Sparrow.	May 7–21.
	Chewink.	Oct. 5–24.
	Red-eyed Vireo.	Sept. 10–Oct. 8.
	Warbling Vireo.	Sept. 4–17.
	Yellow-throated Vireo.	Sept. 10–21.
	Blue-headed Vireo.	May 5–9.
	Black and White Warbler.	Sept. 25–Oct. 4.
	Myrtle Warbler.	May 4–19.

	Black-throated Green Warbler.	Sept. 29–Oct. 21.
	Titlark.	May 1–15.
	Brown Thrasher.	Oct. 5–20.
	House Wren.	Sept. 26–Oct. 15.
May 1–10.	Pigeon Hawk.	May 4–9.
	Yellow-billed Cuckoo.	Sept. 13–Oct. 17.
	Black-billed Cuckoo.	Sept. 4.
	Hummingbird.	Sept. 17.
	Crested Flycatcher.	Aug.–Sept.
	Wood Pewee.	Sept. 21–Oct. 3.
	Bobolink.	Oct. 3–15.
	Baltimore Oriole.	Sept. 8.
	Orchard Oriole.	August.
	Grasshopper Sparrow.	Oct. 20.
	Rose-breasted Grosbeak.	Sept. 1–28.
	Indigo-bird.	Oct. 4–16.
	Scarlet Tanager.	Sept. 24–Oct. 7.
	White-eyed Vireo.	Sept. 15–20.
	Worm-eating Warbler.	August.
	Blue-winged Warbler.	August.
	Golden-winged Warbler	August.
	Nashville Warbler.	Sept. 27.
	Parula Warbler.	Sept. 26–Oct. 6.
	Yellow Warbler.	Sept. 14–23.
	Black-throated Blue Warbler.	May 12–26.
	Black and Yellow Warbler.	May 16–26.
	Chestnut-sided Warbler.	Sept. 5.
	Black-poll Warbler.	May 25–June 3.
	Blackburnian Warbler.	May 13–30.
	Prairie Warbler.	Sept. 21.
	Oven-bird.	Sept. 10–26.
	Water-Thrush.	May 18–27.
	Maryland Yellow-throat.	Oct. 6–16.
	Yellow-breasted Chat.	August.
	Redstart.	Sept. 11–26.

	Catbird.	Oct. 6–14.
	Wood Thrush.	Sept. 18.
	Wilson's Thrush.	Aug.–Sept.
May 10–20.	White-crowned Sparrow.	May 12–22.
	Cliff Swallow.	Aug.–Sept.
	Cape May Warbler.	May 13–16.
	Bay-breasted Warbler.	May 18–27.
	Wilson's Warbler.	May 22–30.
	Canadian Warbler.	May 21–30.
	Gray-cheeked Thrush.	May 11–27.
	Olive-backed Thrush.	May 17–29.
May 20–30.	Yellow-bellied Flycatcher.	May 20–25.
	Mourning Warbler.	May 26.

WINTER BIRDS

Every one knows that the country is full of birds during the migrations; but we do not all realize how many birds are to be seen in winter.

The following lists from Portland, Connecticut, Washington, D. C., and St. Louis, Missouri, suggest what we may expect to find in our own neighborhoods.

The list from Portland has been kindly supplied by Mr. John H. Sage; that from Washington, by Mr. William Palmer; and that from St. Louis, by Mr. Otto Widmann.[1]

Birds that may be seen about Portland, Conn., in Winter.

RESIDENTS.
Bob-white.
Ruffed Grouse.
Mourning Dove.[2]
Sharp-shinned Hawk.
Red-tailed Hawk.
Red-shouldered Hawk.
Sparrow Hawk.
Barred Owl.
Screech Owl.
Great Horned Owl.
Belted Kingfisher.[2]
Hairy Woodpecker.
Downy Woodpecker.
Red-headed Woodpecker.
Flicker.
Blue Jay.
Crow.
Meadowlark.
Purple Finch.

WINTER VISITANTS.
Goshawk.
Rough-legged Hawk.[2]
Pigeon Hawk.[2]
Long-eared Owl.
Acadian Owl.
Snowy Owl.[2]
Pine Grosbeak.
American Crossbill.
White-winged Crossbill.[2]
Redpoll.
Pine Finch.
Snowflake.
Lapland Longspur.[2]
White-throated Sparrow.
Tree Sparrow.
Junco.
Butcherbird.
Yellow-rumped Warbler.[2]
Winter Wren.

[1] These lists include only land birds. [2] Very rare.

WINTER BIRDS

Goldfinch.
Field Sparrow.[1]
Song Sparrow.
Waxwing.
White-breasted Nuthatch.
Chickadee.
Robin.
Bluebird.

Brown Creeper.
Red-breasted Nuthatch.
Golden-crowned Kinglet.
Hermit Thrush.[1]

[1] Very rare.

Birds that may be seen about Washington in Winter.

RESIDENTS.   WINTER VISITANTS.

Of ordinary occurrence and abundance.

Bob-white.
Turkey Vulture.
Red-tailed Hawk.
Red-shouldered Hawk.
Screech Owl.
Downy Woodpecker.
Flicker.[1]
Phœbe.[1]
Blue Jay.[1]
Crow.
Fish Crow.
Meadowlark.[1]
Goldfinch.[1]
Song Sparrow.
Cardinal.
Waxwing.[2]
Carolina Wren.
White-breasted Nuthatch.
Tufted Titmouse.
Carolina Chickadee.
Robin.[1]
Bluebird.

Marsh Hawk.
Pigeon Hawk.
Short-eared Owl.
Horned Lark.
Prairie Horned Lark.
Purple Finch.[1]
American Crossbill.[3]
Pine Finch.[3]
White-throated Sparrow.
Tree Sparrow.
Junco.
Fox Sparrow.
Loggerhead Shrike.
Pipit.[1]
Winter Wren.
Red-breasted Nuthatch.
Golden-crowned Kinglet.
Hermit Thrush.[1]

[1] Most abundant in migrations.
[2] Most abundant in summer.
[3] Of erratic occurrence.

WINTER BIRDS

Not of ordinary occurrence or abundance.

- Ruffed Grouse.
- Mourning Dove.
- Sharp-shinned Hawk.[1]
- Cooper's Hawk.[1]
- Broad-winged Hawk.[1]
- Golden Eagle.[3]
- Bald Eagle.
- Sparrow Hawk.[1]
- Barn Owl.
- Long-eared Owl.
- Barred Owl.
- Great Horned Owl.
- Kingfisher.[1]
- Hairy Woodpecker.
- Pileated Woodpecker.[3]
- Red-headed Woodpecker.[2]
- Red-bellied Woodpecker.
- Cowbird.[4]
- Red-winged Blackbird.[4]
- Vesper Sparrow.[1]
- Field Sparrow.[1]
- Chewink.[2]
- Mockingbird.[3]
- Goshawk.[3]
- American Rough Leg.[3]
- Acadian Owl.
- Snowy Owl.[4]
- Yellow-bellied Sapsucker.[1]
- Pine Grosbeak.[4]
- White-winged Crossbill.[4]
- Redpoll.[3]
- Snowflake.[3]
- Savanna Sparrow.[1]
- Swamp Sparrow.[1]
- Butcherbird.[3]
- Yellow-rumped Warbler.[1]
- Brown Creeper.[1]
- Chickadee.[4]
- Ruby Kinglet.[1]

Birds that may be seen in Winter in St. Louis and St. Charles Counties, Missouri.

Generally distributed.

- Bob-white.
- Downy Woodpecker.
- Blue Jay.
- Crow.
- Tree Sparrow.
- Junco.
- Cardinal.
- Carolina Wren.
- White-breasted Nuthatch.
- Tufted Titmouse.
- Chickadee.
- Carolina Chickadee.

---

[1] Most abundant in migrations.
[2] Most abundant in summer.
[3] Very rare.
[4] Of erratic occurrence.

WINTER BIRDS

Locally distributed.[1]

Mourning Dove.
Marsh Hawk.
Red-tailed Hawk.
Red-shouldered Hawk.
American Rough-legged Hawk.
Golden Eagle.[2]
Bald Eagle.
Sparrow Hawk.
Long-eared Owl.
Short-eared Owl.
Barred Owl.
Screech Owl.
Great Horned Owl.
Hairy Woodpecker.
Yellow-bellied Sapsucker.
Red-headed Woodpecker.
Red-bellied Woodpecker.
Flicker.
Prairie Horned Lark.
Cowbird.
Red-winged Blackbird.
Meadowlark.
Rusty Blackbird.
Crow Blackbird.
Purple Finch.
Redpoll.[3]
Goldfinch.
Lapland Longspur.
Leconte's Sparrow.[3]
White-crowned Sparrow.
White-throated Sparrow.
Song Sparrow.
Swamp Sparrow.
Fox Sparrow.
Chewink.
Waxwing.
Butcherbird.[3]
Loggerhead Shrike.
Yellow-rumped Warbler.
Mockingbird.[3]
Bewick's Wren.[3]
Brown Creeper.[3]
Red-breasted Nuthatch.[3]
Golden-crowned Kinglet.[3]
Ruby Kinglet.[3]
Robin.
Bluebird.

[1] The majority are found in the heavily-timbered bottom-lands along the large rivers.
[2] Very rare.
[3] Of uncertain occurrence.

OUTLINE FOR FIELD OBSERVATIONS

OBSERVATION OUTLINE. — In studying birds in the nesting season, there are many points to keep in mind — in fact, all the questions involved in the life-histories of birds. Observations here, if made with conscientious accuracy, are especially valuable, as few birds have ever been studied exhaustively in the field. The following hints may prove suggestive to the student who is beginning field-work : —

Points to note to assist in identification.

I. Size (compared with Robin, Fig. 5, p. 17).

II. Colors.
  Bright (exs. Oriole, Fig. 25, p. 56 ; Cardinal, Fig. 28, p. 65).
  Dull (ex. Sparrow, Fig. 58, p. 117).

III. Markings.
  Top of head (ex. White-crowned Sparrow, Fig. 93, p. 176).
  Back (ex. Red-headed Woodpecker, Fig. 67, p. 131).
  Breast (ex. Meadowlark, Fig. 45, p. 106).
  Wings (ex. Nighthawk, Fig. 99, p. 189).
  Tail (ex. Kingbird, Fig. 35, p. 83).

IV. Shape.
  1. BODY.
     Long and slender (ex. Cuckoo, Fig. 83, p. 161).
     Short and stocky (ex. Bobolink, Plate VII. p. 104).
  2. BILL.
     Short and stout for cracking seeds (ex. Sparrow, Fig. 119, p. 193).
     Long and slender for holding worms (ex. Oriole, Fig. 112, p. 192).
     Long and heavy for drilling holes in trees or holding fish (exs. Woodpecker, Fig. 108, p. 192 ; Kingfisher, Fig. 114, p. 192).

OBSERVATION OUTLINE

Slender and delicate for probing flower tubes (ex. Hummingbird, Fig. 118, p. 193).

Short, with wide gape for taking insects (exs. Swallows, Fig. 120, p. 193; Goatsuckers, Fig. 113, p. 192).

Hooked for tearing prey (exs. Hawks, Fig. 200, p. 350; Owls, Fig. 199, p. 350).

Crossed for extracting seeds from cones (ex. Crossbill, Fig. 116, p. 193).

Curved for getting insects from tree trunks (ex. Brown Creeper, Fig. 196, p. 350).

3. WING.

Short and round for short flights (exs. Ruffed Grouse and Wren, Fig. 18, p. 45).

Long and slender for sustained flight (exs. Swift, Fig. 19, p. 45; Swallow, Fig. 102, p. 190).

4. TAIL.

Square (ex. White-eyed Vireo, Fig. 208, p. 352).

Notched (ex. Pine Finch, Fig. 209, p. 352).

Fan-shaped (ex. Ruffed Grouse, Fig. 216, p. 353).

Graduated (ex. Mourning Dove, Fig. 12, p. 30).

Pointed for bracing (exs. Brown Creeper, Fig. 212, p. 353; Woodpecker, Fig. 213, p. 353).

Long and forked for steering (exs. Barn Swallow, Fig. 210, p. 352; Swallow-tailed Kite, Fig. 215, p. 353).

Short and tipped with spines for bracing (ex. Chimney Swift, Fig. 214, p. 353).

5. FOOT.

Weak (exs. Kingfisher, Fig. 81, p. 158; Swallow, Fig. 20, p. 50).

  Used only for perching and clinging to walls (ex. Chimney Swift, Fig. 7, p. 25).

  Middle toe greatly elongated (ex. Nighthawk, Fig. 104, p. 191).

Strong.

  Used for walking (exs. Crow Blackbird, Fig. 48,

p. 109 ; Pipit, Fig. 205, p. 351 ; Turkey Vulture, Fig. 206, p. 351).

Used for climbing (exs. Woodpeckers, Fig. 202, p. 351 ; Brown Creeper, Fig. 201, p. 351).

Used for holding and tearing prey (ex. Hawks, Fig. 207, p. 351).

V. Appearance.
Wings and tail drooping.
Crest raised, wings close at sides.

VI. Movements.
Hop (ex. Sparrow); walk (ex. Blackbird).
Creep up trees (ex. Brown Creeper).
Bob head and wag tail (exs. Water-Thrushes and Pipits).
Twitch tail from side to side (ex. Indigo-bird).

VII. Flight.
1. FAST.
   Direct (ex. Robin).
   Abrupt and zigzag (ex. Chimney Swift).
   Smooth and circling (ex. Swallows).
2. SLOW.
   Flapping (exs. Crow and Heron).
   Sailing or soaring (exs. Red-tailed Hawk and Turkey Buzzard).
   Flapping and sailing alternately.
     Oblique flight (ex. Meadowlark).
     Undulating flight (ex. Goldfinch).

Points to note to add to knowledge of life histories.

I. Localities frequented.
Gardens and orchards (exs. Hummingbird and Catbird).
Roadside fences (exs. Kingbird and Vesper Sparrow).
Meadows (exs. Bobolink and Meadowlark).
Thickets (exs. Brown Thrasher and Chat).
Woods (exs. Hermit Thrush and Oven-bird).
Rivers and lakes (ex. Kingfisher).
Marshes (exs. Heron and Marsh Wren).

II. Food.
1. KINDS OF FOOD.
Weed seeds (exs. Finches and Sparrows).
Flies, mosquitoes, etc. (exs. Swallows and Goatsuckers).
Ants (ex. Flicker).
Caterpillars (exs. Cuckoos and Cedar-bird).
Elm leaf-beetles and cankerworms (ex. Cedar-bird).
Eggs and larvæ of cankerworms (exs. Chickadees, Woodpeckers, and Creepers).
Grasshoppers and crickets (exs. Meadowlark and Crow).
Mice and rats, etc. (exs. Hawks and Owls).

2. MANNER OF OBTAINING FOOD.
Lie in wait for prey (exs. Flycatchers and Hawks).
Fall on prey without warning.
Give call of warning.
Take food on wing (exs. Swallows, Swifts, Goatsuckers).

III. Song (by male only, or by female also).
1. MANNER AND TIME OF SINGING.
From a perch (ex. Song Sparrow).
In the air (ex. Bobolink).
In the night (ex. Mockingbird).
Time of joining daybreak chorus.

2. CHARACTER OF SONG.
Plaintive (exs. Wood Pewee and Meadowlark).
Happy (ex. Bobolink).
Long (exs. Mockingbird and Catbird).
Short (exs. Bluebird and Chickadee).

3. VARIETY OF CALL NOTES.

IV. Habits.
1. USE WINGS IN SPECIAL WAYS.
As weapons (ex. Doves).
As musical instruments (ex. Ruffed Grouse).

2. GO IN FLOCKS (exs. Waxwings and Blackbirds).

3. FORM ROOSTS (dates, number of birds in roost, distance birds go to roost).
   Winter roosts (ex. Crow).
   Summer roosts (ex. Robin).
   Migration roosts (ex. Swallows).
4. PERFORM CURIOUS ACTIONS.
   Dances (ex. Prairie Hen).
   Aerial evolutions (ex. Nighthawk).

V. **Nest (in colonies, ex. Swallows — or alone, ex. Thrushes).**
   1. LOCATION OF NEST.
      In or on the ground (exs. Bank Swallows and Oven-bird).
      In tree-trunks (ex. Woodpeckers).
      On branches.
         In crotch.
         On horizontal limb (ex. Robin).
         Pendent from branch (exs. Orioles and Vireos).
   2. SIZE OF NEST (exs. Hummingbird, Robin, and Crow).
   3. FORM OF NEST.
      Cup-shaped (ex. Robin).
      Pocket-shaped (ex. Oriole).
      Basket-shaped (ex. Vireo).
      Wall-pocket-shaped (ex. Swift).
      Dome-shaped (ex. Oven-bird).
      Retort-shaped (ex. Cliff Swallow).
   4. MATERIALS OF NEST.
      Clay (ex. Eave Swallow).
      Vegetable fibres, grasses, rootlets, leaves, twigs (ex. Sparrows).
      Hair (ex. Hairbird, or Chipping Sparrow).
      Fur or feathers (ex. Chickadee).
   5. LENGTH OF TIME NEST IS USED.
      Abandoned after first brood (ex. Vireos).
      Used for successive years (ex. Fish Hawk).

VI. Building.

1. **METHOD OF CONSTRUCTION.**
   Excavating (exs. Woodpeckers and Kingfisher).
   Weaving (ex. Oriole).
   Plastering (ex. Swallow).
2. **NUMBER OF DAYS REQUIRED.**
3. **HABITS OF MALE DURING NEST-BUILDING.**
   Works with female.
   Works alone.
   Sings while female works.
   Brings material to female.
   Absents himself from nest.

VII. Eggs.

Number.
Color.
Markings.

VIII. Incubation.

Interval between completion of nest and beginning of sitting.
Length of incubation.
Habits of male during time.
   Takes place of female on nest.
   Feeds female on nest.

IX. Young.

1. **CONDITION AT HATCHING.**
   Feathered (ex. Quail).
   Naked (exs. Robin and Oriole).
2. **CONDITIONS DURING GROWTH.**
   Position of feather tracts.
   Daily increase in weight.
   Respiration.
   Heart beats.
   Time when eyes open.
   Time spent in nest.
3. **CONDITION ON LEAVING NEST.**

4. CARED FOR BY PARENTS.
Fed in nest.
    Food brought in bill (ex. Sparrows).
    Food regurgitated (ex. Hummingbird).
    Rapidity in feeding, and interval between meals.
Care of young shared by male and female.
All the young kept together on leaving nest, or family separated, each parent feeding its squad.
Young taught to sing.
Notes and actions of young.
Nestling plumage.

X. Problems.

1. COLOR AND MARKINGS.
Protective coloration (exs. Sparrows and Vireos).
    Gradation of tints to counteract light and shade (ex. Grouse).
    Markings to disguise form (exs. Whip-poor-will and Junco).
Sexual coloration (exs. Oriole and Scarlet Tanager).
Relation of color to food.
Manner of seasonal change in plumage.
    Moulting.
    Wearing off of edge of feathers.
    Change in color of feather.
Recognition marks (exs. Junco and Chewink).
Color of eggs.

2. INDIVIDUAL VARIATION.
In song.
In habits.

3. INTELLIGENCE, AS SHOWN BY
Caution.
Curiosity.
Action towards enemies.
Change of habits as result of danger.
Building.
    Choice of sites.

Choice of materials.
Workmanship.
Shape, color, and position to protect from enemies.
Knowledge of number and color of eggs.
Actions toward Cowbird's eggs.
Protection of young.
Discipline of young.
Food obtained by work of other birds (ex. Fish Hawk and Eagle).

4. EMOTION EXPRESSED BY
Use of crest, wings, tail.
Attitudes.
Movements.
Voice.

5. RANGE OF COMMUNICATION.
Calls of signal and warning.
Cries of anger, fear, pain, protest.
Songs of happiness and love.
Display of recognition marks.

OBSERVING IN TOWNS AND VILLAGES

In studying birds closely in the field, their confidence must be won, but in villages and towns they are used to the presence of man, and being less afraid of observers may be watched to peculiar advantage. That a great variety of birds nest in our midst for us to study is shown by the following list from a typical New England town.

BIRDS KNOWN TO NEST IN PORTLAND, CONNECTICUT.

Bob-white.
Ruffed Grouse.
Mourning Dove.[1]
Marsh Hawk.
Sharp-shinned Hawk.
Cooper's Hawk.
Red-tailed Hawk.
Red-shouldered Hawk.
Broad-winged Hawk.
Sparrow Hawk.
Barred Owl.
Screech Owl.
Great Horned Owl.
Yellow-billed Cuckoo.
Black-billed Cuckoo.
Kingfisher.
Hairy Woodpecker.
Downy Woodpecker.
Red-headed Woodpecker.
Flicker.
Whip-poor-will.
Nighthawk.
Swift.
Hummingbird.
Kingbird.
Great-crested Flycatcher.
Phœbe.
Wood Pewee.
Least Flycatcher.
Blue Jay.
Crow.
Bobolink.
Cowbird.
Red-winged Blackbird.
Meadowlark.
Orchard Oriole.
Baltimore Oriole.
Crow Blackbird.
Purple Finch.
Goldfinch.
Vesper Sparrow.
Savanna Sparrow.
Grasshopper Sparrow.
Chipping Sparrow.
Field Sparrow.
Song Sparrow.
Swamp Sparrow.
Chewink.

[1] The Passenger Pigeon formerly bred in Portland.

Rose-breasted Grosbeak.
Indigo Bunting.
Scarlet Tanager.
Purple Martin.
Cliff Swallow.
Barn Swallow.
Tree Swallow.
Bank Swallow.
Rough-winged Swallow.
Waxwing.
Red-eyed Vireo.
Warbling Vireo.
Yellow-throated Vireo.
White-eyed Vireo.
Black and White Creeper.
Worm-eating Warbler.
Blue-winged Warbler.
Golden-winged Warbler.
Nashville Warbler.
Parula Warbler.
Yellow Warbler.
Chestnut-sided Warbler.
Black-throated Green Warbler.
Prairie Warbler.
Oven-bird.
Louisiana Water-Thrush.
Maryland Yellow-throat.
Yellow-breasted Chat.
Redstart.
Catbird.
Thrasher.
House Wren.
Long-billed Marsh Wren.
White-breasted Nuthatch.
Chickadee.
Wood Thrush.
Veery Thrush.
Robin.
Bluebird.

Water Birds.

Wood Duck.
American Bittern.
Least Bittern.
Green Heron.
Black-crowned Night Heron.
Virginia Rail.
Sora.
American Woodcock.
Wilson's Snipe.
Spotted Sandpiper.
Killdeer.

BOOKS OF REFERENCE

For current Government publications apply to Superintendent of Documents, Washington, D. C. For second-hand books, separates, and books that are out of print, look in second-hand bookstores.

KEYS FOR IDENTIFICATION.

Chapman, Frank M. Handbook of Birds of Eastern North America. D. Appleton & Co., New York. $3. Pocket edition. $3.50.

Coues, Elliott. Key to North American Birds. Estes & Lauriat, Boston. $7.50.

Ridgway, Robert. Manual of North American Birds. J. B. Lippincott Company, Philadelphia. $7.50.

STANDARD WORKS OF REFERENCE.

A. O. U. Check-List of North American Birds (1895).[1] $2. Abridged edition. 25 cents.

Audubon, John James. Birds of America;[2] Ornithological Biography.[2]

Baird, S. F., Brewer, T. M., and Ridgway, R. A History of North American Birds; Land and Water Birds. 5 vols. Little, Brown & Co., Boston. $48.

Bendire, Charles E. Life Histories of North American Birds. Smithsonian Institution. 2 vols. $15.

Coues, Elliott. Birds of the Colorado Valley.[2] $2.50. Birds of the Northwest.[2] $2.50.

Nehrling, Henry. Our Native Birds of Song and Beauty. George Brumder, Milwaukee. 2 vols. Unbound, $16; bound, $18–$22.

Newton, Alfred. Dictionary of Birds. Macmillan, New York. $7.50.

---

[1] For sale by L. S. Foster, 33 Pine Street, New York.
[2] Out of print.

Nuttall, Thomas. A Manual of the Ornithology of the United States and of Canada.[2] Chamberlain's Edition, A Popular Handbook of the Ornithology of Eastern North America. Little, Brown & Co. 2 vols. $7.50.

Ridgway, Robert. Nomenclature of Colors. Little, Brown & Co., Boston. $4.

Trumbull, Gurdon. Names and Portraits of Birds. Harper & Brothers, New York. $2.50.

Wilson, Alexander. American Ornithology.[2]

PUBLICATIONS ON SPECIAL SUBJECTS.

FOOD OF BIRDS.

Publications of Massachusetts State Board of Agriculture (Malden, Mass.) : Birds as Protectors of Orchards, Forbush, E. H., Mass. Crop Rept. for July, 1895, pp. 20-32. Birds which feed on the Gypsy Moth, Forbush, E. H., Rept. Gypsy Moth, pp. 20-243. Crow in Massachusetts, Mass. Crop Rept. for Aug. 1896, pp. 24-40.

Publications of the U. S. Department of Agriculture : Crow Blackbirds and their Food, Beal, F. E. L. Food of Woodpeckers, Beal, F. E. L. Four Common Birds of the Farm and Garden, Judd, S. D. Hawks and Owls (Bulletin, No. 3),[2] Fisher, A. K. Hawks and Owls from the Standpoint of the Farmer, Fisher, A. K. Some Common Birds in their Relation to Agriculture, Farmer's Bulletin, No. 54, Beal, F. E. L. The Common Crow of the United States, Barrows, W. B., and Schwarz, E. A. The English Sparrow in America, Merriam, C. H., and Barrows, W. B. The Meadowlark and Baltimore Oriole, Beal, F. E. L. The Blue Jay and its Food, Beal, F. E. L.

MIGRATION OF BIRDS.

Bird Migration. Brewster, William. $0.50.[1]

Bird Migration in the Mississippi Valley. Cooke, W. W. Dept. of Agric.[2]

---

[1] For sale by L. S. Foster, 33 Pine Street, New York.
[2] Out of print.

LOCAL LISTS.

Birds of Connecticut. Merriam, C. Hart.[1]

Birds of Eastern Pennsylvania and New Jersey. Stone, Witmer. $1.

Birds of Hudson Highlands. Mearns, E. A. Bull. Essex (Mass.) Inst. vols. x.–xiii.

Birds of Illinois. Ridgway, Robert. H. W. Rokker, Springfield, Illinois.

Birds of Kansas. Goss, B. F. Geo. W. Crane & Co., Topeka, Kansas. $5.

Birds of Manitoba. Thompson, E. E. Proceedings National Museum (1890).

Birds of Minnesota. Hatch, P. L. Geological Survey of Minnesota, 1892.

Birds of Ohio. Wheaton, J. M. Geological Survey of Ohio.[1]

Birds of Ontario. McIlwraith, Thomas. $2.

Birds of Pennsylvania. Warren, B. H. State Board of Agriculture.[1] $5.

Birds of the Virginias. Rives, W. C. The Newport (R. I.) Nat. Hist. Soc. (1890). $0.60.

List of Birds ascertained to inhabit the District of Columbia: Coues, Elliott, and Prentiss, D. W.[2] Bull. 26, U. S. Natl. Mus. (1883). $0.75.

List of Birds known to occur within Fifty Miles of New York City. Chapman, Frank M. $0.15.[2]

SONGS OF BIRDS.

A Study of the Singing of our Birds. Bicknell, E. P. Estes & Lauriat, Boston. (The Auk, 1884, 1885.[2])

The Evolution of Bird-Song. Witchell, C. A., Adam & Charles Black, London.

Wood Notes Wild. Cheney, S. P. Lee & Shepard, Boston. $2.

---

[1] Out of print.
[2] For sale by L. S. Foster, 33 Pine Street, New York.

POPULAR BIRD BOOKS.

Baskett, J. N. The Story of the Birds. D. Appleton & Co., New York. $0.65.

Bolles, Frank. Land of the Lingering Snow; From Blomidon to Smoky; At the North of Bearcamp Water. Houghton, Mifflin & Co., Boston. $1.25 each.

Burroughs, John. Wake Robin; Fresh Fields; Birds and Poets; Locusts and Wild Honey; Pepacton; Winter Sunshine; Signs and Seasons; Riverby. Houghton, Mifflin & Co., Boston. $1.25 each.

Chamberlain, Montague. Some Canadian Birds. The Copp, Clarke Company, Toronto. $0.30.

Chapman, Frank M. Bird-Life. D. Appleton & Co., New York. $1.75. Edition in colors, $5.

Davis, William T. Days Afield on Staten Island.

Flagg, Wilson. A Year with the Birds. Educational Publishing Company, Boston. $1.00. Birds and Seasons of New England.

Merriam, Florence A. Birds through an Opera-Glass. $0.75. A-Birding on a Bronco, $1.25. Houghton, Mifflin & Co., Boston.

Miller, Olive Thorne. Bird-Ways; In Nesting Time; Little Brothers of the Air; A Bird-Lover in the West; Upon the Tree-Tops. Houghton, Mifflin & Co., Boston. $1.25 each.

Minot, Henry D. Land and Game Birds of New England. (Brewster's Edition.) Houghton, Mifflin & Co., Boston. $3.50.

Robinson, Rowland E. In New England Fields and Woods. Houghton, Mifflin & Co., Boston. $1.25.

Parkhurst, H. E. The Birds' Calendar. $1.50. Song Birds and Waterfowl. $1.50. Scribner, New York.

Thompson, Maurice. John B. Alden. Sylvan Secrets, $0.60. By-Ways and Bird Notes, $0.75. Songs of Fair Weather.

Torrey, Bradford. Birds in the Bush; A Rambler's Lease; The Foot-Path Way; A Florida Sketch-Book; Spring Notes from Tennessee. Houghton, Mifflin & Co., Boston. $1.25 each.

Van Dyke, T. S. Game Birds at Home. Fords, Howard & Hulbert, New York. $1.50.

Wilcox, M. A. Land Birds of New England. Lee & Shepard, Boston. $0.65.

Wright, Mabel Osgood. Birdcraft. $2.50. Tommy-Anne. $1.50. Macmillan Company.

Wright, Mabel Osgood, and Dr. Elliott Coues. Citizen Bird. Macmillan Company. $1.50.

INDEX TO ILLUSTRATIONS

Acadian Flycatcher, Fig. 110, p. 192.

Bald Eagle, Plate XIX, p. 282.
Baltimore Oriole, Fig. 25, p. 56; Fig. 112, p. 192.
Bank Swallow, Fig. 24, p. 55.
Barn Owl, Plate XXVI, p. 294.
Barn Swallow, Plate IV, p. 50; Fig. 47, p. 109; Fig. 102, p. 190.
Barred Owl, Plate XXIV, p. 290.
Bills of
  Blackbird (Crow), Fig. 121, p. 193.
  Blue Jay, Fig. 135, p. 218.
  Bobolink, Fig. 50, p. 110.
  Brown Creeper, Fig. 196, p. 350.
  Chickadee, Fig. 115, p. 193.
  Cowbird, Fig. 42, p. 102.
  Crossbill, Fig. 116, p. 193.
  Crow, Fig. 136, p. 218.
  Dove (Mourning), Fig. 106, p. 192.
  Flycatchers (Acadian), Fig. 110, p. 192.
    (Wood Pewee), Fig. 107, p. 192.
  Goatsucker (Nighthawk), Fig. 113, p. 192.
  Grosbeak (Pine), Fig. 117, p. 193.
  Grouse (Ruffed), Fig. 111, p. 192.
  Hawk (Sparrow), Fig. 200, p. 350.
  Hummingbird, Fig. 118, p. 193.
  Kingfisher, Fig. 114, p. 192.
  Meadowlark, Fig. 43, p. 102.
  Oriole (Baltimore), Fig. 112, p. 192.
  Owl (Screech), Fig. 199, p. 350.
  Shrike (Loggerhead), Fig. 198, p. 350.
  Sparrow (Song), Fig. 119, p. 193.
  Swallow (White-bellied), Fig. 120, p. 193.
  Swift (Chimney), Fig. 9, p. 26.
  Tanager (Scarlet), Fig. 91, p. 170.
  Vireo (White-eyed), Fig. 109, p. 192.
  Vulture (Turkey), Fig. 163, p. 264.
  Woodpecker (Hairy), Fig. 108, p. 192.
  Wren (House), Fig. 197, p. 350.
Black and White Creeper, Fig. 190, p. 347.
Black and Yellow Warbler, Fig. 174, p. 324.

Black-billed Cuckoo, Fig. 86, p. 164.
Blackbirds, Cowbird, Fig. 42, p. 102.
  Crow, Fig. 39, p. 93; Fig. 121, p. 193.
  Red-wing, Plate VI, p. 96; Fig. 48, p. 109; Fig. 54, p. 112.
Blackburnian Warbler, Fig. 185, p. 346.
Black-poll Warbler, Fig. 187, p. 346.
Black-throated Blue Warbler, Fig. 188, p. 347.
Black-throated Green Warbler, Fig. 192, p. 347.
Bluebird, Fig. 16, p. 41.
Blue Jay, Fig. 78, p. 154; Fig. 135, p. 218; Fig. 137, p. 220.
Blue Yellow-backed Warbler, Fig. 189, p. 347.
Bobolink, Fig. 44, p. 103; Plate VII, p. 104; Fig. 50, p. 110; Fig. 51, p. 110; Fig. 53, p. 112.
Bob-white, Fig. 14, p. 37.
Brown Creeper, Fig. 196, p. 350; Fig. 201, p. 351; Fig. 212, p. 353.
Brown Thrasher, Fig. 94, p. 177; Fig. 126, p. 207.

Canada Jay, Plate XII, p. 218.
Canadian Warbler, Fig. 184, p. 346.
Cardinal, Fig. 155, p. 253.
Carolina Wren, Fig. 127, p. 207.
Catbird, Fig. 6, p. 6; Fig. 132, p. 207.
Chat, Yellow-breasted, Fig. 175, p. 331.
Chestnut-sided Warbler, Fig. 183, p. 346.
Chewink, Fig. 95, p. 181; Fig. 153, p. 252.
Chickadee, Fig. 32, p. 74; Fig. 74, p. 153; Fig. 115, p. 193.
Chimney Swift, Plate II, p. 24; Fig. 7, p. 25; Fig. 9, p. 26; Fig. 19, p. 45; Fig. 214, p. 353.
Chipping Sparrow, Fig. 55, p. 113.
Cliff Swallow, Fig. 22, p. 52.
Cooper's Hawk, Fig. 166, p. 270.
Cowbird, Fig. 42, p. 102.
Creeper, Black and White, Fig. 190, p. 347.

INDEX TO ILLUSTRATIONS

Creeper, Brown, Fig. 196, p. 350; Fig. 201, p. 351; Fig. 212, p. 353.
Crossbill, Fig. 116, p. 193.
Crow, Fig. 4, p. 14; Fig. 136, p. 218.
Crow Blackbird, Fig. 39, p. 93; Fig. 121, p. 193.
Cuckoo, Fig. 85, p. 163.
  Black-billed, Fig. 86, p. 164.
  Yellow-billed, Fig. 83, p. 161; Fig. 87, p. 164.

Dickcissel, Fig. 159, p. 253.
Dove, Mourning, Fig. 11, p. 29; Fig. 12, p. 30; Fig. 106, p. 192.
Downy Woodpecker, Fig. 71, p. 139.

Eagle, Bald, Plate XIX, p. 282.
Eave Swallow, Fig. 22, p. 52.

Feet of
  Blackbird (Red-winged), Fig. 48, p. 109.
  Chimney Swift, Fig. 7, p. 25.
  Creeper (Brown), Fig. 201, p. 351.
  Hawk (Fish), Fig. 207, p. 351.
  Kingfisher, Fig. 82, p. 159.
  Nighthawk, Fig. 203, p. 351.
  Pipit, Fig. 205, p. 351.
  Sparrow (Song), Fig. 204, p. 351.
  Swallow (Barn), Fig. 47, p. 109.
  Vulture (Turkey), Fig. 206, p. 351.
  Woodpecker (Hairy), Fig. 202, p. 351.
Fish Hawk, Plate XVIII, p. 280; Fig. 168, p. 281.
Flicker, Fig. 64, p. 127; Fig. 66, p. 130.
Flycatchers, Plate XIII, p. 258.
  Acadian, Fig. 110, p. 192.
  Great-crested Flycatcher, Plate XIII, p. 258.
  Kingbird, Fig. 35, p. 83; Plate XIII, p. 258.
  Least Flycatcher, Plate V, p. 80; Plate XIII, p. 258.
  Phœbe, Fig. 37, p. 88; Plate XIII, p. 258; Fig. 160, p. 260.
  Wood Pewee, Fig. 107, p. 192; Plate XIII, p. 258.
Fox Sparrow, Fig. 143, p. 230.

Gnatcatcher, Blue-gray, Fig. 219, p. 357.
Golden-crowned Kinglet, Fig. 217, p. 356.
Goldfinch, Frontispiece.
Goshawk, Plate XIV, p. 266.
Great-crested Flycatcher, Plate XIII, p. 258.

Great Horned Owl, Plate XXV, p. 292.
Grouse, Ruffed, Fig. 13, p. 33; Plate III, p. 34; Fig. 111, p. 192.
Grosbeak, Pine, Fig. 117, p. 193.
  Rose-breasted, Fig. 89, p. 166; Fig. 151, p. 252.

Hairy Woodpecker, Fig. 69, p. 135; Fig. 108, p. 192; Fig. 133, p. 215.
Hawks, Cooper's, Fig. 166, p. 270.
  Fish, Plate XVIII, p. 280.
  Goshawk, Plate XIV, p. 266.
  Marsh, Plate XVII, p. 278.
  Red-tailed, Plate XVI, p. 272.
  Sharp-shinned, Plate XV, p. 268.
  Sparrow, Fig. 167, p. 277.
Hermit Thrush, Plate XXVIII, p. 360.
Hooded Warbler, Fig. 180, p. 346.
Horned Lark, Fig. 161, p. 262.
House Wren, Fig. 18, p. 45; Fig. 130, p. 207.
Hummingbird, Fig. 1, p. 1; Fig. 100, p. 190; Fig. 118, p. 193.

Insects.
  Ant, Fig. 65, p. 130.
  Army worm, Fig. 6, p. 20.
  Cankerworm, Fig. 30, p. 69.
  Click beetle, Fig. 26, p. 57.
  Clover leaf-beetle, Fig. 41, p. 97.
  Currant worm, Fig. 57, p. 115.
  Cutworm, Fig. 15, p. 38.
  Grasshopper, Fig. 3, p. 13; Fig. 46, p. 108.
  Gypsy moth, Fig. 88, p. 164.
  May beetle, Fig. 40, p. 95.
  Mosquito, Fig. 23, p. 54.
  Potato beetle, Fig. 90, p. 168.
  Prionus beetle, Fig. 68, p. 133.
  Rose chafer, Fig. 36, p. 85.
  Sphynx moth, Fig. 79, p. 155.
  Tent-caterpillar, Fig. 84, p. 162.
  Wood-boring larva, Fig. 70, p. 139.

Jay, Blue, Fig. 78, p. 154; Fig. 135, p. 218; Fig. 137, p. 220.
  Canada, Plate XII, p. 218.
Junco, Fig. 156, p. 253.

Kentucky Warbler, Fig. 186, p. 346.
Kingbird, Fig. 35, p. 83.
Kingfisher, Fig. 80, p. 157; Fig. 81, p. 158; Fig. 82, p. 159; Fig. 114, p. 192.
Kinglet, Golden-crowned, Fig. 217, p. 356.
  Ruby-crowned, Fig. 218, p. 356.
Kite, Swallow-tailed, Plate XX, p. 284.

INDEX TO ILLUSTRATIONS

Lark, Horned, Fig. 161, p. 262.
Lark Sparrow, Fig. 147, p. 237.
Least Flycatcher, Plate V, p. 80.
Loggerhead Shrike, Fig. 169, p. 298.
Long-billed Marsh Wren, Plate X, p. 202; Fig. 131, p. 207.
Long-eared Owl, Plate XXII, p. 288.
Louisiana Water-Thrush, Fig. 178, p. 336.

Magnolia Warbler, Fig. 174, p. 324.
Marsh Hawk, Plate XVII, p. 278.
Maryland Yellow-throat, Fig. 193, p. 347.
Meadowlark, Fig. 43, p. 102; Fig. 45, p. 106; Fig. 52, p. 112.
Mockingbird, Fig. 27, p. 63; Fig. 128, p. 207.
Mourning Dove, Fig. 11, p. 29; Fig. 12, p. 30.
Myrtle Warbler, Fig. 194, p. 348.

Nighthawk, Fig. 97, p. 188; Fig. 99, p. 189; Fig. 104, p. 191; Fig. 113, p. 192.
Nuthatch, Red-breasted, Fig. 75, p. 153.
  White-breasted, Fig. 32, p. 74; Fig. 76, p. 153.

Oriole, Baltimore, Fig. 25, p. 56; Fig. 112, p. 192.
Osprey, Plate XVIII, p. 280.
Oven-bird, Fig. 176, p. 333.
Owls, Barn, Plate XXVI, p. 294.
  Barred, Plate XXIV, p. 290.
  Great Horned, Plate XXV, p. 292.
  Long-eared, Plate XXII, p. 288.
  Screech, Plate XXI, p. 287.
  Short-eared, Plate XXIII, p. 290.
  Snowy, Plate XXVII, p. 294.

Parula Warbler, Fig. 189, p. 347.
Phœbe, Fig. 37, p. 88.
Pine Finch, Fig. 144, p. 233.
Pipit, Fig. 205, p. 351.
Prairie Warbler, Fig. 181, p. 346.
Purple Finch, Plate IX, p. 148.

Quail, Fig. 14, p. 37.

Red-breasted Nuthatch, Fig. 75, p. 153.
Red-eyed Vireo, Fig. 61, p. 121; Fig. 173, p. 305.
Red-headed Woodpecker, Fig. 67, p. 131; Fig. 134, p. 216.
Redpoll, Fig. 157, p. 253.
Redstart, Fig. 195, p. 348.
Red-tailed Hawk, Plate XVI, p. 272.
Red-winged Blackbird, Plate VI, p. 96; Fig. 48, p. 109; Fig. 54, p. 112.
Robin, Fig. 5, p. 17.
Rose-breasted Grosbeak, Fig. 89, p. 166; Fig. 151, p. 252.
Rough-winged Swallow, Fig. 123, p. 195.
Ruby-crowned Kinglet, Fig. 218, p. 356.
Ruffed Grouse, Fig. 13, p. 33; Plate III, p. 34; Fig. 111, p. 192.

Sapsucker, Plate XI, p. 208; Fig. 213, p. 353.
Scarlet Tanager, Fig. 91, p. 170.
Screech Owl, Plate XXI, p. 287.
Sharp-shinned Hawk, Plate XV, p. 268.
Sharp-tailed Sparrow, Fig. 148, p. 239.
Short-eared Owl, Plate XXIII, p. 290.
Shrike, Loggerhead, Fig. 169, p. 298.
Snowbird, Fig. 158, p. 253.
  Slate-colored, Fig. 156, p. 253.
Snowflake, Fig. 158, p. 253.
Snowy Owl, Plate XXVII, p. 294.
Sparrow Hawk, Fig. 167, p. 277.
Sparrows, Chipping, Fig. 55, p. 113.
  Fox, Fig. 143, p. 230.
  Lark, Fig. 147, p. 237.
  Sharp-tailed, Fig. 148, p. 239.
  Song, Fig. 101, p. 190; Fig. 103, p. 191; Fig. 154, p. 252.
  Vesper, Fig. 60, p. 119.
  White-crowned, Fig. 152, p. 252.
  White-throat, Fig. 150, p. 252.
Swainson's Thrush, Fig. 220, p. 361.
Swallows, Bank, Fig. 24, p. 55.
  Barn, Plate IV, p. 50; Fig. 47, p. 109; Fig. 102, p. 190.
  Cliff, Fig. 22, p. 52.
  Eave, Fig. 22, p. 52.
  Rough-winged, Fig. 123, p. 195.
  Tree, Fig. 120, p. 193; Fig. 122, p. 194.
  White-bellied, Fig. 120, p. 193; Fig. 122, p. 194.
Swallow-tailed Kite, Plate XX, p. 284.
Swift, Chimney, Plate II, p. 24; Fig. 7, p. 25; Fig. 9, p. 26; Fig. 19, p. 45; Fig. 214, p. 353.

Tails of
  Barn Swallow, Fig. 210, p. 352.
  Black-billed Cuckoo, Fig. 86, p. 164.
  Bobolink, Fig. 51, p. 110.
  Brown Creeper, Fig. 212, p. 353.
  Mourning Dove, Fig. 12, p. 30.
  Pine Finch, Fig. 209, p. 352.

INDEX TO ILLUSTRATIONS

Ruffed Grouse, Fig. 216, p. 353.
Sapsucker, Fig. 213, p. 353.
Swallow-tailed Kite, Fig. 215, p. 353.
Swift, Fig. 214, p. 353.
Vesper Sparrow, Fig. 60, p. 119.
Vireo, White-eyed, Fig. 208, p. 352.
Yellow-billed Cuckoo, Fig. 87, p. 164.

Tanager, Scarlet, Fig. 91, p. 170.
Thrasher, Brown, Fig. 94, p. 177; Fig. 126, p. 207.
Thrushes, Hermit, Plate XXVIII, p. 360; Fig. 220, p. 361.
Swainson's, Fig. 220, p. 361.
Veery, Fig. 220, p. 361.
Wood, Fig. 220, p. 361.
Tree Swallow, Fig. 120, p. 193; Fig. 122, p. 194.
Tufted Titmouse, Fig. 77, p. 153.
Turkey Vulture, Fig. 163, p. 264; Fig. 164, p. 265.

Veery Thrush, Fig. 220, p. 361.
Vesper Sparrow, Fig. 60, p. 119.
Vireo, Red-eyed, Fig. 61, p. 121; Fig. 173, p. 305.
Warbling, Fig. 172, p. 305.
White-eyed, Fig. 109, p. 192; Fig. 171, p. 305.
Yellow-throated, Fig. 170, p. 305.
Vulture, Turkey, Fig. 163, p. 264.

Warblers, Black and White Creeper, Fig. 190, p. 347.
Black and Yellow, Fig. 174, p. 324.
Blackburnian, Fig. 185, p. 346.
Black-poll, Fig. 187, p. 346.
Black-throated Blue, Fig. 188, p. 347.
Black-throated Green, Fig. 192, p. 347.
Blue Yellow-backed, Fig. 189, p. 347.
Canadian, Fig. 184, p. 346.
Chestnut-sided, Fig. 183, p. 346.
Hooded, Fig. 180, p. 346.
Kentucky, Fig. 186, p. 346.
Louisiana Water-Thrush, Fig. 178, p. 336.
Magnolia, Fig. 174, p. 324.
Maryland Yellow-throat, Fig. 193, p. 347.
Myrtle, Fig. 194, p. 348.
Oven-bird, Fig. 176, p. 333.
Parula, Fig. 189, p. 347.
Prairie, Fig. 181, p. 346.
Redstart, Fig. 195, p. 348.
Water-Thrush, Fig. 177, p. 336.
Wilson's, Fig. 182, p. 346.
Worm-eating, Fig. 179, p. 338.

Yellow, Fig. 191, p. 347.
Yellow-breasted Chat, Fig. 175, p. 331.
Yellow-rumped, Fig. 194, p. 348.
Warbling Vireo, Fig. 172, p. 305.
Waxwing, Plate VIII, p. 142; Fig. 72, p. 144.
Weeds, Amaranth, Fig. 96, p. 184.
Crab grass, Fig. 56, p. 114.
Foxtail, Fig. 142, p. 228.
Pigweed, Fig. 59, p. 117.
Ragweed, Fig. 139, p. 222.
Thistle, Fig. 73, p. 147.
Whip-poor-will, Fig. 98, p. 188.
White-bellied Swallow, Fig. 120, p. 193; Fig. 122, p. 194.
White-breasted Nuthatch, Fig. 76, p. 153.
White-crowned Sparrow, Fig. 152, p. 252.
White-eyed Vireo, Fig. 171, p. 305; Fig. 109, p. 192.
White-throated Sparrow, Fig. 150, p. 252.
Wings of
Barn Swallow, Fig. 102, p. 190.
Chimney Swift, Fig. 19, p. 45.
House Wren, Fig. 18, p. 45.
Hummingbird, Fig. 100, p. 190.
Nighthawk, Fig. 99, p. 189.
Song Sparrow, Fig. 101, p. 190.
Waxwing, Fig. 72, p. 144.
Woodpeckers, Downy, Fig. 71, p. 139.
Flicker, Fig. 64, p. 127; Fig. 66, p. 130.
Hairy, Fig. 69, p. 135; Fig. 108, p. 192; Fig. 133, p. 215.
Red-headed, Fig. 67, p. 131; Fig. 134, p. 216.
Yellow-bellied, Plate XI, p. 208; Fig. 213, p. 353.
Wood Pewee, Fig. 107, p. 192.
Wood Thrush, Fig. 220, p. 361.
Wrens, Carolina, Fig. 127, p. 207.
House, Fig. 18, p. 45; Fig. 130, p. 207.
Long-billed Marsh, Fig. 131, p. 207; Plate X, p. 202.
Winter, Fig. 129, p. 207.

Yellow-bellied Woodpecker, Plate XI, p. 208; Fig. 213, p. 353.
Yellow-billed Cuckoo, Fig. 83, p. 161; Fig. 87, p. 164.
Yellow-bird, Frontispiece.
Yellow-breasted Chat, Fig. 175, p 331.
Yellow-rumped Warbler, Fig. 194, p. 348.
Yellow-throated Vireo, Fig. 170, p 305.
Yellow Warbler, Fig. 191, p. 347.

INDEX

Acadian Flycatcher, 254.
Acanthis linaria, 236-237.
Accipiter atricapillus, 266-267.
   cooperi, 269-271.
   velox, 268-269.
Adaptation, shown by
   bill, 5, 25, 57, 59, 70, 86, 110-111, 123, 139, 190, 191, 214, 234-235, 264, 349.
   foot, 24-25, 35, 50, 159, 264, 282, 349.
   mucilaginous saliva, 26, 130, 140.
   power of regurgitation (see Regurgitation).
   protective coloration, 5, 26, 33-35, 44, 56, 67, 104-105, 107-108, 122, 130, 146, 171, 183, 185, 190, 262, 294, 318, 348, 349.
   tail, 25, 110, 140, 240, 283, 350.
   tongue, 139, 140, 214.
   wing, 5, 24, 35, 44-45.
Agelaius phœniceus, 96-98.
Alder Flycatcher, 258.
Ammodramus caudacutus, 239-240.
   maritimus, 240-241.
   sandwichensis savanna, 225-226.
   savannarum passerinus, 226-227.
Ampelis cedrorum, 141-144.
Anthus pensilvanicus, 348.
Antrostomus vociferus, 185-187.
Asio accipitrinus, 290-291.
   wilsonianus, 288-289.

Bachman's Sparrow, 242.
Bald Eagle, 281, 282-283.
Baltimore Oriole, 56-61, 62.
Bank Swallow, 54-55, 159, 195.
Barn Owl, 293-294.
Barn Swallow, 49-51, 53, 54.
Barred Owl, 291-292.
Bewick's Wren, 201.
Bird boxes, xxv, 42-43, 46, 48-49, 72, 288.
Bird psychology, 46-47, 107-108, 255, 318-320.
   association of ideas, 72, 87.
   courage, 28, 29, 32, 71, 200, 267.
   dissimulation, 32, 39-40, 160, 172.
   expression of emotions and ideas,
      — by use of crests, attitudes,
and movements, 3, 9, 129, 141-142, 288, 332. By voice, — calls of warning, 40, 50; cries of anger, distress fear, pain, 9, 121, 150, 172, 180; scoldings, 60, 316; songs, 18, 99, 104, 169, 232, 238, 316, 332, 334.
   individuality, 10-11, 14-15, 59, 201, 255, 302, 318-320.
   inherited instincts, 27.
   intelligence shown in
      building, 52, 55, 136, 318; bringing up young, 18; coöperation, 18, 46-47, 157, 281; discrimination between eggs, 87; getting food, 282, 295; protecting young, 39-40, 99; protective attitudes, devices, and movements, 27, 142, 161, 255-256, 289; strategy, 39-40, 49, 160, 161, 255, 269; turning to man for help, 46, 81-82, 238.
   play impulse, 75.
   storing habit, 133, 218-219, 299.
Birds,
   agents in cross-fertilization and fruit-planting, 4-5, 123.
   anecdotes about, 107-108, 142, 157; appealing to man for help, 46-47, 238; defense of nest, 87; devotion to young, 28-29, 36-37, 39-40, 71, 172; feeding neighbor's children, 100-101, 318-320; friendliness when well treated, 9, 10-11, 46-47, 81-82, 113-115, 124-125, 129, 302; originality of Crow, 14-15.
   as guides to water, 30-31.
   bills, feet, tails, wings of (see Adaptation).
   comparisons of groups of, 40, 79, 91-92, 109-111, 143-144, 173, 181-182, 190-191, 196, 204-205, 214-216, 219, 242-246, 258-259, 271-272, 284-285, 295, 297, 302-303, 306-307, 339-342, 350, 361-363.
   destruction of, 3, 31-32, 37, 64-65, 78-79, 117-118, 122-123, 137, 138, 236.
   domestic life of, as parents, 2-3, 8-9, 15, 18, 19, 28-29, 32, 36-37,

INDEX

39–40, 71, 98–99, 100, 172, 318–320; companionship of mates, 18, 31, 76, 142, 146, 169, 316; courtship, 43–44, 128–129, 136, 149, 180, 186–187, 210, 255, 279–280, 288; defense of nest and young, 9, 32, 36–37, 39–40, 71, 87, 160, 161, 187; family government, 18; habits of male at nest, — absent from, 3–4; helps build, 39, 76, 136, 210; mated through life, 15, 60, 136, 288.
economic status of (see Economic status).
eyesight of, 84–85.
flight of, 72, 84, 178, 186, 189, 195, 213, 272–273, 276–278, 280, 283–284, 299.
flocks of, 19, 24, 51, 55, 66, 73, 78, 111, 141, 144, 145, 148, 175, 189, 194, 221, 231, 233, 234, 317, 339, 354.
food of (see Food of birds).
how and what to observe about, xiv–xv, 4, 12, 14, 18–20, 23–24, 26–27, 141–142, 144, 149, 160–161, 199–200, 352, 367–368, 380–388.
how to find name of, xiii, 79–80.
how to protect, attract, and feed, xx–xxi, xxiv–xxviii, 36, 40, 42–43, 46, 48–49, 53, 58, 68, 81, 113, 124–125, 146, 154, 194, 235, 281.
how to protect crops from, xx–xxi, 7, 8, 13, 21, 58, 105, 143, 209.
human companionship sought by, 10–11, 218.
keys to (see Keys).
migration of (see Migration).
sleeping places of, 28, 51, 75, 139–140.
songs (see Songs and calls of birds).
winter, xxvi–xxviii, 376–379.
young (see Young birds).
Black and White Creeper, 314.
Black and Yellow Warbler, 324–325.
Blackbirds, 12, 101–102, 109–111, 144.
Cowbird, 98–101, 102, 110.
Crow, 93–96, 101, 110.
Key to, 111–112.
Red-wing, 96–98, 101, 102, 110.
Rusty, 101–103, 110.
Blackbirds and Orioles, 109–111.
Key to, 111–112.
Blackburnian Warbler, 326.
Black-poll Warbler, 321–322.
Black-throated Blue Warbler, 312–313, 326.

Black-throated Bunting, 224.
Black-throated Green Warbler, 311, 326.
Bluebird, 41–44, 59, 140.
Blue-gray Gnatcatcher, 357.
Blue Jay, 154–157.
Blue Yellow-backed Warbler, 317–318.
Bobolink, 103–106, 107, 110.
Bob-white, 37–40, 57, 80.
Bonasa umbellus, 32–37.
Broad-winged Hawk, 275.
Brown Creeper, 349–352.
Brown Thrasher, 177–180, 182.
Bubo virginianus, 292–293.
Butcherbird, 300.
Buteo borealis, 271–273.
  latissimus, 275.
  lineatus, 273–274.
Buzzard, Turkey, 263–265, 266.

Canada Jay, 217–219.
Canadian Warbler, 322.
Cardinal, 65–66, 151, 171, 199, 200.
Cardinalis cardinalis, 65–66.
Carolina Chickadee, 71–72, 151.
Carolina Wren, 199–200.
Carpodacus purpureus, 148–149.
Catbird, 6–11, 92.
Cathartes aura, 263–265.
Cats, xxv, 118.
Cedar-bird, 141–144.
Ceophlœus pileatus, 212–213.
Certhia familiaris americana, 349–352.
Ceryle alcyon, 157–160.
Chætura pelagica, 23–29.
Chat, Yellow-breasted, 331–333.
Chebeck, 80–82, 92.
Chelidon erythrogaster, 49–51.
Cherry-bird, 141–144.
Chestnut-sided Warbler, 318–320.
Chewink, 181–183.
Chickadee, 67–71, 79, 95, 138, 152.
  Carolina, 71–72, 151.
Chimney Swift, 23–29, 45, 92.
Chipping Sparrow, 113–116.
Chondestes grammacus, 237–238.
Chordeiles virginianus, 188–190.
Circus hudsonius, 278–280.
Cistothorus palustris, 202–204.
Clay-colored Sparrow, 241.
Cliff Swallow, 50, 52–54.
Clivicola riparia, 54–55.
Coccyzus americanus, 160–163.
  erythropthalmus, 163–164.
Cock-of-the-Woods, 212–213.
Colaptes auratus, 127–131.
Colinus virginianus, 37–40.
Columbigallina passerina terrestris, 31–32.
Compsothlypsis americana, 317–318.

INDEX

Contopus borealis, 257.
  virens, 90–93.
Cooper's Hawk, 269–271.
Corvus americanus, 11–15.
  ossifragus, 16.
Cowbird, 98–101, 102, 110.
Creeper, Brown, 349–352.
Crossbill, American, 234–235.
Crow, American, 11–15.
  Fish, 16.
Crow Blackbird, 93–96, 101, 110.
Crows and Jays, 156, 219.
  Key to, 220.
Cuckoos, 162, 177–178.
  Black-billed, 163–164.
  Yellow-billed, 160–163.
Cuckoos and Kingfishers, 164.
  Key to, 165.
Cyanocitta cristata, 154–157.

Dendroica æstiva, 307–308.
  Blackburniæ, 326.
  cærulescens, 312–313.
  coronata, 310.
  discolor, 325–326.
  maculosa, 324–325.
  palmarum hypochrysea, 316–317.
  pensylvanica, 318–320.
  striata, 321–322.
  virens, 311.
Dickcissel, 224.
Dolichonyx oryzivorus, 103–106.
Doves, 45, 79–80, 94.
  Ground, 31–32.
  Key to, 80.
  Mourning, 29–31.
  Passenger Pigeon, 78–79.
Downy Woodpecker, 137–140.
Dryobates borealis, 210–211.
  pubescens, 137–140.
  villosus, 135–137.

Eave Swallow, 50, 52–54.
Economic status of
  Bald Eagle, 282–283.
  Barn Owl, 293–294.
  Barn Swallow, 53, 54.
  Barred Owl, 291.
  Black-poll Warbler, 322.
  Bluebird, 43.
  Blue Jay, 154–156.
  Bobolink, 105–106.
  Bob-white, 37–38.
  Broad-winged Hawk, 275.
  Brown Thrasher, 179.
  Butcherbird, 300.
  Catbird, 7–8.
  Chewink, 182–183.
  Chickadee, 69–70.
  Chimney Swift, 25.
  Chipping Sparrow, 115–116.
  Cooper's Hawk, 269–271.
  Crow, 12–14.
  Crow Blackbird, 12, 95–96.
  Cuckoos, 162–164.
  Dickcissel, 224.
  Downy Woodpecker, 138–139.
  Eave Swallow, 54.
  Field Sparrow, 184.
  Flicker, 130–131.
  Goldfinch, 146–147.
  Goshawk, 266–267.
  Great Horned Owl, 292–293.
  Hairy Woodpecker, 136–137.
  Horned Lark, 262–263.
  Junco, 221–222.
  Kingbird, 85–86.
  Kingfisher, 159.
  Loggerhead Shrike, 299.
  Long-eared Owl, 289.
  Marsh Hawk, 279.
  Meadowlark, 108–109.
  Nighthawk, 188.
  Nuthatch, 75.
  Orioles, 57–59, 61–62.
  Osprey, 280.
  Phœbe, 89–90.
  Pileated Woodpecker, 213.
  Pine Finch, 233.
  Red-bellied Woodpecker, 212.
  Red-headed Woodpecker, 132–133.
  Redpoll, 237.
  Red-shouldered Hawk, 273–274.
  Red-tailed Hawk, 272.
  Red-winged Blackbird, 96–97.
  Robin, 20–21.
  Rose-breasted Grosbeak, 167–168.
  Sapsucker, 208–209.
  Savanna Sparrow, 225–226.
  Screech Owl, 287.
  Sharp-shinned Hawk, 268.
  Short-eared Owl, 290–291.
  Song Sparrow, 117.
  Sparrow Hawk, 276.
  Swallow-tailed Kite, 284.
  Thrushes, 358.
  Tree Sparrow, 229.
  Tufted Titmouse, 152.
  Vireos, 122, 304.
  Warblers, 307.
  Waxwing, 142–143.
  Whip-poor-will, 187.
  White-throated Sparrow, 175.
  Woodpeckers, 12, 133, 213–214.
Ectopistes migratorius, 78–79.
Elanoides forficatus, 283–284.
Empidonax minimus, 80–82.
  traillii alnorum, 258.
  virescens, 254.
English Sparrow, xix, 42, 46, 49.

Falcons, Hawks, and Eagles, 284–285.

INDEX

Key to, 285-287.
Falco sparverius, 276-278.
Field Sparrow, 183-185.
Finch, Pine, xxvii, 233.
　Purple, xxvii, 148-149.
Finches and Sparrows, 242-246.
　Key to, 246-251.
Fish Hawk, 280-282.
Flicker, 127-131, 140.
Flycatchers, 91-93, 116, 258-259.
　Acadian, 254.
　Alder, 258.
　Great-crested, 255-256.
　Key to, 260-261.
　Kingbird, 83-87.
　Least, 80-82, 92.
　Olive-sided, 257.
　Phœbe, 53, 87-90, 91.
　Traill's, 258.
　Wood Pewee, 90-93.
Food of birds, xv-xxiv, 6-8, 12-13
　(see Economic status).
　Ants, xxii, 130, 209.
　Army worms, xxiv, 20, 116.
　Asparagus beetles, 85.
　Beet caterpillars, 97.
　Cabbage worms, 115, 117.
　Cankerworms, xvii, 69.
　Caterpillars, 57, 122, 162, 163.
　Chinch bugs, xxiii.
　Cotton worms, xxiii.
　Elm leaf-beetles, 143.
　Field mice and rats, 14, 272, 274,
　　275, 279, 287, 289, 290, 293.
　Grasshoppers, xxiv, 7, 13, 108,
　　132, 155, 276.
　Gypsy moth, xvi, xxiii, xxiv, 14,
　　164.
　Insects, xvii.
　May beetles, xxii, 95, 132, 133,
　　179.
　Mosquitoes, 54, 188.
　Potato beetles, xxi, 38, 167-168.
　Rose chafers, 85.
　Scale insects, xxii.
　Sphynx moths, 155, 156.
　Squash beetles, 54, 89.
　Tent-caterpillars, xxi, 14, 162.
　Thistle seeds, 147.
　Weed seeds, xviii, 96, 97, 115,
　　123, 146, 175, 184, 221, 229, 262.
　Weevils, xxii, 89.
　Wire worms, xxiii, 57.
　Wood-borers, 137, 139.
Food of young birds, 2, 8, 14, 48, 72,
　142, 147.
Fox Sparrow, 230-231.

Galeoscoptes carolinensis, 6-11.
Geothlypis formosa, 329-330.
　trichas, 315-316.

Gnatcatcher, Blue-gray, 357.
Goatsuckers and Swifts, 190-191.
　Key to, 193.
Golden-crowned Kinglet, 356.
Goldfinch, 145-147.
Goshawk, 266-267.
Grackle, Purple, 93-96, 101, 110.
Grass Finch, 119-120.
Grasshopper Sparrow, 226-227.
Great-crested Flycatcher, 255-256.
Great Horned Owl, 292-293.
Grosbeak, Pine, 231-233.
　Rose-breasted, 166-169.
Grouse, Ruffed, 32-37, 39, 40, 92.
Grouse and Quail, 45.
　Key to, 40.

Hairy Woodpecker, 135-137, 140.
Haliæetus leucocephalus, 282-283.
Harporhynchus rufus, 177-180.
Hawks, 284-285, 297.
　Broad-winged, 275.
　Cooper's, 269-271.
　Fish, 280-282.
　Goshawk, 266-267.
　Key to, 285-287.
　Marsh, 278-280.
　Red-shouldered, 273-274.
　Red-tailed, 271-273.
　Sharp-shinned, 268-269.
　Sparrow, 276-278.
　Swallow-tailed Kite, 283-284.
Hawks and Owls, 263-297.
Helminthophila rubricapilla, 322-
　323.
Helmitherus vermivorus, 337-339.
Hermit Thrush, 360.
High-hole, 127-131, 140.
Hooded Warbler, 327-328.
Horned Lark, 261-263.
House Wren, 44-48.
Hummingbird, Ruby-throated, 1-5,
　25, 50.

Icteria virens, 331-333.
Icterus galbula, 56-61.
　spurius, 61-62.
Indigo Bunting, 149-150.

Jay, Blue, xxvii, 154-157.
　Canada, 217-219.
Junco, Slate-colored, xxvii, 221-
　222.
Junco hyemalis, 221-222.

Kentucky Warbler, 329-330.
Keys to
　All birds mentioned in book,
　　xxix-xlix.
　Blackbirds and Orioles, 111-112.

INDEX

Crows and Jays, 220.
Falcons, Hawks, and Eagles, 285–287.
Finches and Sparrows, 246–251.
Flycatchers, 260–261.
Goatsuckers and Swifts, 193.
Grouse and Quail, 40.
Kinglets and Gnatcatchers, 357.
Nuthatches and Titmice, 152.
Owls, 296–297.
Shrikes, 300.
Swallows, 196–197.
Tanagers, 174.
Thrashers and Wrens, 205–206.
Thrushes and Bluebirds, 360–361.
Vireos, 304.
Warblers, 342–345.
Woodpeckers, 216–217.
Kingbird, 83–87.
Kingfisher, Belted, 157–160.
Kinglets, Golden-crowned, 356.
Key to, 357.
Ruby-crowned, 354–355.
Kinglets and Gnatcatchers.
Key to, 357.
Kite, Swallow-tailed, 283–284.

Lanius borealis, 300.
ludovicianus, 298–299.
Lark, Horned, 261–263.
Shore, 261–263.
Lark Sparrow, 237–238.
Least Flycatcher, 80–82.
Loggerhead Shrike, 298–299.
Long-billed Marsh Wren, 202–204.
Long-eared Owl, 288–289.
Louisiana Water-Thrush, 336–337.
Loxia curvirostra minor, 234–235.

Magnolia Warbler, 324–325.
Marsh Hawk, 278–280.
Martin, Purple, 48–49.
Maryland Yellow-throat, 315–316.
Meadowlark, 101, 106–109.
Megascops asio, 287–288.
Melanerpes carolinus, 211–212.
erythrocephalus, 131–134, 144.
Melospiza fasciata, 116–119.
georgiana, 229–230.
Merula migratoria, 17–22.
Migration, xv, 116, 123, 148, 342, 367–376.
Mimus polyglottos, 63–65.
Mniotilta varia, 314.
Mockingbird, 63–65, 298–299.
Molothrus ater, 98–101.
Moose Bird, 217–219.
Mourning Dove, 29–31.
Myiarchus crinitus, 255–256.
Myrtle Warbler, 310.

Nashville Warbler, 322–323.
Nests,
methods of building, 24, 27, 46, 52, 53, 59, 60, 70, 76, 91, 136, 159, 255.
types of, 59.
Bank Swallow, 55.
Barn Swallow, 53.
Bewick's Wren, 201.
Bluebird, 140.
Catbird, 9.
Chickadee, 140.
Chimney Swift, 26.
Cuckoo, 161.
Eave Swallow, 52.
Hummingbird, 2.
Kingfisher, 159.
Orioles, 59, 62.
Oven-bird, 335.
Parula Warbler, 317.
Red-eyed Vireo, 124.
Winter Wren, 198.
Wood Pewee, 91.
Wood Thrush, 22.
Yellow-throated Vireo, 301.
unusual sites, 47–48, 172, 201, 212.
Nighthawk, 188–190.
Notebooks, xiii, xiv.
Nuthatches, 92.
Red-breasted, xxvii, 76–77.
White-breasted, xxvii, 73–76.
Nuthatches and Titmice, 152.
Key to, 152.
Nyctea nyctea, 294–295.

Olive-backed Thrush, 359.
Olive-sided Flycatcher, 257.
Orchard Oriole, 58, 61–62.
Orioles, xxvii, 109–111, 122.
Baltimore, 56–61, 62.
Orchard, 58, 61–62.
Osprey, 280–282.
Otocoris alpestris, 261–263.
Oven-bird, 333–335.
Owls, 295, 297.
Barn, 293–294.
Barred, 291–292.
Great Horned, 292–293.
Key to, 296–297.
Long-eared, 288–289.
Screech, 287–288.
Short-eared, 290–291.
Snowy, 294–295.

Pandion haliaëtus carolinensis, 280–282.
Parula Warbler, 317–318.
Parus atricapillus, 67–71.
bicolor, 151–152.
carolinensis, 71–72.
Passerella iliaca, 230–231.

INDEX

Passerina cyanea, 149–150.
Perisoreus canadensis, 217–219.
Petrochelidon lunifrons, 52–54.
Peucæa æstivalis bachmanii, 242.
Pewee, Wood, 90–93.
Phœbe, 53, 87–90, 91, 92.
Pigeon, Passenger, 78–79.
Pigeons and Doves, 79–80.
Pileated Woodpecker, 212–213.
Pine Finch, 233.
　Grosbeak, 231–233.
Pinicola enucleator, 231–233.
Pipilo erythrophthalmus, 181–183.
Pipit, American, 348.
Piranga erythromelas, 170–172.
Plectrophenax nivalis, 223.
Polioptila cærulea, 357.
Poocætes gramineus, 119–120.
Prairie Warbler, 325–326.
Progne subis, 48–49.
Purple Finch, 148–149.
　Grackle, 93–96, 101, 110.
　Martin, 48–49.

Quail, 37–40, 57, 80.
Quiscalus quiscula, 93–96.

Red-bellied Woodpecker, 211–212.
　-cockaded Woodpecker, 210–211.
　-eyed Vireo, 120–125, 126.
　-headed Woodpecker, 131–134.
Redpoll, xxvii, 236–237.
　Warbler, 316–317.
Red-shouldered Hawk, 273–274.
Redstart, 309–310, 318–320.
Red-tailed Hawk, 271–273.
　-winged Blackbird, 96–98, 101, 102, 110.
Reed Bird, 103–106.
Regulus calendula, 354–355.
　satrapa, 356.
Regurgitation
　of food for young, 2, 32, 130, 136, 142.
　of indigestible food, 93, 159.
Rice Birds, 103–106.
Robin, xxvii, 17–22.
Roosts, 19–20, 24, 51, 66, 78, 194–195.
Rose-breasted Grosbeak, 166–169, 170.
Ruby-crowned Kinglet, 354–355, 356.
Ruffed Grouse, 32–37, 39, 40, 92.
Rusty Blackbird, 101–103, 110.

Sapsucker, 208–210.
Savanna Sparrow, 225–226.
Sayornis phœbe, 87–90.
Scarlet Tanager, 170–172.
Scolecophagus carolinus, 101–103.
Screech Owl, 287–288.
Seaside Sparrow, 239, 240–241.
Seiurus aurocapillus, 333–335.

Seiurus motacilla, 336–337.
　noveboracensis, 335–336.
Setophaga ruticilla, 309–310.
Sharp-shinned Hawk, 268–269.
　-tailed Sparrow, 239–240.
Shore Lark, 261–263.
Short-eared Owl, 290–291.
Shrikes.
　Butcherbird, 300.
　Key to, 300.
　Loggerhead, 298–299.
Sialia sialis, 41–44.
Siskin, 233.
Sitta canadensis, 76–77.
　carolinensis, 73–76.
Snowbird, 223.
　Slate-colored, 221–222.
Snow Bunting, 223.
Snowflake, 223.
Snowy Owl, 294–295.
Song Sparrow, 100, 116–119.
Songs and calls of Birds, 98, 136, 166–167, 182, 358, 360.
　alarm notes, 40, 50.
　comparisons in songs, 23, 45, 90, 92.
　flight songs, 104, 316, 332, 334.
　seasonal calls, 10, 146.
　variations in song, 18, 60–61, 119, 315, 332, 334.
Sparrow Hawk, 276–278.
Sparrows, 99, 116, 122, 242–246.
　Bachman's, 242.
　Chipping, 113–116.
　Clay-colored, 241.
　English, 42, 46, 49.
　Field, 183–185.
　Fox, xxvii, 230–231.
　Grasshopper, 225–226.
　House, 42, 46, 49.
　Key to, 248–251.
　Lark, 237–238.
　Savanna, 225–226.
　Seaside, 239, 240–241.
　Sharp-tailed, 239–240.
　Song, xxvii, 100, 116–119.
　Swamp, 229–230.
　Tree, xxvii, 227–229.
　Vesper, 119–120.
　White-crowned, 176–177.
　　-throated, 174–175.
Sphyrapicus varius, 208–210.
Spinus pinus, 233.
　tristis, 145–147.
Spiza americana, 224.
Spizella monticola, 227–229.
　pallida, 241.
　pusilla, 183–185.
　socialis, 113–116.
Stelgidopteryx serripennis, 195–196.
Sternella magna, 106–109.
Strix pratincola, 293–294.

INDEX

Swainson's Thrush, 359.
Swallows, 53, 109, 196.
  Bank, 54–55, 159.
  Barn, 49–51, 53, 54.
  Cliff, 50, 52–54.
  Eave, 50, 52–54.
  Key to, 196–197.
  Purple Martin, 48–49.
  Rough-winged, 195–196.
  Tree, 194–195.
  White-bellied, 194–195.
Swallow-tailed Kite, 283–284.
Swamp Sparrow, 229–230.
Swift, Chimney, 23–29, 45, 92.
Syrnium nebulosum, 291–292.

Tachycineta bicolor, 194–195.
Tanagers,
  Key to, 174.
  Scarlet, 170–172.
  Summer, 173.
Thistle-bird, 145–147.
Thrasher, Brown, 177–180, 182.
Thrushes, xxvii, 358.
  Hermit, 360.
  Key to, 360–361.
  Olive-backed, 359.
  Swainson's, 359.
  Veery, 358–359.
  Wilson's, 358–359.
  Wood, 22–23.
Titlark, 348.
Titmice, 72.
  Tufted, 151–152, 199, 200.
Towhee, 181–183.
Traill's Flycatcher, 258.
Tree Sparrow, xviii, 227–229.
  Swallow, 194–195.
Trochilus colubris, 1–5.
Troglodytes aëdon, 44–48.
  hyemalis, 197–198.
Thryothorus bewickii, 201.
  ludovicianus, 199–200.
Tufted Titmouse, 151–152, 199.
Turdus aonalaschkæ pallasi, 360.
  fuscescens, 358.
  mustelinus, 22–23.
  ustulatus swainsoni, 359.
Turkey Buzzard, 263–265, 266.
  Vulture, 263–265, 266.
Turtle Dove, 29–31.
Tyrannus tyrannus, 83–87.

Veery Thrush, 358–359.
Vesper Sparrow, 119–120.
Vireo flavifrons, 301.
  gilvus, 126.
  noveboracensis, 302.
  olivaceus, 120–125.
Vireos, 122, 144, 159, 302–304.
  Key to, 304.
  Red-eyed, 120–125, 126.
  Warbling, 126, 149.
  White-eyed, 302.
  Yellow-throated, 301.
Vultures, Black, 265–266.
  Key to, 266.
  Turkey, 263–265, 266.

Warblers, 306–307, 339–342.
  Black and White Creeper, 314.
  Black and Yellow, 324–325.
  Blackburnian, 326.
  Black-poll, 321–322.
  Black-throated Blue, 312–313, 326.
    Green, 311, 326.
  Blue Yellow-backed, 317–318.
  Canadian, 322.
  Chestnut-sided, 318–320.
  Hooded, 327–328.
  Kentucky, 329–330.
  Key to, 342–345.
  Louisiana Water-Thrush, 336–337.
  Magnolia, 324–325.
  Maryland Yellow-throat, 315–316.
  Myrtle, 310.
  Nashville, 322–323.
  Oven-bird, 333–335.
  Parula, 317–318.
  Prairie, 325–326.
  Red-poll, 316–317.
  Redstart, 309–310, 318–320.
  Water-Thrush, 335–336.
  Wilson's, 339.
  Worm-eating, 337–339.
  Yellow, 307–308.
    -breasted Chat, 331–333.
    -rumped, 310.
Warbling Vireo, 126, 149.
Water-Thrush, 335–336.
  Louisiana, 336–337.
Waxwing, 141–144.
Whip-poor-will, 185–187, 188.
Whiskey Jack, 217–219.
White-bellied Swallow, 194–195.
  -crowned Sparrow, 176–177.
  -eyed Vireo, 302.
  -throated Sparrow, 174–175, 176.
Wilsonia canadensis, 322.
  mitrata, 327–328.
  pusilla, 339.
Wilson's Thrush, 358–359.
Wilson's Warbler, 339.
Winter Wren, 197–198.
Woodpeckers, 12, 133, 140, 214–216.
  Downy, 137–140.
  Hairy, xxvii, 135–137, 140.
  Flicker, 127–131, 140.
  Key to, 216–217.
  Pileated, 212–213.

INDEX

Woodpecker, Red-bellied, 211-212.
   -cockaded, 210-211.
   -headed, 131-134, 144.
  Sapsucker, 208-210.
  Yellow-bellied, 208-210.
Wood Pewee, 90-93.
  Thrush, 22-23.
Worm-eating Warbler, 337-339.
Wrens, 57, 67-68, 92, 204-205.
  Bewick's, 201.
  Carolina, 199-200.
  House, 44-48.
  Key to, 205-206.
  Long-billed Marsh, 202-204.
  Winter, 197-198.
Wrens and Thrashers, 204-205.
  Key to, 205-206.

Yellow-bellied Woodpecker, 208-210.
  -bird, 145-147.
  -breasted Chat, 331-333.
  -hammer, 127-130.
  Palm Warbler, 316-317.
  Red-poll Warbler, 316-317.
  -rumped Warbler, 310.
  -shafted Woodpecker, 127-131, 140.
  -throated Vireo, 301.
  Warbler, 307-308.
  -winged Sparrow, 226-227.
Young birds — brought back to nest at night, 27-28; fed by regurgitation, 2; first flights, 28; length of time spent in nest, 2, 27, 160; taught to follow parents, 19, 51.

Zamelodia ludoviciana, 166-169.
Zenaidura macroura, 29-31.
Zonotrichia albicollis, 174-175.
  leucophrys, 176-177.

PLATE XXVIII. — HERMIT THRUSH

Upper parts olive-brown; *tail reddish brown;* throat and breast
spotted. *Length,* about $7\frac{1}{4}$ inches.

Date Due

DEC 1 0 2009

DEC 1 0 2009